ANOTHER 366 DAYS

MORE STORIES FROM THIS DAY IN HISTORY

SCOTT ALLSOP

Also by Scott Allsop

366 Days

Published by L & E Books

www.mrallsophistory.com   www.historypod.net

ISBN: 978-0-9956809-2-0

In memory of my dad

Kevin Allsop

PREFACE

There are some historical events – the Battle of Hastings; the assassination of Archduke Franz Ferdinand; the invention of the World Wide Web – that had an enormous and tangible effect on our world. Yet there are millions of other pieces of the past that are less well remembered. Though they may not be as obvious as the glaring spotlights of conquest and invention, these candle flames of history still provide a valuable and fascinating illumination of the past.

One of the greatest challenges in writing this book was deciding which event to focus on for a particular day. Equally as difficult was the decision over which events to ignore. I assume that, when Billy Joel composed his 1989 hit song 'We Didn't Start the Fire', he faced a similar problem. The song tells the history of the world he had grown up in through a broadly chronological list of 119 events, inventions, and personalities.

The first thing that probably jumps out to anyone listening to the song is that Billy Joel's view of the modern world is dominated by America. Yet that shouldn't be much of a surprise. We are all affected by cultural and geographical proximity, which means we are more likely to assign significance to those things that have tangibly affected our existence or have similarities to those things that are familiar. Billy Joel, who grew up in the Bronx in the 1950s, demonstrates this perfectly in his song by featuring major international events alongside references to cultural milestones such as baseball, pop music, and cinema that we part of his life as he grew up. Through those 119 historical references, Billy Joel tells his story of the world. However, it's important to emphasise that it is *his* world. The lyrics were obviously affected by the ability to fit within a rhythm and rhyme structure, but more than anything they were affected by his judgements of historical significance.

The case is similar with this book. I have made a concerted effort to write about a diverse range of events, times, and places. Nevertheless, my ability to judge an event's significance and explain it in a clear and accessible way has relied on me having some existing knowledge and understanding of the context. It therefore sometimes proved best to write confidently about an event I already had some contextual understanding of, rather than one from a culture, or a period of history, of which I had only limited existing knowledge.

Assessing the historical significance of events also relies heavily on personal judgement, and I readily admit that my decisions may be different to those of someone else. While there are a range of recognised criteria for historical significance, the decisions regarding events in this book have often been based on how much impact the event had on people at the time, and since – whether directly or indirectly.

The decision to include, or exclude, events has also relied on a more practical aspect: the need to find those that are known to have occurred on a specific day. In practice, the Romano-Christian calendar dominates such a chronologically. Consequently, some historic cultures and regions of the world are dramatically underrepresented as it is impossible to pinpoint the precise modern equivalent date on which events in those places occurred.

In the case of the pre-Islamic Arabian Peninsula, the Muslim calendar has been used since what the Romano-Christian calendar would call the 7th century. However, it took another 400 years for Islamic astronomers to successfully align the start of that calendar to a fixed date on the Western calendar. Furthermore, since an Islamic month is a lunar month – and can therefore vary in length – Arab scholars had to do their calculations by creating a 'tabular' Islamic calendar using arithmetical rules to determine the length of the months. They then projected this backwards to the foundation of the Islamic calendar in order to identify the equivalent date on the Christian calendar.

The fact that this was a later mathematical calculation means that the earliest Islamic dates are unlikely to be completely accurate, since the mathematical month may not truly align with the lunar observations that were made at the time. Attempting to pinpoint *pre*-Islamic events to a specific date on the modern calendar is therefore virtually impossible, and this sadly means that they are underrepresented in this book.

The reason that we don't face this problem with ancient European events is due to the Roman Empire. Virtually all modern scholars draw on the work of ancient Roman scholar Marcus Terentius Varro, who calculated that the city of Rome was founded on precisely the 21st April 753 BCE. He backdated a timeline of Roman history by using a list of Roman consuls, together with some historical license to allow for periods of dictatorial rule. Varro's timeline is therefore known to contain some inaccuracies, but nobody has ever provided sufficiently trustworthy evidence to propose a different calendar. His system is the standard chronology and, due to the long-lasting impact of the Roman Empire, the calendar system that it spawned continues to dominate the world to this day.

This book is therefore a single snapshot of one person's judgements of historical significance, which have been influenced by a multitude of different factors. I hope that that, for each of the 366 events featured in the book, you go away feeling that the account was both interesting and enlightening. Moreover, I hope that the book helps you to add extra threads to the rich and colourful tapestry of world history to binds us all together.

Scott Allsop
Bucharest, 2019

JANUARY

JANUARY
1
1772

The first traveller's cheques, in the form of a 'circular note' issued by a bank, went on sale in London.

Devised by the Scottish banker Robert Herries, circular notes were an immediate hit with young British aristocrats who needed to obtain foreign currency while exploring Europe on the Grand Tour. They needed an easy way to access to their British-based wealth, and Herries' creation provided it.

Having secured the cooperation of a number of continental banks, Herries was able to ensure that his customers could withdraw local currency in more than 80 European cities. The notes were issued against the payment of cash to the bank in London, meaning that the customer was freed from the burden of travelling with gold. Since the notes had to be countersigned by the recipient they also provided much greater security. Any unused notes could be returned to the issuing bank in London and the cash refunded.

A century later, and just two years after the first round-the-world tour, the British company Thomas Cook began issuing their own circular notes to help customers manage the constant change of currencies. This idea was developed further by American Express, who launched the first branded Travelers Cheque in 1891. It is said that the system was developed by American Express employee Marcellus Flemming Berry after the company's founder, J. C. Fargo, experienced problems obtaining funds on a European trip.

The popularity of traveller's cheques has declined in recent years due to the creation of pre-paid currency cards alongside debit and credit cards. Yet their fundamental aim remains the same as the circular notes introduced by Robert Herries in 1772. They all allow travellers to access funds while away from home.

JANUARY

2

1980

In response to Soviet military intervention in Afghanistan, Jimmy Carter brought the period of détente to an end.

President Carter had come to power in January 1977 in the midst of a period of a reduction in tensions between the USA and the USSR. The Strategic Arms Limitation Talks that began under Richard Nixon and resulted in the Anti-Ballistic Missile Treaty are often presented as one of détente's greatest achievements. This led to a second round of talks that sought to build on the original agreement and begin physically reducing the number of nuclear weapons held by each country.

Despite such shows of cooperation, there continued to be tension between East and West that manifested itself through involvement in proxy wars. At the same time Carter openly criticised the Soviet Union's human rights record, but it wasn't until the USSR's invasion of Afghanistan in December 1979 that the relationship critically deteriorated.

Hoping to send a strong message to the USSR that military intervention in Afghanistan was unacceptable, on 2 January 1980 Carter formally requested the Senate postpone ratification of the SALT II treaty that he and Brezhnev had signed in June. He also recalled the US ambassador from Moscow while Jody Powell, the White House Press Secretary, described the Soviet action as 'a serious threat to peace.'

The Soviet refusal to withdraw resulted in the imposition of US trade sanctions, alongside a boycott of the 1980 Summer Olympics that were held in Moscow. At the same time the CIA began to covertly fund and train anti-Soviet fighters in Afghanistan, which directly contributed to the later rise of the repressive Taliban regime.

JANUARY

3

1870

Construction began on the Brooklyn Bridge.

Although numerous suspension bridges had been built prior to the Brooklyn Bridge, nothing came close to the almost 1,600 foot span across the East River from Brooklyn to Manhattan. German immigrant John Augustus Roebling was attracted to the challenge after he developed a system to stabilise large span bridges using a steel web truss down each side. He was appointed chief engineer but, six months before construction began, died of a tetanus infection after a boat crushed his toes while he was surveying the site.

Roebling's son Washington took over the project but he too suffered a terrible injury while inspecting the foundations. In order to secure a stable foundation for the towers of the bridge, large watertight timber caissons were sunk to the river bed. These enormous upside down boxes were filled with compressed air to keep out the water, and men known as sandhogs then entered to dig away the sediment until they reached bedrock.

The compressed air inside the caissons gave the workers terrible headaches but, more dangerously, dissolved high levels of gases into their bloodstream. Exiting the caisson caused these gases to expand, leading to incredible pain, paralysis, and even death. Washington Roebling himself was struck down with 'caisson disease', now better known as 'the bends', and was confined to his home for much of the bridge's construction. His wife, Emily, took over many of his duties and successfully oversaw the completion of the project.

The bridge was officially opened on May 24, 1883, 13 years after construction began. The total cost was over $15 million, more than twice the original estimate, but well over a century later it still remains a vital link for New Yorkers.

American inventor Samuel Colt received the first order for his revolver firearms from the US government.

Samuel Colt was born into a wealthy Connecticut family and, by the time he was eighteen, had developed a keen interest in science and technology. Inspired by the capstan ratchet mechanisms he had seen while on board the brig *Corvo*, he later created his indexing revolver mechanism that allowed a single-barrelled firearm to hold and fire multiple rounds.

Having developed his fortune by touring the United States delivering nitrous oxide demonstrations, in 1835 Colt travelled to Britain where he patented the prototype revolver he had commissioned gunsmith John Pearson to build. After securing the European patent he then returned to America where he was granted his United States patent.

Despite having exclusive rights to manufacture the first practical revolver, Colt initially struggled to sell his new weapon. However, the outbreak of the Mexican-American War saw Captain Samuel Walker of the Texas Rangers approach Colt with an order for 1,000 revolvers on 4 January 1847. This was dependent on a number of changes to the original design, including increasing the capacity from 5 to 6 shots and being powerful enough 'to kill a man with a single shot'.

This new design, known as the Colt Walker, proved immensely popular and helped Colt finance a new factory in Hartford. Working with his chief mechanic, Elisha K. Root, he developed precision moulds and workshop equipment that ensured each component was an exact replica of every other. This meant that parts were interchangeable, resulting in one of the world's first industrial assembly lines.

JANUARY

5

1066

A succession crisis was sparked following the death of Edward the Confessor, the last Anglo-Saxon king of England.

Edward was crowned King of England in 1042 and earned a reputation as a pious and gentle ruler largely thanks to later religious writers in Westminster who lobbied for his canonisation. The term 'Confessor' was consequently applied to recognise him having lived a saintly life but dying without martyrdom.

Edward's death instead came about after a period of illness that began sometime after the Northumbrian revolt of October 1065 that led to the exile of Tostig, one of the king's favourites. Assumed by many to have been the effect of a series of strokes, Edward died on 5 January the following year having missed the consecration of his new church, Westminster Abbey, on 28 December.

His death was problematic because Edward and his wife, Edith, had never had any children. Numerous explanations for this have been put forward, but ultimately the fact that he died without an obvious heir produced a succession crisis that was to bring about the end of Anglo-Saxon rule in England.

At the time there were no clear rules for royal succession and, although the opinion of the previous king was a factor in deciding the next ruler, it relied just as much on support from the Church and the nobility and the contender's own military might. While Harold Godwinson, the strongest of England's earls, claimed that Edward had entrusted the kingdom to him while on his deathbed, William of Normandy maintained that Edward had previously promised the throne to him. Along with Harald Hardrada, a Dane with direct links to the kings who had ruled England before Edward, the stage was set for a series of battles that culminated at Hastings in October 1066.

JANUARY
6
1975

Rock band Led Zeppelin were banned from Boston after fans rampaged through the Boston Garden arena.

Led Zeppelin were due to release their sixth studio album, *Physical Graffiti*, in February and the announcement of the supporting tour generated incredible excitement among fans. Determined to get their hands on a ticket to the Boston show on 4 February, more than 2,000 fans began queueing along Causeway Street outside the Boston Garden venue from 5pm on 6 January in anticipation of the sale windows opening the next morning.

Such lines were not unusual but, as the temperature began to drop towards freezing, it became evident that the blue denim jeans and jean jackets worn by the waiting fans would not keep them warm. In response, ticket-office manager Steven Rosenblatt decided to open the hall's lobby and allow people to wait there instead.

Author Stephen Davis, who wrote two books about Led Zeppelin's 1975 tour, reveals that the crowd began to grow increasingly boisterous as they passed around cheap alcohol. Then around midnight, during a security shift change, some of those waiting broke through the doors to the concert hall itself. They broke into the beer concession stands and set fire to the wooden bleachers, the rampage only beginning to calm down when the venue opened the ticket windows hours ahead of schedule at 2.30am.

To disperse the remains of the crowd riot police were called in, and by 6am the venue was an empty but smouldering mess. Boston mayor Kevin H. White subsequently cancelled the concert and banned Led Zeppelin from performing in Boston for five years. They ended up never playing in the city again, since the band broke up after the death of drummer John Bonham in 1980.

JANUARY

7

1785

The first aerial crossing of the English Channel was conducted by Frenchman Jean-Pierre Blanchard and American John Jeffries in a gas-filled balloon.

Born to a peasant family in Normandy, Blanchard fled to Paris as a teenager. Here he developed an interest in science and, following the Montgolfier brothers' successful flight of a hot air balloon in 1783, turned his attention to the new craze. On 2 March the following year Blanchard made his first successful flight at the Champs de Mars in Paris using a hydrogen-filled balloon.

Desperate to achieve fame and fortune, Blanchard moved to London in August 1784 where the population had not yet become caught up in 'balloonomania'. Blanchard quickly convinced a group of financiers to support him and, alongside the wealthy Dr John Jeffries, Blanchard planned the first aerial crossing of the Channel.

Having provided the necessary funds, Jeffries insisted that he should accompany Blanchard on the flight from Dover to Calais. Unwilling to share the certain fame Blanchard concealed lead weights in his clothes in an attempt to persuade Jeffries that the balloon would be too heavy to carry both of them, but the American discovered the deception and was able to take his place on board.

Soon after departing England, the pair were forced to throw out their ballast and cargo. This included a propeller and a set of oars with which they had hoped to 'row' through the air. Barely skimming the tops of the waves, they later urinated over the side in an attempt to reduce the weight before opting to discard their clothes. When they touched down in a forest near Calais, they were wearing nothing but their underwear and the cork life jackets that they had brought in case they crashed into the sea.

JANUARY

8

1790

American President George Washington delivered the very first State of the Union address to Congress.

Washington's presidency began on 30 April 1789, and he believed it was vital to quickly establish precedents implementing the terms of the Constitution. His address, which at the time was referred to as the Annual Message to a Joint Session of Congress, was designed to fulfil the Constitution's requirement that the President 'shall from time to time give to the Congress Information of the State of the Union, and recommend to their Consideration such Measures as he shall judge necessary and expedient'.

Washington knew the importance of establishing the role of the president in the new nation, and was initially wary of appearing to be too monarchical. Consequently the address he delivered on 8 January was carefully balanced to praise the work of Congress while recommending the issues he wished them to address in the near future. These included establishing a uniform system of currency and weights, formalising naturalisation to encourage foreigners to become American citizens, and even the cautious suggestion to create a standing army.

In his address the President also highlighted the importance of the welfare of existing citizens through promoting public education, while encouraging Congress to address the pressing financial issues of public credit and the national debt.

Washington's speech was well received by both the Senate and the House, while many newspapers printed the address in full and wrote positively about it. The annual message only became known as the State of the Union Address under President Harry Truman, but Washington's precedent nevertheless continues to this day.

JANUARY

9

1349

The Jewish population of Basel were massacred amidst accusations that they were responsible for causing the Black Death.

The Black Death, which is estimated to have killed between 75 and 200 million people in the middle of the fourteenth century, arrived in central and western Europe in 1348. The pandemic spread through Savoy and soon began to kill people in the city of Basel.

Convinced that the Jews of the city were dying of the disease less frequently than the Christians, the local population soon began to accuse the Jews of poisoning the wells. Although accurate statistical evidence is lacking, numerous theories have been put forward to explain why Jews may have appeared to have suffered less from the disease. While one of these is based on the simple observation that Christians were less likely to see Jewish victims due to the fact they were buried in separate cemeteries, another suggests that strict Jewish dietary rituals meant that Jewish homes were much less appealing to the rats that are believed to have carried the plague.

Under pressure from the powerful guilds, many of whom had obtained confessions from local Jews under torture, the City Fathers responded with extraordinary ruthlessness. Having separated children from their parents, the adult Jews were taken to a specially constructed wooden barn on an island in the Rhine. Here they were shackled together and the structure set on fire, leaving the victims to burn alive. The surviving children were forcefully converted to Christianity, while Jews were banned from the city for 200 years.

The Black Death itself continued to ravage Europe for around another four years, killing between 30 and 60 per cent of the entire population of the continent.

JANUARY

10

49 BCE

Julius Caesar crossed the Rubicon with the 13th Legion during his march on Rome that led to the Roman Civil War.

Julius Caesar had joined with Pompey and Crassus in 60 BCE to form a political alliance known as the First Triumvirate, in an attempt to put pressure on the Senate to pass bills in their favour. The following year he was elected Consul and began to push laws through with the support of his political allies.

After his consulship ended in 58 BCE, Caesar was able to secure for himself the governorship of a number of provinces that brought at first four legions of troops under his control. By 50 BCE he had conquered Gaul, but the First Triumvirate had collapsed. In Rome, the Senate had made Pompey sole consul and ordered Caesar to disband his army and return to Rome as a regular citizen.

Concerned that he would be prosecuted for historic crimes from his time as consul, Caesar instead chose to make his way to Rome with the 13th Legion. The small Rubicon River marked the border between Cisalpine Gaul and Italy, and crossing this with an army was a capital offence. Caesar knew that doing so would be seen as an act of war, and the phrase 'to cross the Rubicon' is now used to refer to actions that commit a person to a specific course.

In Caesar's case he crossed the Rubicon on 10 January 49 BCE, though the exact circumstances are widely debated. The Roman historian Suetonius later claimed that Caesar deliberated until a supernatural apparition prompted him to cross. Sources disagree over what he said next, though all versions involve a die being cast.

As Caesar approached Rome, Pompey and the Senate fled south. The subsequent civil war lasted for over four years, ending with Caesar's victory and him being declared dictator for life.

JANUARY
11
1569

The first recorded lottery in England was drawn.

The concept of a lottery, in which lots were drawn to determine a winner, had been around for centuries before Queen Elizabeth I chartered a prize draw to raise money for the 'reparation of the havens and strength of the Realme, and towardes such other publique good works'. The scheme itself was announced in 1566, at a time when England was seeking to expand its international trade. Income from the lottery was therefore used to fund improvements to the country's coastal infrastructure and the construction of new ships.

Unlike most modern lotteries, which seek to produce a profit, the value of Elizabeth's prize fund equalled the money raised through ticket sales. Each ticket was also guaranteed to win one of the available prizes, which ranged from silver plate and tapestries to a jackpot of £5,000. However, the fact that the draw didn't take place until nearly three years after the scheme's introduction effectively meant that the Crown benefited from a 3 year interest free loan.

400,000 tickets were put on sale at the cost of 10 shillings each, a cost that was far out of the reach of most ordinary people at the time, and which led to some forming syndicates in which they purchased a share of a single ticket. To entice purchases, all ticket holders were promised that they would be exonerated from any crimes they had committed other than murder, felonies, piracy or treason.

The draw itself was made outside the west wing of the old St Paul's Cathedral in London. Sadly the name of the grand prize winner has been lost, but ultimately the lottery paid off for Elizabeth. She was able to invest heavily in her navy and coastal defences, which proved vital in 1588 and the successful defeat of the Spanish Armada.

JANUARY
12
1967

Dr James Hiram Bedford became the first human to be cryonically preserved.

James Bedford had been a psychology professor at the University of California before developing kidney cancer that later metastasized to his lungs. He died, aged 73, in the early afternoon of 12 January 1967 at which point his body was packed in ice while the nursing home staff located the President of the Cryonics Society of California, Robert Nelson.

Nelson and the two other members of the cryonic 'suspension team', Robert Prehoda and Dr Dante Brunol, arrived around an hour after Bedford's death. They proceeded to inject him with dimethyl sulfoxide, a cryoprotectant chemical intended to protect his tissue from freezing damage, after which they transferred his body to a box insulated with foam.

Nelson later revealed how he initially kept Bedford's body, frozen using blocks of dry ice, in a garage in Topanga Canyon since his 'cryonic capsule' was not ready. Bedford was subsequently moved to the Cryo-Care Equipment Corporation in Phoenix, Arizona and then to a number of other locations before finally arriving at the Alcor Life Extension Foundation in 1982.

In the interim Bedford's wife and son faced lengthy and expensive legal challenges from other relatives over the contents of his will and his cryopreservation. The $100,000 Bedford had set aside for cryonics research was spent many times over and so, following the death of his wife Ruby in 1987, the Alcor Foundation assumed all financial responsibilities associated with his continued cryonic suspension. His frozen body remains with them now while research into reviving cryopreserved humans continues.

JANUARY
13
1842

Dr William Brydon of the British East India Company Army was the only survivor of an army of 4,500 men and 12,000 camp followers to reach safety at Jalalabad in Afghanistan.

Although it later emerged that a further 115 British officers and soldiers, along with their wives and children, had survived as hostages Brydon was the only Briton to have escaped from Kabul without being captured.

Part of the First Anglo-Afghan War, British troops had maintained a garrison in Kabul since 1839 following the restoration of the British-supported Shuja Shah. On 2 November 1841 a group of locals, under the leadership of Akbar Khan, launched an uprising against the occupying forces. The British commander General William Elphinstone, who had been called 'the most incompetent soldier who ever became general' by his contemporary General William Nott, did little to re-establish control and instead agreed to the British withdrawal to the garrison at Jalalabad.

Having handed over gunpowder, new muskets and canon to Akbar Khan in return for safe passage approximately 16,000 British soldiers and civilians left Kabul on 6 January 1842. They were soon set upon by Afghan tribes, and within three days 3,000 people had died while the column had only moved 25 miles. Freezing conditions and desertions further increased the losses so that by 11 January the army had been reduced to just 200 men. A final standoff at the Gandamak pass finished off much of the rest of the British army leaving only Brydon, who had earlier become separated from the remnants of the army, to make it to Jalalabad alone despite his own life-threatening injuries. On being asked what had happened to the rest of the army Brydon is said to have responded, 'I am the army'.

JANUARY
14
1973

Elvis Presley became the first solo entertainer to broadcast a live performance via satellite with *Aloha From Hawaii*.

Elvis Presley was renowned for his demanding schedule of live performances throughout the United States. By the early 1970s his manager, Colonel Tom Parker, had received numerous offers to stage international tours but turned down them all down since he was in America illegally and feared deportation if he ever attempted to leave.

Recognising the demand to see Elvis perform, Parker conceived the idea of an international broadcast after seeing Nixon's visit to China transmitted via satellite. While international satellite broadcasts had therefore taken place previously, such as the 1967 *Our World* special on which The Beatles performed 'All You Need is Love', *Aloha From Hawaii* was the first to feature a single headline performer.

Parker sold the rights to RCA who owned the NBC television network and, importantly, had access to satellites such as the recently-launched Intelsat IV F-4. NBC appointed experienced telecast director Marty Pasetta to oversee the project, whose criticism of previous Elvis concerts persuaded the star to lose weight and install a stage set that would make the performance more exciting.

The concert began at 12:30am on the morning of 14 January 1973. The 6,000 audience members at the Honolulu International Center received their tickets for free, but donated $75,000 towards the Kui Lee Cancer Fund. Elvis and his band then performed a combination of 23 classic songs and newer hits for an hour.

Contrary to the legends surrounding the concert, it was only shown live in six countries. Others broadcast a recording of the spectacular days or even months later, with NBC itself not airing the concert until April 4 due to a scheduling clash with the Super Bowl.

JANUARY
15
1919

21 people were killed and a further 150 were injured after 2.3 million gallons of molasses swept through North End in Boston, Massachusetts after a storage tank collapsed.

The 50 ft (15 m) tall tank on Commercial Street had been built in 1915 by the Purity Distilling Company to store molasses that were then fermented to produce industrial alcohol for liquor and munitions manufacturing. Demand for the latter had soared following the outbreak of the First World War, and the company had rushed to take advantage. The storage tank was built quickly and was already known to leak, since the metal used for its construction was poor quality and only half as thick as it needed to be to hold the intended quantity of molasses.

A warm shipment of molasses was added to the tank two days before the disaster, decreasing the overall viscosity of the contents and enabling it to flow faster while also increasing the pressure on the tank walls. It has since been suggested that the dramatic increase in air temperate from -17 to 5.0 °C over the course of the previous day may have also increased the speed of fermentation within the tank, adding further pressure from carbon dioxide.

The tank collapsed shortly after noon, and witnesses later recalled feeling the ground shake and hearing a variety of loud crashes followed by a sound similar to gunfire as the rivets shot out of the tank. A wave of molasses measuring over 15 feet swept down the street at 35 miles an hour, smashing houses and seriously damaging the support girders of a nearby elevated train track. Many of the victims were either crushed by the force of the wave or drowned in the sticky syrup. The youngest victims were just ten years old.

JANUARY

16

1412

Antipope John XXIII made the Medici Bank the official bank of the Papacy.

The upper-class Medici family had a history in banking that stretched back to the middle of the 14th Century, although the founding of the Medici Bank is usually dated to 1397 when Giovanni de' Medici opened his operation in the city state of Florence while maintaining an office in Rome.

Giovanni soon set about developing a close business relationship with Baldassarre Cossa, Pope Boniface IX's papal treasurer. Meanwhile the Catholic Church was mired in the Western Schism that saw multiple concurrent popes claiming to be St Peter's rightful successor. As Cossa secured further promotions the Medici Bank was never far away and, following Cossa's election as Pope John XXIII in 1410, Giovanni's bank became an important source of loans for the new pope.

Although John was acknowledged as pope by numerous European states including France, England, Bohemia, and Portugal, he was based in Pisa and faced competition from the Roman claimant Gregory XII. Keen to establish his authority, John borrowed thousands of florins from the Medici Bank to finance a military campaign. By January 1412 John had been forced to take out further loans and made the Medici the official bank of the Papacy.

In Rome, Gregory XII was protected by King Ladislaus of Naples who defeated John's army in 1413 and forced him to sign a peace treaty involving the payment of 95,000 florins. This transaction was, unsurprisingly, again handled by the Medici Bank which went on to become one of Europe's most powerful and influential institutions during the late medieval period.

JANUARY

17

1944

The Battle of Monte Cassino began when Allied forces launched the first of four attacks against the Gustav Line in Italy.

The Gustav Line, which together with the Bernhardt and Hitler lines formed a series of defences known as the Winter Line, had been established by the Germans and Italians to defend Rome from a northern advance by the Allies. The Allied forces had secured a foothold in Italy in Operation Avalanche the previous September, having first captured Sicily.

By early January 1944 the Allies had advanced a long way north, but their progress had been stopped by poor weather that forced them to approach Rome along Highway 6 that ran from Naples through the Liri valley. The southern entrance to the valley was dominated by the town of Cassino and overlooked by the Benedictine abbey of Monte Cassino.

Although the German army did not position defensive units in the abbey itself, the natural topography gave them a notable advantage over the Allies. Combined with minefields that had been laid in advance, the strong German position withstood the first assault that lasted for two and a half weeks and involved troops under British, American and French command attacking the position from three sides.

German forces finally withdrew on 17 May, and the following morning soldiers from the Polish 12th Podolian Cavalry Regiment raised a Polish flag over the ruins. The four assaults that made up the Battle of Monte Cassino had led to 55,000 Allied causalities and destroyed the ancient abbey. The treasures it contained had been evacuated to Rome in November 1943.

JANUARY

18

1919

The Paris Peace Conference convened to establish the terms of the peace after the First World War.

Fighting in the First World War ended on 11 November 1918 with the signing of the Armistice of Compiègne, but it wasn't until January that representatives of the victorious powers began formal peace negotiations. The delay was primarily due to the British Prime Minister, David Lloyd George, who called a general election prior to the negotiations. Consequently the conference began on the 48th anniversary of the proclamation of the German Empire. This was not lost on President Poincaré of France, who welcomed the delegates with a bitter verbal assault at Germany's expense.

While 27 nations were officially involved in the peace negotiations, the conference was dominated by the Big Four of Britain, France, the USA and Italy. However, each came with sometimes dramatically different demands, meaning the negotiators were regularly forced to compromise in order to agree the final terms. The hundreds of diplomats in Paris were divided into 52 commissions, and altogether held 1,646 sessions to discuss the terms of the peace treaties. Meanwhile the defeated nations were excluded from the conference until the draft treaties had been prepared.

The Paris Peace Conference is perhaps best known for producing the Treaty of Versailles that dealt with Germany, but the delegates created a total of five separate treaties that affected all the defeated nations. After the Treaty of Versailles in June 1919 came the treaties of Saint-Germain with Austria and Neuilly with Bulgaria. Trianon with Hungary, and Sèvres with Turkey were not completed until 1920, by which time the inauguration of the League of Nations had brought the conference to an end.

JANUARY

19

1917

A munitions factory in Silvertown in the East End of London exploded, killing 73 people and injuring over 400 more.

The Brunner Mond chemical factory had been built in 1893 to manufacture caustic soda and soda crystals. However, declining demand for caustic soda meant that production ceased in 1912 and parts of the factory stood idle. Due to a crippling shell shortage following the onset of the First World War, the War Office chose to use the spare capacity at the Silvertown site to purify TNT for explosive shells.

The chief scientist at the factory described the purification process as 'manifestly very dangerous' and the company bosses themselves tried to dissuade the government for going ahead with the plan. Despite these concerns, and the fact that the factory was situated in a highly populated area, the Silvertown plant began to produce TNT in September 1915 at a rate of approximately 9 long tons per day.

At 6.52pm on the evening of 19 January 1917, a fire that had broken out in another part of the factory reached the stores of TNT. Approximately 50 tonnes exploded, completely destroying the factory and many nearby buildings. The blast could be heard as far away as Sandringham in Norfolk while molten metal was strewn across several miles, some of which damaged a gasometer in Greenwich and caused a giant fireball as 200,000 cubic metres of gas caught fire.

Over 60,000 properties suffered some form of damage from the blast, but the loss of life was fortunately a lot lower than it could have been. The explosion took place in the early evening when there were not many people in the factory, and people had not yet gone to bed in the upstairs rooms of their homes that suffered the most damage.

JANUARY
20
1850

Robert McClure departed England with HMS *Investigator* to lead the first expedition to transit the Northwest Passage.

The Northwest Passage is the sea route linking the Atlantic and Pacific oceans through the Arctic. Europeans had sought to establish the presence of such a passage since the late medieval period as an alternative route to Asia and, by the middle of the 18th century, dozens of expeditions had tried but failed to find a route.

In 1845 the English explorer Sir John Franklin led a disastrous attempt to navigate the Northwest Passage. After his ships failed to return, further expeditions were sent to find him. Consequently, on 20 January 1850, the ships *Enterprise* and *Investigator* departed Plymouth for the Pacific to conduct their search from west to east.

The two ships became separated after navigating the Straits of Magellan. *Investigator*, under the command of Robert McClure, continued northwards and entered Arctic waters alone through the Bering Strait in August. Within a month the ship was trapped by ice and the crew began sledge expeditions. On 31 October, McClure confirmed he had sighted the Northwest Passage.

Investigator was trapped in the pack ice for three years before contact was made with a search party from HMS *Resolute* which had approached the Arctic from the east. *Investigator* was subsequently abandoned and the crew made their way to *Resolute* by sledge. Although *Resolute* itself was later abandoned to the ice, the crew managed to return to Britain where McClure received a knighthood.

The abandoned *Resolute* was later recovered by an American crew and given to Britain as a gesture of goodwill. When it was salvaged in 1879, the timbers were used to build the Resolute Desk that was given to the US President and currently resides in the Oval Office.

JANUARY

21

1981

The first DeLorean DMC-12 sports car, the car later used as the time machine in Back to the Future, rolled off the production line.

The DeLorean Motor Company was founded by engineer and automobile executive John DeLorean in 1975. The prototype DeLorean Safety Vehicle was completed in October 1976 with initial investment from celebrities including Johnny Carson and Sammy Davies Jr. Meanwhile DeLorean secured significant financial incentives from the Northern Ireland Development Agency to build the manufacturing plant in Dunmurry, a suburb of Belfast, in an attempt to cut unemployment and curb sectarian violence.

The factory was built in 1978 with production of the car scheduled to begin the following year. Subsequent engineering delays and budget overruns meant that work on the first units didn't officially begin until 1981. Built by an enthusiastic but largely inexperienced workforce, the first of the distinctively shaped DeLorean DMC-12s was completed on 21 January. Fitted with gull-wing doors and finished with stainless-steel body panels, the car's appearance was expected to be a unique selling point.

However, by the time the first cars were available a recession had hit the United States that had a devastating effect on new car sales. Combined with mediocre reviews and customer complaints about the quality of the finished vehicles, at least half of the 7,000 cars produced by February 1982 had not been sold. Although the company limped on for a few more months, the DeLorean Motor Company went bankrupt shortly after its owner was charged by the US government with trafficking cocaine. He was later acquitted, but DeLorean's reputation was irreparably damaged.

JANUARY

22

1808

The Portuguese royal family and more than 10,000 courtiers relocated to Brazil to escape the advancing Napoleonic forces.

The War of the Third Coalition, which had begun in 1803, saw the British government instigate a naval blockade of Napoléon's coastline. Following the collapse of the Holy Roman Empire in 1806 a new coalition was formed but, following the French defeat of Prussia at the Battle of Jena, Napoléon issued the Berlin Decree that created the Continental System to starve Britain of European trade.

Meanwhile the prince regent of Portugal, the future Dom João VI, refused to join the Continental System against Britain with whom the country had been allies since 1386. Frustrated, Napoléon ordered his army to invade. Under the command of French general Jean-Andoche Junot, a combined force of French and Spanish troops crossed the border into Portugal on 19 November.

Having anticipated the invasion, and on hearing that Napoléon planned to depose the ruling House of Braganza, the prince regent settled on a plan to escape to the Portuguese colony of Brazil. Sailing under protection of the British navy, the Portuguese fleet departed Lisbon on the morning of 29 November.

The royal family and their chests of royal treasures were joined by approximately 10,000 other people ranging from ministers to merchants. When their ships arrived at the port of Salvador in Brazil on 22 January the passengers were finally able to escape from the squalor that had plagued their 4,500 mile journey.

The royals stayed in Brazil until after the Liberal Revolution of 1820. Since then the changes made to Brazil's status following the royal family's relocation have been interpreted as representing 'the first step toward Brazilian independence'.

JANUARY
23
1900

British troops mounted a night-time attack on Spion Kop during the Second Boer War.

The Second Boer War saw the British Empire fight against the Afrikaans-speaking Dutch settlers of the South African Republic and the Orange Free State. The early months of the war saw the Boers inflict successive defeats on the British. After they began a crippling siege against the British at Ladysmith, a plan was made to attack the Boers and relieve the garrison.

The Boers had established a defensive line along the Tugela River approximately 20 miles outside Ladysmith. The centre of their line was overlooked by a 430 metre high hill known as Spion Kop, which roughly translates as 'Spy Hill'. The British planned to seize the hill under cover of darkness, and establish a commanding position over the Boer line and the route to Ladysmith.

General Sir Charles Warren selected Lieutenant Colonel Alexander Thorneycroft to lead the assault, which took place late on 23 January in thick mist. The British overwhelmed a small group of Boers on the hill and began to dig trenches on what they believed was the summit, though the rocky terrain on the hilltop meant they were very shallow and offered little protection.

When the mist began to lift the next morning the British were dismayed to find that they had only seized a plateau. They were surrounded on three sides by the Boers on higher terrain, and they began to bombard the British with ten shells every minute. Vicious fighting continued for the whole day but, shortly after nightfall, the Boers abandoned their positions on the summit. Thorneycroft was unaware that victory was in his grasp and ordered his own retreat. The Boers reoccupied the hilltop the following morning.

JANUARY

24

1908

The first instalment of Robert Baden-Powell's *Scouting for Boys* was published, triggering the Boy Scout movement.

Robert Baden-Powell had become a national hero as a result of his successful defence of the South African town of Mafeking during the Second Boer War. Baden-Powell's garrison survived the 217-day siege in part thanks to his recruitment of boys aged 12–15 who were trained to form the Mafeking Cadet Corp.

On his return to England, Baden-Powell found that his military field manual *Aids to Scouting* had found an audience amongst teachers and youth organisations who had begun to use it to train boys in skills such as tracking and observation. Encouraged by his friends, and inspired by Ernest Thompson Seton's *The Birchbark Roll of the Woodcraft Indians*, Baden-Powell subsequently decided to write a non-military version of his book specifically for boys.

Before *Scouting for Boys* was published, Baden-Powell first tested his approach with a diverse group of 21 boys on Brownsea Island in Poole Harbour, Dorset. The week-long camp in the summer on 1907 saw the first trials of what was to become the Patrol System as Baden-Powell and his assistants taught the boys a broad range of skills such as woodcraft, observation, and lifesaving techniques.

Following the success of the Brownsea camp, *Scouting for Boys* was published in six fortnightly instalments by Baden-Powell's friend, the newspaper magnate Sir Arthur Pearson. Beginning on 24 January 1908, it proved to be an immediate sensation and, within a matter months, Scout Troops had begun to form throughout Britain and its empire. The six instalments were then combined into a single book that went on sale in May and, with regular revisions, it has become one of the best-selling books of all time.

A patent for the first interactive electronic game was filed by physicists Thomas T. Goldsmith Jr. and Estle Ray Mann.

Goldsmith was the director of research at DuMont Laboratories in New Jersey where he was exploring the use of cathode ray tubes in television sets. It was during this period that he and Mann created their game, which was directly influenced by Second World War radar displays. The two scientists combined a cathode ray tube with an oscilloscope to allow a player to simulate launching an explosive shell at enemy targets in what they called The Cathode Ray Tube Amusement Device.

The patent stated that targets needed to be physically positioned on the screen of the device using transparent overlays. The player then used the controls of the oscilloscope to position a spot of light created by the CRT, much like the controls on an Etch A Sketch toy, in order to hit the target. When a switch was flicked the spot would move in a parabolic arc, mimicking the flight of a shell, at the end of which the light would become unfocused in imitation of an explosion. If the spread of the beam hit the target, the player scored a hit. Additional controls allowed the player to change the angle and trajectory of the light beam, and change the time delay before detonation.

Despite securing a patent for the device, the game never went into commercial production. The parts were too expensive and DuMont Laboratories were more interested in advancing television technology. Consequently The Cathode Ray Tube Amusement Device's place in video game history is negligible, and it is likely that later developers created their own games without any knowledge of the work done by Goldsmith and Mann.

JANUARY

26

1564

Pope Pius IV issued a Papal bull confirming the decrees of the Council of Trent that defined Catholic doctrine in the face of the Protestant Reformation.

In the aftermath of Martin Luther publishing his Ninety-Five Theses that challenged the practices of the Catholic Church, the German monk burned the Papal response, the bull *Exsurge Domine*, in 1520. Although Luther called for an ecumenical council to resolve the theological disputes, the idea wasn't seriously pursued until the election of Pope Paul III in 1534. With the support of the Holy Roman Emperor Charles V, a council eventually met for the first time in the Italian city of Trent or Trento on 15 March 1545.

The council met twenty-five times over the course of the next eighteen years, spanning the rule of three different Popes. During this time the council reached many decisions regarding Church doctrines, although Protestants were generally excluded from the proceedings. Even when they were permitted to attend they did not have the right to vote, further deepening the divisions.

By the time the council finally closed on 5 December 1563, all the Protestant disputes had been addressed and numerous ambiguities in Catholic doctrine and practice had been clarified. The resulting decisions, which had been agreed by the two hundred and fifteen members of the final session, were then sent to the Pope for confirmation.

Pope Pius IV issued the bull *Benedictus Deus* on 26 January 1564 in which he ratified the decrees and definitions of the council. In its wake the Roman Catholic Church began to eradicate the abuses that had motivated the early Protestants, propelling the Counter-Reformation and the resurgence of Catholicism.

JANUARY

27

1967

The Outer Space Treaty, which provides the basic framework on international space law, was opened for signatures in the United States, the Soviet Union, and the United Kingdom.

The full name of the agreement is 'Treaty on Principles Governing the Activities of States in the Exploration and Use of Outer Space, including the Moon and Other Celestial Bodies'. The document was drawn up by the Legal Subcommittee of the UN Committee on the Peaceful Uses of Outer Space that had been established by the United Nations General Assembly shortly after the Soviet Union launched its Sputnik 1 satellite in 1957.

The treaty consists of just 17 articles, all of which were intended to be flexible in order to adapt to new advances in space technology. At its core, though, are the key principals that underline all modern space exploration. These include an agreement that all exploration should be done 'for the benefit and in the interests of all countries' and that nobody has the right to claim celestial bodies as their own, in an attempt to avoid the frenetic imperialism of the nineteenth century. To avoid space becoming a new frontier for war, the treaty banned countries from placing weapons of mass destruction in space – though doesn't forbid conventional weapons.

107 countries are currently party to the treaty, although another 23 have signed it but not completed ratification. This makes it, in the words of Christopher Johnson, the space law adviser for the Secure World Foundation, 'the most important and most fundamental source of international space law'. Nations subsequently create their own specific legislation, but this draws on the 17 principles laid out in the Outer Space Treaty. As a result space exploration has remained entirely peaceful – for the time being at least.

JANUARY

28

1393

Charles VI of France danced in the *Bal des Ardents* in which four people died after their costumes caught fire.

Charles VI of France inherited the throne when he was 11 years old, but the government was dominated by his regents for a decade before he took up personal rule. The return of his father's trusted advisors brought renewed prosperity and respect for the crown, but Charles soon began experiencing extreme episodes of psychosis.

In response to the king's mental illness his doctor, Guillaume de Harsigny, stated that 'pleasure and forgetfulness will be better for him than anything else.' In response, the court began to organise extravagant festivities that included an elaborate masquerade to celebrate the third marriage of Charles' wife Queen Isabeau's lady-in-waiting, Catherine de Fastaverin.

Tradition dictated that a woman's remarriage should be marked with a charivari or mock-serenade and, on the suggestion of Huguet de Guisay, six nobles performed a frenzied dance while dressed as wood savages. They wore linen costumes soaked in resin or pitch and covered with flax and frazzled hemp to give the appearance of being covered in shaggy hair. These materials were highly flammable, so guests were forbidden from carrying torches close to the dancers.

Despite this decree the king's brother, Louis of Orléans, and Phillipe de Bar entered the hall carrying torches after the performance had begun. The exact details are unclear, but it is recorded that a spark ignited one of the dancers which quickly set fire to others. The king was saved by Joan, Duchess of Berry, who covered him with her skirt to shield him from the sparks while a second dancer jumped into an open vat of wine to extinguish the flames. The remaining four dancers died horrific deaths.

JANUARY

29

1942

Desert Island Discs, **Britain's longest-running radio programme, was first broadcast by the BBC.**

Devised by the English radio broadcaster and producer Roy Plomley in November 1941, each episode of *Desert Island Discs* features an interview with a celebrity who imagines that they have been cast away on a desert island with only a limited number of home comforts. In the early years they were permitted to choose eight songs to take with them, although a few years after the programme's inception castaways were also allowed to take one book and one luxury item, in addition to a copy of the *Complete Works of Shakespeare* and an appropriate religious or philosophical work such as the Bible.

Plomley was commissioned to create the new radio programme by the BBC's Head of Popular Record Programmes, Leslie Perowne. Just two months after he pitched the idea, he found himself in the bomb-damaged studio at Maida Vale conducting the very first interview with popular entertainer Vic Oliver who chose Chopin's Étude No.12 in C minor, 'Revolutionary', as his first piece of music.

The first series was originally commissioned to run on the BBC Forces Programme for eight weeks but, excluding a break between 1946-51, has remained on air for 42 weeks a year ever since. Plomley himself presented the programme until his death in 1985, in which time he recorded 1,791 episodes. He was succeeded as presenter by Michael Parkinson.

Desert Island Discs still features the same theme music, 'By the Sleepy Lagoon' by Eric Coates which is overlaid with sounds of herring gulls to conjure up the feeling of being by the sea. Some listeners, however, continue to take issue with this sound effect since herring gulls are not known to congregate near tropical islands.

Adolf Hitler was appointed Chancellor of Germany by President Paul von Hindenburg.

Hitler's rise to power was neither immediate nor particularly expected, especially as he had been imprisoned for a treasonous attempt to overthrow the Weimar Government in 1923. His incarceration in Landsberg Prison gave him the opportunity to redraw his blueprint for seizing power and, on his release, he set about rebuilding the Nazi Party as a legitimate political organisation.

It wasn't until the Great Depression that the Nazis truly emerged as a mainstream force. Germany faced a particularly dire economic situation which the Weimar government, under Chancellor Brüning, responded to by cutting government spending and benefits. Rather than solving the problem this actually made the situation worse and seriously damaged the public's trust in the government. By 1932 six million Germans were out of work.

This desperate situation saw a dramatic increase in support for the Nazis. In 1932 Hitler capitalised on this growing national appeal to stand in the Presidential election against Hindenburg. Although Hitler lost the election with 13 million votes to Hindenburg's 19 million, the election campaign had secured the Nazis enormous publicity. Meanwhile the beleaguered government struggled on.

By the end of 1932, ex-Chancellor Franz von Papen began arguing that Hitler and the 196 Nazis in the Reichstag could form a majority and get government moving again. Hindenburg reluctantly agreed to make Hitler the Chancellor based on the assumption that, by ensuring only a few Nazis were in the Cabinet and von Papen himself was Vice Chancellor, the Nazis could be controlled. Hitler was formally appointed German Chancellor on 30th January 1933.

JANUARY

31

1983

It became compulsory for all drivers and front-seat passengers in the United Kingdom to wear seat belts.

The modern 3-point seat belt was created by Swedish inventor Nils Bohlin, who was a safety engineer for car manufacturer Volvo. His creation was first fitted as a standard item to the Volvo 122 in 1959, after which the company made the patent available to other car manufacturers for free.

Australia was the first country to mandate the wearing of seat belts. While all British cars manufactured after 1967 had to have seat belts fitted, it took twelve attempts for legislation to be passed through parliament to make it a requirement to actually wear them.

Figures released at the time placed the number of road deaths in Britain at 6,000. William Rodgers, who served as the Secretary of State for Transport in the previous government, claimed that wearing seat belts could have saved upwards of 1,000 of these lives. Yet even in the face of these figures, which were not widely disputed, critics of the new law accused the government of infringing on personal freedoms and operating a nanny state.

The government, along with organisations such as the Automobile Association and the Royal Society for the Prevention of Accidents, invested heavily in pre-legislation advertising campaigns. These are believed to have increased the voluntary seat belt wearing rate to around 50%, while surveys conducted in the days after the law came into force showed that over 90% of people were now wearing them. The penalty for not doing so was a £50 fine.

The first year of the law also saw the number of road deaths drop by nearly 500 and, having been trialled for three years, the compulsory wearing of seat belts was made permanent in 1986.

FEBRUARY

FEBRUARY

1

1960

The Greensboro sit-ins began when four black students sat at the 'whites only' lunch counter in the Woolworth department store.

In 1960 over a quarter of the population of the North Carolina city of Greensboro was black. The state had a range of segregation laws in place that generally left them with poorer quality facilities than their white counterparts and denied many the right to vote. This segregation permeated throughout daily life thanks to numerous Jim Crow laws. Determined to draw attention to the injustice of the situation, students Ezell Blair, Jr., Franklin McCain, Joseph McNeil, and David Richmond planned their simple yet effective protest.

After buying some small items from the Woolworth department store in Greensboro, the four students then took seats at the segregated lunch counter. The counter staff, in line with company policy, refused to serve them and later called the police after the Greensboro Four, as they became known, refused to leave. However, as the men had not taken any provocative action the police were unable to intervene, and they stayed seated at the counter until the store closed that evening.

The sit-in continued the next day as more black students joined the protest. Encouraged by local press coverage that soon became national, similar protests soon broke out at other segregated lunch counters across America. Despite this pressure, many stores refused to change their policies and it wasn't until 25 July that the lunch counter at Woolworth's in Greensboro was finally integrated. The protests had been front-page news around the country and went on to spur the desegregation of hundreds of public spaces across the United States.

A potential diphtheria epidemic in Alaska was avoided after a dogsled relay transported vials of antitoxin 674 miles in five and a half days in the 'Great Race of Mercy'.

The town of Nome lies just 2 degrees south of the Arctic Circle and, at the time of the diphtheria outbreak, approximately 10,000 people lived in and around the town. The town's sole doctor, Curtis Welch, had ordered diphtheria antitoxin to replace the expired stocks in the hospital, but the shipment did not make it to Nome before the port on the Bering Sea closed for the winter.

In December 1924 Dr Welch diagnosed a young boy with tonsillitis, having originally dismissed the possibility of it being diphtheria since nobody else had displayed symptoms of this highly contagious disease. The child died soon after, but his mother refused to allow Welch to perform an autopsy, meaning that other children caught and died of the disease before Welch was formally able to diagnose diphtheria in mid-January.

On 21 January the town council imposed a quarantine and put out an urgent call for antitoxin, which was in Anchorage. With the fierce winter conditions making aircraft delivery impossible, the decision was made to transport the valuable cargo using a dogsled relay. The first of twenty mushers involved in the relay, 'Wild Bill' Shannon collected the package at 9pm on 27 January and immediately set off on the first leg in a temperature of −46°C. The longest and most hazardous leg, stretching 91 miles, was completed by Norwegian-born Leonhard Seppala and his lead dog Togo.

At 5.30am on 2 February the serum arrived in Nome with Gunnar Kaasen and his lead dog Balto. Every ampule remained intact, and within three weeks the quarantine was lifted.

FEBRUARY

3

1961

Operation Looking Glass began flying an Airborne Command Post above the United States 24 hours a day.

As Cold War tensions between the USA and the USSR intensified at the start of the 1960s, the American military created an intricate failsafe system to coordinate its strategic and nuclear arsenal in case of a nuclear attack. While multiple facilities existed on the ground, Looking Glass provided an additional airborne node in case all these ground centres were somehow wiped out.

The name Looking Glass was chosen since the airborne fleet mirrored operations on the ground. Consisting of specially equipped EC-135 aircraft, Looking Glass flew out of Offutt Air Force Base in Nebraska, the headquarters of the Strategic Air Command. From the moment the first aircraft took off on 3 February 1961, a Looking Glass plane flew above the United States 24 hours a day for the next 29 years, except for a brief interruption in March 1980.

Each aircraft was crewed by one of seven operational teams consisting of up to 20 skilled individuals known as battle staff. In the event of a devastating nuclear attack that wiped out all ground control centres, the Airborne Emergency Action Officer (AEAO) could assume full authority to coordinate a counterattack. This included the ability to direct bombers and launch intercontinental ballistic missiles using the radio-controlled Airborne Launch Control System. This ability to retaliate was well known to the Soviets, and consequently served as an additional deterrent to any potential attack.

Although Looking Glass's continuous airborne alert was discontinued on 24 July 1990, the planes and crews continued their 24-hour alert from the ground but with the ability to take off at a moment's notice. A similar system continues to function today.

FEBRUARY

4

1555

John Rogers became the first English Protestant martyr under Mary I after he was burnt at the stake.

John Rogers was educated at Cambridge, after which he became a Catholic priest. As the Reformation began to take hold, Rogers questioned his vocation and subsequently resigned his ministry. He moved to Antwerp in 1534 where he met William Tyndale who had published his English translation of the New Testament a few years earlier.

Tyndale was instrumental in converting Rogers to Protestantism, after which he married Adriana de Weyden with whom he had several children. Just a few months later his friend Tyndale was arrested and executed for heresy, and Rogers continued his friend's work to produce a complete edition of the Bible in English. Rogers combined Tyndale's New Testament with the parts of the Old Testament that he had been able to translate before his arrest, and used the translation of Myles Coverdale for the remaining books of the Old Testament and the Apocrypha.

The completed Bible was published in 1537 under the pseudonym Thomas Matthew, and immediately gained the support of Thomas Cranmer who managed to persuade Chancellor Thomas Cromwell to secure a license for it from King Henry VIII. Rogers stayed in Europe, including time at the University of Wittenberg, for a number of years afterwards.

He returned to England in 1548 but, following the accession of the Catholic Mary I, he became an outspoken proponent of Reformation principals. Having been sent to Newgate Prison in 1554, Rogers was sentenced to death the following January. He was burned at the stake at Smithfield, the first victim of the Marian persecutions.

FEBRUARY

5

1958

An American Mark 15 thermonuclear bomb was lost off Tybee Island near Savannah, Georgia following an in-air collision.

On the afternoon of 4 February 1958, two B-47 bombers took off on a routine Cold War training mission from Homestead Air Force Base in Florida. The aircraft, under the command of Major Howard Richardson, each carried a Mark 15 thermonuclear hydrogen bomb to ensure the handling of the planes reflected what pilots would experience in a real situation.

The simulated combat mission saw the crew fly for more than ten hours over the United States. During this time, they refuelled over the Gulf of Mexico before activating an electronic signal over a predetermined target in Georgia to imitate the release of their deadly payload. Having completed their mission, they turned for home.

At around 2am on the morning of 5 February, the B-47s were intercepted by three F-86 aircraft on their own training mission. One of the fighter planes collided with the B-47 flown by Major Richardson, forcing the pilot of the F-86 to eject while the B-47 was seriously damaged. Struggling to control his aircraft, and fearful of the risk of a catastrophic explosion in case of a hard emergency landing with the Mark 15 still on board, Richardson was given permission to jettison the bomb, which he did from around 7,000 feet over Tybee Island in Savannah.

While there are conflicting claims over whether the bomb was a fully functional weapon or had been fitted with a dummy lead core, it still contained 400-pounds of conventional explosives and a quantity of weapons-grade uranium that could have caused significant damage. All attempts to locate the bomb have proven unsuccessful, so its final resting place – and its condition – remain a mystery.

FEBRUARY

6

1778

France and the United States signed the first two treaties ever negotiated by the American government, and which formally recognised the independence of the United States.

Keen to exact revenge on Britain for the Seven Years' War, France had begun to send secret military aid to the American Continental Army even before the Continental Congress declared independence. With French finance and equipment coming in through the fictitious Roderigue Hortalez and Company, founding Father John Adams began to draft a possible future treaty with France. Confident of securing a formal alliance with King Louis XVI, the Continental Congress sent a delegation to France under Benjamin Franklin in late 1776.

Franklin first met with the French Foreign Minister, the Comte de Vergennes, on 28 December where he sought to obtain further French support for the fledgling American government. However, he struggled to secure a formal alliance due to French concerns over recent British victories in the New York and New Jersey campaign.

The British defeat at the Battle of Saratoga in October the following year caused the French government to reconsider their position and reopen talks with the United States. These negotiations led to the Treaty of Amity and Commerce and the Treaty of Alliance. Signed in Paris on 6 February 1778, the first of these documents formally recognised the independence of the United States and established a trading relationship that defied the Navigation Acts which had restricted colonial trade to England. The Treaty of Alliance was consequently signed to provide mutual military support in case the Treaty of Amity and Commerce caused Britain to break its existing peace agreement with France and go to war.

FEBRUARY

7

1495

Dominican friar Girolamo Savonarola led the burning of thousands of objects in the Bonfire of the Vanities.

Savonarola became one of the Renaissance's most influential clerics after Lorenzo de' Medici, the *de facto* ruler of Florence, invited him to the city in 1490. He had already established himself as a passionate preacher who championed the need for reform and repentance, and he soon began drawing enormous crowds who gathered to hear him speak out against the corruption and excesses of the Renaissance.

Savonarola's growing power coincided with the decline of the Medici family who were effectively overthrown in 1494. In the absence of the city's most powerful political dynasty, Savonarola assumed the position of leader and soon turned his attention to ridding the city of luxuries and vice.

As part of his program of reform, he urged the public to surrender luxurious objects to be destroyed. In the weeks leading up the Bonfire of the Vanities, thousands of works of art and other items were collected including paintings, manuscripts, and musical instruments. Some sources even suggest that the renowned artist Sandro Botticelli handed over some of his own work.

This collection of items, while considered objectionable by Savonarola, included priceless and irreplaceable works of art. Yet, despite their cultural significance, they were all consigned to the flames in the Piazza della Signoria on 7 February 1495.

Over the next two years Savonarola's sermons grew increasingly critical of the Church in Renaissance Italy, attracting the attention of Pope Alexander VI who had already banned him from preaching. He was excommunicated in 1497 and executed the following year.

FEBRUARY

8

1904

Japanese destroyers began preparations for a torpedo attack on the Russian Far East Fleet in Port Arthur that sparked the Russo-Japanese War.

Port Arthur was a fortified naval base in the south of Manchuria that had been leased to Russia since 1898. After crushing the Boxer Rebellion as part of an eight-nation coalition, Russia infuriated Japan, which claimed parts of Manchuria within its own sphere of influence, by refusing to remove its troops. Japan was willing to recognise Russian dominance in Manchuria in return for access to Korea, but an agreement could not be reached. Japan broke off diplomatic relations on 6 February 1904.

Three hours before the Russian government received the declaration of war on 8 February, the Japanese Imperial Navy conducted a pre-emptive strike. Japanese Admiral Tōgō sent ten destroyers to Port Arthur where their torpedoes damaged two of the Russian fleet's most powerful battleships as well as a cruiser. Although none of the ships were sunk due to the effectiveness of torpedo nets in the port, the Russian fleet was seriously weakened as the ships that had been hit were put out of action. The attack was halted at around 2am the following morning after the Russians turned on their searchlights and began to return fire.

At around 8am Admiral Tōgō sent a reconnaissance mission through the morning mist to inspect Port Arthur. With his observers reporting that the Russian fleet had been crippled by the previous night's attack, the Japanese fleet were ordered to launch an attack on the port. In reality the reconnaissance was wrong, and the Russians were prepared for battle. The Battle of Port Arthur resulted in ships on both sides suffering damage before the Japanese fleet retreated.

FEBRUARY

9

1895

Volleyball was invented by William G. Morgan, the Director of Physical Education at the YMCA in Holyoke, Massachusetts.

Morgan had attended the YMCA's Springfield College where he had met James Naismith, the inventor of basketball. After graduating Morgan continued to work for the YMCA and soon took the position of Director of Physical Education in nearby Holyoke.

Having noticed that the speed of basketball made it too challenging for weaker men and older athletes, Morgan set about devising a new game. Drawing on basketball's original aims of being a sport that could be played inside with minimal physical contact, Morgan later wrote that 'tennis occurred to me, but this required rackets, balls, a net and other equipment, so it was eliminated – but the idea of a net seemed a good one'.

Naming his game 'mintonette', Morgan took a year to refine the rules before staging an exhibition match. This took place at the 1896 YMCA Physical Directors Conference at Springfield after Morgan impressed the director of the professional physical education training school, D. Luther Gulick. The game received a positive reception from the delegates including Dr Alfred T. Halstead who suggested renaming it to Volley Ball to better reflect the objective of the game. The two words were eventually combined to form Volleyball in 1952.

After the positive response to the exhibition game Morgan continued to experiment with the rules, firstly by raising the height of the net and then by trying different types of balls to achieve the optimum weight and speed. Sporting goods company A.G. Spalding & Bros. eventually created a new type of ball that achieved the perfect balance he was seeking and, within just a few years, Morgan's game had begun to spread around the world.

FEBRUARY

10

1355

The St Scholastica's Day Riot began, leading to the deaths of 63 students and around 30 townspeople in Oxford.

Tensions between university students and the locals of Oxford had been building for some time before violence broke out. The townspeople were frustrated with the University's privileges, while students felt that local businesses exploited them by charging higher prices for rents, goods, and services.

On 10 February 1355 a group of students were drinking in the central Swindlestock Tavern. When they complained to the landlord about the quality of the drinks he had brought them, he responded with 'stubborn and saucy language' which prompted the two sides to exchange 'snappish words'. One of the students, who may have been either Walter Spryngeheuse or Roger de Chesterfield, then threw a tankard of wine at the landlord's head.

This prompted a pub brawl that expanded into a city-wide riot after one of the townsfolk called for assistance by ringing the bells of St Martin's church, while the students rang those at St Mary's, the University Church. Weapons that even included bows and arrows were used by both sides and, the next day, people from the local area joined the carnage with cries of, 'Havoc! Havoc! Smyt fast, give gode knocks!'

The riot lasted for three days and left more than 90 people dead. The townsfolk were found to be responsible and were ordered to attend Mass for the souls of the dead students every year on the anniversary of the riot. They were also required to swear an oath acknowledging the University's privileges and pay a fine of 63 pence – one for each dead student. This continued until 1825 when the Mayor refused. It was only rescinded by Parliament in 1955.

Massachusetts Governor Elbridge Gerry signed a bill that redrew electoral boundaries in the first example of 'gerrymandering'.

Elbridge Gerry was an established politician who had signed both the Declaration of Independence and the Articles of Confederation, and served in the House of Representatives, before being elected Governor of Massachusetts in 1810.

During his second term, the state legislature was dominated by the Democratic-Republican Party of which Gerry was a member. Seeking to weaken the Federalist Party in the forthcoming senatorial elections, the legislators redrew the district boundaries to concentrate the Federalist vote in a few districts and spread their own across many. Having consequently sliced up the Federalist stronghold of Essex County, the final bill presented strangely-shaped districts that later became the target for criticism and ridicule.

According to his son-in-law, Gerry himself was reluctant to sign the bill into law but did so on 11 February 1812. Six weeks later on 26 March the *Boston Gazette* published a picture, believed to be by the illustrator Elkanah Tisdale, which portrayed a map of the new Essex South district as a monstrous salamander with teeth and claws.

The term 'gerrymander' is therefore a portmanteau of Elbridge Gerry's surname and salamander. The cartoon appeared with 'Gerry-mander' as its title, though who coined the term itself is unknown. It has nevertheless become the common way to describe the redrawing of electoral boundaries to give an advantage to a particular political party. Such redistricting continues to be a popular way to dictate electoral outcomes. In the case of Gerry's party in 1812, they won twenty-nine seats to the Federalists' eleven.

FEBRUARY

12

1924

George Gershwin's *Rhapsody in Blue* was performed for the first time at a concert by Paul Whiteman and his Palais Royal Orchestra called *An Experiment in Modern Music.*

Whiteman had previously worked with Gershwin when he conducted the original performance of *Blue Monday*, a one-act 'jazz opera' composed by Gershwin with lyrics by Buddy DeSylva. Although it was a Broadway flop, Whiteman was impressed by *Blue Monday* and had a conversation with Gershwin in which they discussed the idea of composer writing a jazz concerto.

According to legend Gershwin forgot about the conversation until early January 1924 when his brother, Ira, read an article in the *New York Tribune* that said Whiteman would perform a jazz concerto by Gershwin at a concert on 12 February. His musical *Sweet Little Devil* was due to open in Boston at the end of the month, yet Whiteman was able to persuade Gershwin to write the piece after promising he only needed to submit a piano score. Whiteman's arranger Ferde Grofé orchestrated the piece, while the band added their own touches such as clarinettist Ross Gorman who turned the opening solo into an extended *glissando* that has since become the accepted way to open the piece.

Gershwin himself played piano when the piece was premiered at Aeolian Hall in New York City. He hadn't scored the piano part and so performed from memory, improvising some parts. The audience, which included composers such as John Philip Sousa and Sergei Rachmaninoff, responded enthusiastically to the piece but critics were divided. It has since gone on to become one of Gershwin's most famous pieces and a vital part of American musical history that proved how jazz elements could be used in so-called 'serious' music.

FEBRUARY

13

1542

Catherine Howard, the fifth wife of King Henry VIII of England, was executed in the Tower of London.

Catherine Howard, who was a cousin of Henry's second wife Anne Boleyn, spent much of her childhood in the household of her father's stepmother, the Dowager Duchess of Norfolk. Here she experienced little in the way of discipline and, after moving to the Dowager Duchess' household in Lambeth, began a relationship with Francis Dereham that ended after the Duchess was informed through an anonymous letter from her former her music teacher.

Shortly after King Henry VIII's marriage to Anne of Cleves, Catherine's uncle the Duke of Norfolk arranged for her to become a lady-in-waiting to the new queen. Here, in the face of Henry's well-documented disappointment with Anne's appearance, the young Catherine soon found herself the focus of the king's affections.

The two were married on 28 July 1540, less than three weeks after the annulment of Henry's marriage to Anne. Yet, despite Henry showering her with gifts, allegations of Catherine having an affair with the courtier Thomas Culpepper soon began to surface along with accounts of her sexual indiscretions while at Lambeth.

Thomas Cranmer, the Archbishop of Canterbury, ordered an investigation that turned up a love letter from Catherine in Culpepper's chambers. Her previous relationship with Dereham was discovered, so both he and Culpepper were executed for treason.

Catherine was stripped of her title of queen and was later found guilty of treason for failing to disclose her sexual history to the king. She was beheaded with one blow from an axe on the morning of 13 February 1542, and her body was buried in the chapel of St Peter-ad-Vincula within the walls of the Tower of London.

Pale Blue Dot, the furthest photograph ever taken of Earth, was created by the Voyager 1 space probe.

Voyager 1 was launched in September 1977 to study the outer Solar System including flybys of Jupiter and Saturn. Having completed the mission for which it had been created in November 1980, the spacecraft was allowed to continue its flight and leave the Solar System.

Carl Sagan, the astronomer and author, was a member of the Voyager imaging team and suggested that *Voyager 1* should take a last photograph of Earth before the cameras were deactivated to allow their power to be used for the flight into interstellar space. NASA scientists were concerned that such a photograph, in which the Earth would be relatively close to the sun, could permanently damage *Voyager 1's* Imaging Science Subsystem. They consequently held off turning the cameras around until 14 February 1990, by which time the spacecraft was approximately 6 billion kilometres from Earth.

Known as the *Family Portrait* series of images, *Voyager 1* transmitted 60 frames back to Earth where NASA stitched them together to create a mosaic of the Solar System. Three of the images, each taken with a different colour filter, were combined to produce the *Pale Blue Dot* image, in which the tiny dot of Earth fills less than 1 pixel of the 640,000 pixels that make up the rest of the frame.

Barely visible within the vastness of space, Sagan reflected on the 'pale blue dot' at a public lecture at Cornell University and later wrote about it in his book that drew its name from the image.

'Look again at that dot. That's here. That's home. That's us. On it everyone you love, everyone you know, everyone you ever heard of, every human being who ever was, lived out their lives.'

FEBRUARY
15
1949

The first professional archaeological excavation began in the Qumran Caves, the location of the Dead Sea Scrolls.

The Qumran Caves are a series of natural and man-made caves in the limestone cliffs above the ancient settlement of Qumran in the modern West Bank. Although a series of excavations of the area were conducted in the 19th century, these all focused on the settlement itself and its large cemetery of over one thousand graves.

It wasn't until late 1946 or early 1947 that Bedouin shepherd Muhammed edh-Dhib happened upon the first of eleven caves that contained what we now know as the Dead Sea Scrolls. While searching for a lost animal he ventured into one of the caves where he found a number of clay jars containing seven ancient documents.

Over the next few months the existence of the scrolls was shared with local parties, and finally became public knowledge after Mar Samuel of the Monastery of Saint Mark sought a professional appraisal. Academics excited by the scriptural similarities to *The Nash Papyrus*, the oldest known biblical manuscript at the time, soon set about trying to locate the original cave but found it difficult to gain access to the area due regional unrest in the aftermath of the establishment of the state of Israel.

The Arab Legion was eventually given permission to search the area and, on 29 January 1949, Cave 1 was located. Less than three weeks later, on 15 February, Gerald Lankester Harding and Roland de Vaux began the first archaeological excavation. In the cave they found fragments of other scrolls alongside other artefacts including cloth and pottery. By 1956 the archaeologists and local Bedouin had found over 200 more caves, eleven of which contained scroll fragments that date back as far as the 3rd century BCE.

The DuPont company's organic chemist Wallace Carothers received a patent for linear condensation polymers, the basis of the material better known as nylon.

Carothers joined DuPont from Harvard University, where he had taught organic chemistry. He was initially reluctant to move due to concerns that his history of depression would be a problem in an industrial setting, but DuPont executive Hamilton Bradshaw persuaded him otherwise and he took up his role in February 1928.

Having thrown himself into researching the structure and synthesis of polymers, Carothers and his team were responsible for creating the first synthetic replacement for rubber which was later named neoprene. Their laboratory, which was nicknamed 'Purity Hall', then began to focus on producing synthetic fibres that could be used in place of silk as this was becoming harder to source due to declining relations with Japan following the Great Depression.

On 28 February 1935 Carothers produced a fibre initially referred to as polyamide 6-6 as its components had six carbon atoms. Although the manufacturing process was complicated, DuPont were excited by the new material's strength and elasticity and ordered the laboratory to press ahead with their research. However, plagued by depression, Carothers committed suicide in a hotel room in April 1937 by drinking potassium cyanide dissolved in lemon juice.

DuPont continued to refine the manufacturing process and revealed women's stockings made of nylon, as it became known, at the 1939 New York World's Fair. By the time the first pairs were made commercially available in 1940, the company had invested $27 million into the development of a material that is now found in everything from guitar strings to medical implants.

FEBRUARY

17

1864

H. L. Hunley became the first submarine to sink an enemy ship when it attacked the Union Navy warship USS _Housatonic._

The 40 feet (12 metre) long submarine was named after its main financier Horace Lawson Hunley for the Confederacy in the American Civil War. Powered by a hand-cranked propeller, the vessel carried a crew of eight.

Early tests of the submersible had resulted in the deaths of thirteen crewmen. Nevertheless, testing continued and led to the installation of a spar torpedo that would be rammed into the enemy ship's hull and detonated as the submarine reversed away.

Meanwhile the Union navy had begun a blockade around Confederate ports to prevent them from trading. In response the Confederate forces mounted numerous attempts to break the blockade using torpedo boats, but these were generally ineffective. Consequently _H. L. Hunley_ was launched against the Union sloop-of-war ship _Housatonic_ that guarded the entrance to Charleston Harbor on the evening of 17 February 1864.

The exact details of the _Hunley_'s approach are unclear, but the historical consensus is that it was spotted too late by the _Housatonic_'s crew. Despite the blockade vessel being equipped with twelve large guns, these were not able to be used against the submarine as they could not be tilted low enough to hit the dark shape in the water.

Having jammed the spar torpedo into the starboard side of the _Housatonic_'s hull the _Hunley_ retreated. Following the explosion, the Union ship sank in just a few minutes with the loss of two officers and three men from its crew of 150. The _Hunley_ also sank that night with the loss of all eight crew members, with recent research suggesting that its proximity to the blast caused their deaths.

FEBRUARY
18
1885

Mark Twain's *Adventures of Huckleberry Finn* was published in the United States.

Samuel Langhorne Clemens, under his pen-name Mark Twain, had previously published the novel *The Adventures of Tom Sawyer* in which the character of Huckleberry 'Huck' Finn is introduced for the first time. Eight years after its release, the sequel was published in the United Kingdom in December 1884 and was followed by the American version two months later.

Adventures of Huckleberry Finn, which was originally published without the definite article at the start of its title, is set in the antebellum South when the economy was fuelled by plantations using slave labour. The novel follows Huck's journey down the river Mississippi with Jim, a slave who ran away from his owner Miss Watson.

Notable as one of the first American novels to be written in vernacular English, it is told in the first person by Huck himself. This is said to have revolutionised American literature, with Ernest Hemingway later claiming that 'All modern American literature comes from…*Huckleberry Finn*.'

Despite such later acclaim, the book was greeted with mixed reviews on its release and within just a month it had been banned by the library in Concord, Massachusetts for being 'trash…suitable only for the slums'. Other libraries in the late 19th and early 20th century followed suit, and the novel continues to divide opinion due to its frequent use of the n-word and its portrayal of black characters. However, defenders of the book instead interpret Twain's creation as a masterpiece of American literature that uses satire to present a powerful attack on racism.

FEBRUARY

19

1913

Pedro Lascuráin began the shortest presidential term in history when he became President of Mexico for less than an hour.

Mexico had been governed by Francisco Madero since the collapse of the Díaz regime in 1911. Madero had won the Presidential election with nearly 90% of the vote, but soon faced opposition from both sides of the political spectrum. Rebellions around the country grew, and the inexperienced president eventually turned to General Victoriano Huerta of the Federal Army to deal with the insurrection.

By early 1913, however, Huerta had joined a conspiracy against Madero that saw the President imprisoned and threatened with death unless he resigned. With few options available to them, both Madero and his vice president, José María Pino Suárez, resigned. They were murdered a few days later while being transferred to a prison.

In the meantime Pedro Lascuráin, who had served as Madero's Secretary of Foreign Affairs, assumed the Presidency. The Mexican constitution stated that in the absence of the president, the vice president, and the Attorney General (who had also been forced out by Huerta) control passed to the Foreign Minister. Lascuráin thus became President, appointing Huerta as the Interior Minister before promptly resigning and passing control to the General.

Sources are unclear on exactly how long Lascuráin held the presidency. The shortest place it at just 15 minutes, but all agree the total time was less than an hour. Huerta's militaristic regime went on to face significant opposition, plunging the country further into civil war. With the Federal Army unable to defeat the revolutionaries he was forced to resign and flee the country just 17 months after assuming the presidency. Meanwhile Lascuráin retired from politics and returned to his previous career as a lawyer.

FEBRUARY
20
1472

The Orkney and Shetland Isles were given to Scotland by Norway in place of a wedding dowry for Margaret of Denmark.

The Northern Isles, which consist of the two island groups of Shetland and Orkney, have been inhabited since prehistoric times but were formally annexed by the Norwegian king Harald Hårfagre in around 875 after he subdued the Vikings who used the islands as a base from which to raid Norway and Scotland.

The islands remained under Norwegian control for almost 600 years, despite increased Scottish interest from the 13th century onwards. Scottish influence began to grow following the death of Jon Haraldsson, the last of an unbroken line of Norse jarls or earls, in 1231 after which the Jarldom passed to ethnic Scots noblemen with permission of the Norwegian King Håkon Håkonsson.

By the time the Scottish noble Henry Sinclair was appointed to the Jarldom of Orkney in 1379, Norway was in decline as a result of the devastating effects of the Black Death that had struck in 1349. The Kalmar Union of 1397 then joined the kingdoms of Denmark and Norway with Sweden under a single monarch.

By the time Margaret of Denmark, the daughter of King Christian I of Denmark and Norway, was betrothed to James III of Scotland in 1468 the Scandinavian monarchy was in a dire financial situation. Unable to raise the dowry payment of 50,000 Rhenish Florins, Christian pledged the islands as security until he could pay. As it became increasingly clear that the dowry was unlikely to be paid, James declared Orkney and Shetland forfeit and they were formally annexed to Scotland on 20 February 1420 through an act of parliament. Although later Danish monarchs attempted to regain the islands by paying the debt, the Scottish kings resisted their efforts.

FEBRUARY

21

1613

The Romanov dynasty began after Michael Romanov was elected Tsar of Russia by the Zemsky Sobor national assembly.

Michael was related to Fyodor I, the last Tsar of the Rurik dynasty, through his grandfather who had also been an advisor to Ivan the Terrible. Following Fyodor's death and the election of Tsar Boris Godunov in 1598, the two-year-old Michael and his mother were forced in to exile. By the time of Michael's election as Tsar in 1613, his mother had become a nun and was living with her teenage son at the Ipatiev Monastery near Kostroma around 300km northeast of Moscow.

Godunov's reign was the first of a period known as the Time of Troubles in which Russia faced numerous internal and external threats. Desperate to restore stability, the Zemsky Sobor, a national assembly made up of the three feudal classes, considered handing the throne to members of both the Polish and Swedish royal families before eventually settling on Michael Romanov in an election on 21 February 1613. Michael himself hadn't been involved in the discussions, and only accepted the position in March after a delegation visited him and his mother in the monastery.

Although he became Tsar when he was only 16 years old, Michael oversaw a period of Russian expansion and renewed prosperity. Much of this was achieved after his father, Patriarch Filaret of Moscow, returned from imprisonment in Poland and assumed *de facto* control of the country.

Michael died in 1645 and left the throne to his son Alexis who, like his father, became Tsar when he was just 16 years old. Nevertheless, the Romanov dynasty continued for more than 250 years until the abdication of Nicholas II in 1917.

FEBRUARY

22

1797

The last invasion of Britain by a hostile foreign force began when French troops under the command of the Irish-American Colonel William Tate landed near the Welsh town of Fishguard.

Britain joined the War of the First Coalition against Revolutionary France in 1793. Three years later the French General Lazare Hoche devised a plan to invade Britain in support of the Republican Society of United Irishmen under Wolfe Tone.

Two of the three intended invasion forces were stopped by poor weather, leaving only the 1,400 troops of *La Legion Noire* (The Black Legion) to launch their attack on Bristol. Since the professional French army was serving under Napoléon in Europe, *La Legion Noire* included 800 irregular soldiers ranging from republicans to recently-released Royalist prisoners. Well-equipped and dressed in dyed captured British uniforms that gave them their name, they arrived off the English coast in four warships. Unable to land in Bristol due to adverse weather, Colonel Tate instead anchored at Carregwastad Head near the Welsh town of Fishguard late on 22 February.

Soldiers and equipment were put ashore as darkness fell, faced only by a small force of volunteers under Lieutenant-Colonel Thomas Knox. When dawn came Knox realised that he was heavily outnumbered and retreated to meet up with reinforcements led by Lord Cawdor. By this time the undisciplined French troops had begun looting local settlements where they became increasingly drunk after finding wine from a recently-wrecked Portuguese vessel.

Local people soon joined the defence, including cobbler's wife Jemima Nicholas who single-handedly rounded up 12 Frenchmen and locked them in a church. With his troops in disarray, Tate submitted to an unconditional surrender on 24 February.

FEBRUARY

23

303

Emperor Diocletian ordered the destruction of the new church in the ancient city of Nicomedia, marking the start of the 'Great Persecution' of Christians.

Diocletian was declared Emperor of the Eastern Roman Empire in 284. Within two decades he had established a powerful 'tetrarchy' of four rulers who began to restore order and wealth to an empire that had suffered a range of internal and external threats over the previous century.

Christians were perceived by many in traditional Roman society to be a threat to the established order. Not only was the religion seen as a foreign cult, it was built on a monotheistic belief that directly undermined traditional Roman religion. Contemporary sources say that Diocletian himself was broadly tolerant of Christians in the early years of his rule and indicate that it was the tetrarch Galerius who encouraged the introduction of persecutory policies.

On 23 February 303 Diocletian ordered that the newly-built church in Nicomedia should be destroyed, along with its scriptures. The following day he published the first of four edicts that went on to strip Christians of their legal rights and the freedom to assemble to worship, and later demanded that they conform to established Roman religious practices such as performing sacrifices to the gods.

The persecutions continued for eight years, during which time thousands of Christians were killed for their faith. Nevertheless, the religion survived and, shortly after Diocletian's death in 311, Galerius himself issued the Edict of Toleration which legalised Christianity in the Eastern Empire. Constantine and Licinius went further in 313 and, following the former's emergence as sole Emperor in 324, Christianity quickly began to spread across the Empire.

FEBRUARY
24
1868

United States President Andrew Johnson was impeached by the House of Representatives.

Having previously served as a senator and later military governor for the state of Tennessee, Andrew Johnson was chosen by Abraham Lincoln to be his running mate in the election of 1864. He had been the only senator from a seceding state to remain loyal to the Union at the outbreak of the Civil War, so secured the support of 'Union Democrats' and consequently became Vice President.

Johnson's inauguration took place on 4 March 1865, but exactly six weeks later he became President of the United States after Lincoln was assassinated by John Wilkes Booth. This coincided with the end of the Civil War, leaving him to introduce a lenient Reconstruction policy towards the defeated South that was vehemently opposed by the Radical Republicans in Congress. They passed laws to protect the rights of freed slaves, but the President vetoed them. In response Congress passed the Tenure of Office Act that stopped the president removing opponents from the cabinet by stating that the Senate had to approve the dismissal of officials.

Johnson defied the act in 1867 when he sought to replace the Republican Secretary of War, Edwin M. Stanton, with General Ulysses S. Grant. The change was not approved, and Stanton returned to the post after Grant resigned. On 21 February 1868 Johnson again dismissed Stanton and this time appointed General Lorenzo Thomas in his place, but Stanton refused to go and locked himself inside his office.

Although effectively a test of the constitutionality of the Tenure of Office Act, Johnson's actions saw him impeached on 24 February. He was acquitted on 16 May by just one vote.

FEBRUARY

25

1570

Pope Pius V issued the Papal bull *Regnans in Excelsis* which excommunicated Queen Elizabeth I of England for heresy.

Elizabeth's older sister Mary had reconciled England with the Papacy following her father Henry VIII's break with Rome and the subsequent introduction of Protestantism under her younger brother Edward. The revival of the Heresy Acts resulted in the execution of hundreds of Protestants, which in turn exacerbated anti-Catholic sentiment among the Protestant population.

Elizabeth became queen following Mary's death in 1558 and, the following the year, Parliament passed the Act of Supremacy through which the new queen assumed the position of the Supreme Governor of the Church of England. This abolition of Papal authority, alongside a series of Protestantising policies, led many English Catholics to lend their support to Elizabeth's imprisoned cousin Mary, Queen of Scots.

The Rising of the North in 1569, which sought to depose Elizabeth in favour of Mary, was greeted with support from Pope Pius V. Although the rebellion failed, he issued the papal bull *Regnans in Excelsis* on 25 February 1570 in which he excommunicated Elizabeth and freed her subjects from allegiance to her. The bull also excommunicated anybody who continued to follow 'the pretended Queen of England and the servant of crime'.

The pope's approach did little to improve the situation for Catholics in England. Conversely it hardened the attitude of Elizabeth's government, and heralded increasing repression of the religion. Nevertheless, the new laws were unable to completely crush opposition to the queen and arguably encouraged future attempts to achieve her overthrow such as the Ridolfi assassination plot in 1571.

FEBRUARY

26

1935

Adolf Hitler formally defied the Treaty of Versailles by re-establishing a German Air Force, known as the _Luftwaffe_, under the command of Hermann Goering.

The German Empire established its first air force, the _Fliegertruppe_, in 1910 which saw extensive action in the First World War. Following Germany's defeat and the signing of the Treaty of Versailles, Germany was banned from possessing an air force and the _Fliegertruppe_ was dissolved.

Despite the ban, the German military established a secret flight school at Lipetsk in the Soviet Union that began training fighter pilots and ground crew from 1926. This meant that there were already up to 120 trained pilots by the time Hitler came to power in January 1933. Senior Nazi, and former First World War pilot Hermann Goering, was named Reich Commissioner of Aviation.

On 15 May 1933 the Reich Ministry of Aviation took control of all military flying operations. Although often considered by many to be the 'birth' of the _Luftwaffe_, the development of military aircraft continued in secret. Having formally approved its position as a third military service alongside the army and navy on 26 February 1935, Hitler and Goering began to reveal the _Luftwaffe_.

Germany's expansion of its air force was protested by both France and Britain, the latter of which had begun to strengthen the Royal Air Force in March. However, neither country nor the League of Nations attempted to sanction this blatant defiance of the Treaty of Versailles. Consequently, the _Luftwaffe_ continued to grow, and the following year the Condor Legion saw action for the first time as part of the Nationalist forces in the Spanish Civil War. As a result, up to 20,000 members of the _Luftwaffe_ gained valuable combat experience.

Pokémon, **the world's highest-grossing media franchise, was launched in Japan with** ***Pocket Monsters: Red*** **and** ***Green.***

Created by the video game designer Satoshi Tajiri at Game Freak, *Pokémon* was inspired by his childhood hobby of collecting insects. Instead of insects, however, the game would allow players to collect electronic creatures. The idea developed further after he saw how a link cable could be used to connect two Nintendo Game Boys together and allow players to trade creatures with each other.

Over a five-year period the game and its creatures went through various stages of development, before Tajiri settled on the name *Pocket Monsters.* Having convinced Nintendo to publish the game, two different version were released on 27 February 1996. *Pocket Monsters: Red* and *Green* were an immediate and unexpected success. Together with the special edition *Pocket Monsters: Blue* that was released via mail-order in October more than 1 million units were sold in the first year alone. The themes of collecting, training, and battling different species of creatures soon turned *Pocket Monsters* into the best-selling game in Japan and began earning overwhelmingly positive reviews from critics.

In 1998 *Pokémon Red* and *Blue* were the first versions of the game to be released outside Japan where a $50 million-dollar marketing campaign convinced the public they 'Gotta Catch 'Em All'. The same year the name *Pokémon*, a phonetic version of the Japanese *Pocket Monsters,* was also adopted for the media franchise management company set up jointly by Nintendo, Game Freak and Creatures. The Pokémon Company now oversees the highest-grossing media franchise of all time with products ranging from video games to trading cards and soft toys to motion pictures.

The Waco siege began in Texas after agents from the Bureau of Alcohol, Tobacco and Firearms raided the Branch Davidian church.

The Branch Davidians originated in the late 1950s as a sub-group of the Davidian Seventh-Day Adventist Church. Under the leadership of Benjamin Roden, they took control of the Mount Carmel religious settlement 10 miles outside the Texan town of Waco where they prepared for the Second Coming of Jesus Christ.

The mid-1980s saw a power struggle from which Vernon Howell, who later renamed himself David Koresh, emerged as the new leader of the group. Shortly after this Howell announced that God had told him that he should take multiple wives, with reports stating that some of these were as young as 11 years old.

The Bureau of Alcohol, Tobacco and Firearms had already been watching the Mount Carmel compound due to concerns that Koresh and his followers were stockpiling illegal weapons. They began making plans to raid the compound in late February but were prompted to action after the *Waco Tribune-Herald* newspaper began to publish a series of articles that included allegations of child abuse within the cult.

More than 70 agents raided the property on the morning of 28 February, but Koresh had already received a tip-off and had made preparations. Gunfire consequently broke out, although it is still unclear who fired first. The fighting lasted for almost two hours and resulted in the deaths of four agents from the Bureau of Alcohol, Tobacco and Firearms as well as a similar number of Davidians. The resulting siege lasted until 19 April when it was ended by the FBI in a raid that saw the compound destroyed by fire.

FEBRUARY

29

1504

Christopher Columbus used knowledge of a forthcoming lunar eclipse to fool Jamaican natives into providing his stranded crew with provisions.

Columbus embarked on his fourth transatlantic voyage in May 1502 but, after sustaining significant damage in a series of storms, his fleet beached in St Ann's Bay, Jamaica where they remained stranded for a year. The native peoples were initially welcoming to the Europeans and traded food and shelter in return for trinkets. However, as time went on, their hospitality began to wane. After some of Columbus' crew mutinied and attacked the locals, food supplies were stopped and Columbus' crew faced possible starvation.

Desperate to save himself and his crew, Columbus devised a plan that would fool the natives into providing more supplies. After consulting an almanac of astronomical tables, he noticed that a lunar eclipse would occur in the near future. In a meeting with the local leader, Columbus said that his God was angry that the natives had stopped providing food and would show his displeasure by making the moon appear 'inflamed with wrath'.

Three nights later, on 29 February 1504, the moon turned dark red. According to Columbus' son Ferdinand who had accompanied his father, the natives greeted the sight with 'great howling and lamentation' and soon returned 'laden with provisions and beseeching the admiral to intercede with his god on their behalf'.

Columbus retired to his cabin where he used an hourglass to time the eclipse, emerging shortly before the almanac's predicted end of totality. Informing the natives that he had prayed to his god to forgive them, the moon soon reappeared. Columbus and his men remained well-supplied before being rescued at the end of June.

MARCH

MARCH
1
1872

Yellowstone became the first national park in the world after President Ulysses S. Grant signed *The Act of Dedication* law.

The modern Yellowstone National Park, which covers an area of almost 3,500 square miles around the Yellowstone Caldera, lies on the border of Wyoming, Montana, and Idaho. The region had been known to humans for around 11,000 years prior to the arrival of members of the Lewis and Clark Expedition at the start of the 19th century. John Colter is widely recognised as the first white person to witness geothermal activity in the region, but it wasn't until the Cook–Folsom–Peterson Expedition of 1869 that the area was explored and recorded in detail.

This was followed by two more expeditions over the next two years, the most notable arguably being the Hayden Geological Survey of 1871. Partially funded by the government, the detailed report that emerged from this expedition helped to persuade the US Congress to protect the area through law. Supported by field sketches, paintings, and photographs, expedition leader Ferdinand V. Hayden presented the report to as many politicians and other people in positions of power as he could.

Hayden's determination paid off. On 18 December 1871 a bill was introduced in both the Senate and in the House of Representatives to set the area aside as 'a great national park or pleasure-ground for the benefit and enjoyment of the people'. The bill passed with comfortable victories, and President Grant signed it into law on 1 March 1872.

Yellowstone is now a popular tourist destination with more than 4 million visitors a year taking advantage of numerous outdoor recreational opportunities in one of the world's most beautiful areas.

MARCH

2

1791

French scientist Claude Chappe sent the first message by semaphore machine, establishing a communication system that was faster than a messenger on horseback.

Chappe was born into a wealthy family in 1763 and originally trained as a member of the church. However, the turmoil of the French Revolution meant that he was unable to continue in his position and he returned home to focus on science. Working with his brothers, Chappe began to experiment with optical telegraph designs.

Chappe was not the first person to attempt to create a system of long-distance communication. The English scientist Robert Hooke had presented a proposal a century earlier, but his idea was never implemented. Consequently the Chappe brothers were the first to successfully transmit a message when they demonstrated their system on 2 March 1791, covering more than 16km from Brûlon to Parcé.

Using what became known as the Synchronized System, Chappe was able to transmit the phrase 'If you succeed, you will soon bask in glory' in just four minutes. Two pendulum clocks had their faces modified with a series of symbols and, after being synchronised, were placed in the two locations alongside a telescope that pointed to the other. The transmitting station used black and white panels to alert the receiver to when the second hand of the clock was passing over the appropriate symbol, which they then recorded. The string of symbols, when decoded, produced the message.

Chappe soon abandoned synchronised clocks in favour of mechanical arms to portray the different symbols. When mounted on top of a tower, the arms could be seen through a telescope and their alignment either recorded or relayed onwards. A 230km semaphore line of these towers between Paris and Lille was installed in 1792.

MARCH

3

1861

Tsar Alexander II of Russia signed the Emancipation Manifesto.

By the middle of the 19th century, an estimated 38% of all Russians were serfs. Although different to slaves, who were property themselves, serfs were tied to privately owned land and consequently to the owner of that land who exercised enormous control over their lives. There were also large numbers of state serfs who came under the control of the Ministry of State Property.

In the aftermath of Russia's humiliating defeat in the Crimean War, the new Tsar Alexander II was determined to dramatically reform Russia's social structure. He believed that Russia's reliance on inefficient and antiquated systems such as serfdom meant the country would never be able to compete with the more developed Western powers.

Just a year after his coronation, Alexander made his views clear in a speech to the Marshalls of the Nobility. He invited the landowning nobles themselves to propose a way to successfully abolish serfdom, after which their suggestions were reviewed and combined to form a draft law.

Five years after he first announced his desire to free the serfs, Alexander signed the Emancipation Manifesto on 3 March 1861. Serfs became free and were given the right to own property. In practical terms, however, it was the landlords who were the main beneficiaries. They often kept the best land for themselves, selling on poorer land for more than its market value. The peasants, who had no savings, were forced to take out high-interest government loans. These redemption payments saddled much of the peasantry with debt that was often inherited by next generation.

The Forth Bridge in Scotland, which featured the longest cantilever bridge span in the world at the time, was opened by the future King Edward VII.

The Forth Bridge stretches almost 2.5km across the Firth of Forth, a large estuary area to west of Edinburgh. The bridge, which features two main spans of over 500m each, continues to operate as vital rail link between Fife and the Lothians. The bridge was designed by the English engineers Sir John Fowler and Sir Benjamin Baker using the cantilever principle in which a central span is supported by the tension and compression of supporting arms that are only anchored at one end.

Before construction even began on the bridge in 1882, the contractor Sir William Arrol & Co. landscaped the shores on each side. They then constructed buildings such as workshops, as well as huts and houses to accommodate the more than 4,500 workers who worked on the bridge. Of these, 73 are known to have died in work-related accidents.

The bridge was finally completed in December 1889 and was tested the following month to ensure that it operated properly under load. Satisfied that the bridge was safe, the chairmen of the various railway companies involved in funding the £3.2 million construction travelled over it several times on 24 February. A week later the future King Edward VII formally opened the bridge and secured the last of 6.5 million rivets.

The bridge continues to carry more than 200 trains a day, and is an important symbol of Scotland. Thanks to the development of a new coating, it is also no longer necessary to continuously paint the bridge, a task that takes 10 years to complete.

MARCH

5

1046

The Persian poet and philosopher Nasir Khusraw began a seven-year journey through the Islamic world that he recorded in the *Safarnama*.

Khusraw was born in modern Tajikistan in 1004 and worked for the Seljuk sultanate as a financial administrator until 1046 when he was inspired to undertake the Hajj pilgrimage to Mecca. Departing on 5 March he did not return home until October 1052, almost seven years after he set out, by which time he had compiled a detailed journal of his travels through the Islamic world.

Khusraw's 19,000 kilometre journey saw him travel to the Islamic holy city of Mecca four times, in addition to visiting the major cities of Jerusalem and Cairo. In Egypt he became particularly drawn to the Shi'a doctrines of the ruling Fatimid dynasty and, although he attempted to introduce these beliefs on his return to Persia, he was met with significant opposition from the Sunni population.

Having settled in Yamgan in the Badakhshan mountains of present-day Afghanistan, Khusraw set about compiling his extensive notes into the *Safarnama*. Known in English as the *Book of Travels*, Khusraw's travelogue is respected as one of the most influential pieces of Persian travel writing and remains a valuable historical source for its detailed descriptions of the places he visited.

Written in eloquent prose, rather than the verse that makes Khusraw one of the most important poets in Persian literature, the *Safarnama* presents accounts of both the architecture and the daily life of the places he visited. Interspersed with both anecdotes and spiritual reflections, the book is still read by modern-day Persian speakers.

The United States Supreme Court issued its ruling in the *Dred Scott v. John F.A. Sandford* case.

Dred Scott was a slave owned by John Emerson, an army surgeon from the slave state of Missouri. Emerson took Scott with him when he moved to the free state of Illinois in 1834 and to the free Territory of Wisconsin in 1836. Emerson died in 1843 and his widow, Irene, inherited Scott and his wife and child. Scott later attempted to buy his family's freedom by offering Irene $300 but she refused. In response the Scotts sued for freedom, with legal advisors arguing that their residence in a free state and a free territory meant they must have been emancipated.

Drawing on the Missouri precedent of 'once free, always free' the case was not fully heard until 1850. Although the jury ruled in Scott's favour, the Missouri Supreme Court reversed the decision after Irene Emerson appealed. She then transferred the Scotts to her brother, John F. A. Sanford, in New York.

In 1853 the case went to the Federal Courts, which found in Sanford's favour. Scott subsequently appealed this ruling to the Supreme Court, which mis-spelled Sanford's name due to a clerical error and didn't deliver the majority opinion until 6 March 1857. Chief Justice Roger B. Taney wrote the decision, which said that black people could never be citizens of the United States and so did not have right to bring a case to the Federal Courts. Furthermore, the decision stated that Congress did not have the right to regulate slavery in the territories meaning that, as private property, slaves could not be taken away from their owners. The decision increased tensions within the United States and contributed to both the election of Abraham Lincoln and the outbreak of Civil War.

The German ocean liner SS *Kaiser Wilhelm der Grosse* became the first vessel to transmit a ship-to-shore wireless message.

Named after Wilhelm I, the first Emperor of the German nation that was created in 1871, SS *Kaiser Wilhelm der Grosse* is regarded as the first superliner and was the first vessel in the world to be fitted with four funnels or 'stacks'.

Launched in 1897 by Wilhelm I's grandson, Wilhelm II, *Kaiser Wilhelm der Grosse* established the North German Lloyd shipping company as a direct competitor to the British-dominated transatlantic maritime trade. Wilhelm II was particularly enthusiastic about the fact that the ship could easily be converted into an auxiliary cruiser thanks to strengthened decks that could accommodate artillery guns in times of conflict.

Just a few months after her launch, *Kaiser Wilhelm der Grosse* was awarded the Blue Riband award for the fastest transatlantic crossing, usurping the British liner *RMS Lucania* and firmly establishing Germany as a powerful maritime force. Keen to maintain the ship's reputation for speed and safety, in 1900 her owners sent her for a refit that included the installation of a commercial wireless telegraphy system by the Marconi Company. Despite the relative infancy of this new technology *Kaiser Wilhelm der Grosse* conducted a series of demonstrations, making her the first ship to send a ship-to-shore message on 7 March.

With the outbreak of the First World War in 1914, the ship was requisitioned by the German navy and fitted with guns as an auxiliary cruiser. Under the command of Captain Reymann, she sank a number of Allied vessels before being defeated in the Battle of Río de Oro off the North African coast on 26 August 1914.

French pilot Raymonde de Laroche became the first woman to be awarded a pilot's license.

Elise Raymonde Deroche was the daughter of a Parisian plumber. After becoming an actress she adopted the stage name Raymonde de Laroche. Having been introduced to aviator Charles Voisin in 1909, she convinced him to teach her how to fly. Although initially reluctant, Voisin invited her to his airfield at Chalons.

It was there, on 22 October 1909, that de Laroche flew for the first time. The aircraft she trained in had been designed for stunt displays and could only seat one person, so the instructor was obliged to run alongside the aircraft. Having mastered taxiing de Laroche later took off, flying around 300 yards (270m) before touching down again. There are conflicting accounts of this flight, with aviation journalist Harry Harper claiming in 1953 that it took place after little training whereas contemporary reports suggest that de Laroche had already had a number of lessons before going airborne.

De Laroche was awarded her pilot's license five months later on 8 March 1910. Issued by the Aero-Club of France, her license was the first to be awarded to a woman and led to her being invited to take part in numerous international aeronautical meetings and displays where she flew as part of Voisin's team. At the Egyptian Grand Prix later that year she came sixth, a position that she improved on when she flew again in St Petersburg.

De Laroche was never a member of the nobility. However, in an October 1909 report the contemporary British aviation magazine *Flight* captioned a photograph of her as 'Baroness de la Roche'. She was even addressed as 'baroness' in an audience with the Russian Tsar Nicholas II after her flight in St Petersburg.

Mattel's iconic Barbie doll made its debut at the New York Toy Fair.

Barbie, whose full name is Barbara Millicent Roberts, was invented by Mattel's co-founder Ruth Handler. She was inspired to create a doll with adult features after seeing her own daughter make paper dolls depicting a mature shape.

During a family holiday to Europe, Handler bought three German-created Bild Lilli dolls. These were based on the sassy adult comic-strip character Lilli and had originally been created as novelty toys for men. However, Handler saw the potential to adapt Lilli's features and market the doll to children.

Alongside designer Jack Ryan she redesigned the doll, and employed fashion designer Charlotte Johnson to create a wardrobe for the new 'Teen-age Fashion Model'. According to Mattel it was due to the bulky material and the necessary waistbands and fastenings on Barbie's clothes that the doll was given such a famously narrow waist.

Barbie was unveiled at the New York Toy Fair on 9 March 1959 wearing a black and white striped swimsuit. The doll was met with scepticism from both within Mattel and from the toy industry at large. Parents also expressed concern at Barbie's mature body. In response Mattel adopted a marketing strategy that completely bypassed the need to win parents over by launching an extensive television advertising campaign directed solely at children themselves. This made Mattel the first company to successfully exploit youth television advertising and harness the power of 'kid consumerism', resulting in the creation of a modern toy icon that went on to sell over 300,000 units its first year alone.

MARCH

10

2000

The NASDAQ Composite stock market index peaked at the height of the dot-com bubble.

The economic bubble that is also referred to as the 'dot-com boom' was the result of investors speculatively pouring money into the numerous internet companies that were founded in the mid- to late-1990s. The exponential growth witnessed by the stock market was primarily based on overconfidence in new online businesses, many of which had a '.com' suffix. A large number of these companies raised enormous funds by selling shares in initial public offerings, despite the fact that some of them had not even begun to generate income, let alone make a profit.

Driven by a mixture of private investors and venture capitalists, both of whom hoped to make massive gains from the rapid growth of the internet, the stock value of many of the new dot-com companies increased exponentially. The party couldn't last and the market quickly declined after the NASDAQ Composite index, which includes many technology companies, peaked at 5,132.52 during trading on 10 March 2000.

Around this time some of the companies began to report huge losses. This bad news, combined with large sell orders of stocks by some of the larger tech companies, led to panic selling that made the stock market lose 10% of its value within just a few weeks. Without access to previously abundant capital other companies folded, bursting the dot-com bubble.

The dot-com crisis was exacerbated by a stock market downturn following the September 11 attacks in 2001. Yet, despite the broader collapse in the tech sector, a number of companies including Amazon, eBay, and Google, managed to survive and later flourish.

MARCH

11

1702

The Daily Courant, the first daily English-language newspaper, was published in London.

The Daily Courant was established by E. Mallet at offices on Fleet Street, which had been an important centre for printing since the early 16th century. The government's strict control over printing had only ended with the end of the Licensing of the Press Act in 1695, and British society took time to adapt to the new press freedoms. Consequently there is some dispute over who exactly E. Mallet was, but most sources agree that the paper was established by Elizabeth Mallet, the wife of the deceased printer David Mallet. It would have been jarring for many people at the time to have seen the name of a woman on the by-line, so it is understood that she instead used a single initial and referred to herself as 'he' when necessary.

The single-sheet newspaper carried digests of foreign newspapers on the front page and adverts on the reverse. Mallet herself claimed to 'give news daily and impartially' while promising 'Nor will [the Author] take it upon himself to give any Comments or Conjectures of his own, but will relate only Matter of Fact; supposing other People to have Sense enough to make Reflections for themselves'.

By 1703 Mallet had sold *The Daily Courant* to the printer and bookseller Samuel Buckley who continued to produce the daily editions after relocating the offices to another area of the city. Buckley later launched the *Spectator* (not to be confused with the current weekly magazine that began in the 19th century), but this new publication lasted for less than two years. Meanwhile *The Daily Courant* continued to be printed until 1735 when it merged with the *Daily Gazetteer* that survived in various forms until 1797.

Andrew Watson became the world's first black international football player when he captained Scotland to a 6-1 victory over England.

Andrew Watson's father, Peter Miller Watson, was the manager of a sugar plantation in British Guiana while his mother was a local woman called Anna (or Hannah) Rose. Having been born illegitimately, accurate details of Watson's early life are virtually non-existent. It was only after his father moved the young Andrew and his sister Annetta to Scotland in the early 1860s that any reliable evidence began to appear.

Peter Watson died in 1869 while his son was enrolled at a boarding school in Halifax in West Yorkshire. He and his sister inherited a significant amount of money that secured their financial futures and, after attending King's College School in Wimbledon, Watson took up a place to study mathematics, engineering and natural philosophy at the University of Glasgow. With his existing interest in football flourishing and, having left university after just one year to take up an engineering apprenticeship, Watson's talents as a full back saw him join a succession of increasingly bigger clubs.

By 1880 Andrew Watson was playing for Queen's Park – Britain's leading team – and the next year he was called up to captain the Scottish national side in a match against England on 12 March 1881. Played at the Oval in London, which currently serves as an international cricket venue, the Scots defeated England by an incredible 6 goals to 1 in a match that is still the heaviest defeat ever suffered by England on home soil. He later moved to London where he became the first black player in the English FA Cup when he joined Swifts in 1882.

MARCH

13

1920

The right-wing Kapp Putsch attempted to overthrow the Weimar Republic.

The Weimar Republic was established in the aftermath of Germany's defeat in the First World War and the abdication of Kaiser Wilhelm II. Unpopular with both the political left and right, the government faced several threats from the left in early 1919 prior to their reluctant signing of the Treaty of Versailles. In its aftermath the *Freikorps* volunteer paramilitary units, on whom the government had relied to put down the previous uprisings, were to be disbanded.

In early March 1920 two leading *Freikorps* units refused the order to dissolve. Already opposed to the democratic Weimar government, the unit under the command of Captain Herman Ehrhardt occupied Berlin with the cooperation of General Walther von Lüttwitz, the district army commander.

Two days earlier Lüttwitz had approached right-wing journalist Wolfgang Kapp and some other leading military figures in preparation for taking over the government. They swiftly occupied government buildings and met no opposition from regular troops stationed in the city, while officials generally accepted the coup.

However, the putsch was far less popular with the general population. After the Weimar government fled to Dresden, President Ebert issued a cabinet proclamation calling for a general strike to defeat the putsch. Supported by the major trade unions and leftist parties, the people of Berlin refused to cooperate with the Kapp government and services ground to a halt. More than 12 million workers went on strike from 14 March, paralysing essential services ranging from water to transportation. Less than a week later, with the putsch a failure, Kapp was forced to flee to Sweden.

MARCH

14

1958

Perry Como was awarded the first gold record by the Recording Industry Association of America for his song 'Catch a Falling Star'.

Gold records were originally presented to artists by their own label, primarily as a form of self-congratulatory publicity. The very first framed gold record of this type was presented to the American bandleader Glenn Miller by RCA Victor in February 1942. This was in recognition of the sale of 1.2 million copies of his single 'Chattanooga Choo Choo'. In 1956 Elvis Presley later received a gold record after selling 1 million copies of 'Don't Be Cruel', but this was again a company award.

The Recording Industry Association of America was formed in 1952 to develop the burgeoning recording industry, and introduced its own industry-wide award program six years later. Issued to recognise any single that sold over a million copies (or an album that achieved one million dollars in sales), the first gold record was awarded to Perry Como for 'Catch a Falling Star' that later won him the Grammy Award for Best Male Vocal. Como had previously awarded the McGuire Sisters with a company gold record on the Gisele MacKenzie Show for their million-selling song Sugartime. He was in turn presented with his RIAA gold record on live television by announcer Frank Gallop who erroneously referred to 'Chase a Falling Star' before Como performed a comedy arrangement of the song.

Increasing record sales in the 1970s led to the introduction of the platinum award to recognise singles that sold more than two million units, but the number of required sales was eventually halved in 1989 to its current level of 500,000 for gold and one million for platinum.

MARCH
15
1906

Rolls-Royce Limited was established by Charles Rolls and Henry Royce.

Englishman Frederick Henry Royce had established an electrical engineering firm in 1884 but, by the start of the twentieth century, he was facing increasing competition from German and American manufacturers. In response he turned his attention to designing his own motor car, and he completed the first of three two-cylinder Royce 10 prototypes at his Manchester factory in 1904.

Based on a 1901 two-cylinder Decauville, one of the cars was sold to Henry Edmunds who was friends with Charles Rolls of the C.S. Rolls & Co. car dealership in London. Despite specialising in imported French and Belgian vehicles, Rolls was impressed by the Royce 10 and Edmunds subsequently arranged for him to meet Royce at the Midland Hotel. This led to an agreement on 23 December through which Rolls would sell every car Royce manufactured. These ranged from the original 10 hp two-cylinder up to a 30 hp six-cylinder model.

The manufacturer-salesman partnership between the two men proved to be an incredible success and, on 15 March 1906, they formalised their relationship with the establishment of Rolls-Royce Limited. With increased sales thanks to the combination of Royce's high quality engineering and Rolls' business expertise, the company soon opened a dedicated factory in Derby in 1908.

It was from this base that Rolls-Royce later established a reputation for the development of aero engines. In the Second World War their V-12 Merlin engine powered the iconic British Supermarine Spitfire and Hawker Hurricane, while modern Rolls-Royce jet engines are fitted to aircraft such as the Airbus A380.

The entire Jewish population of the northern English city of York was massacred in a pogrom.

Jews first began to arrive in England following the Norman Conquest. Primarily serving as moneylenders due to strict Catholic laws about usury, anti-Jewish sentiment had begun to grow by the time of Richard I's coronation on 3 September 1189. The day witnessed anti-Semitic rioting that led to the deaths of around 30 Jews after they were denied entry to the coronation banquet. Although Richard later explicitly stated that Jews in England should not be harmed, violence surfaced again and slowly spread north after he departed for the Holy Land on the Third Crusade.

In March the anti-Semitic attacks reached York. In the midst of a raging fire, the cause of which is unknown, a mob looted the house and killed the family of Benedict, a wealthy Jew who had been mortally wounded in the London pogrom. Fearing for their lives, the rest of the Jewish population of the city, numbering in the region of 150 people, fled to the well-defended Clifford's Tower.

Having been granted access by the warden, the fearful Jews later locked him out while an armed mob surrounded the tower. Trapped inside, and faced with either forced conversion to Christianity or death at the hands of the angry crowd, most of the Jews chose to die at their own hand. Many fathers killed their wives and children before committing suicide. The tower was then set on fire.

Although some Jews took up the offer of safe passage in return for their conversion, they were all killed by the crowd. Led by Richard Malebisse and other members of the local gentry, the mob then moved to York Minster where they burned the records of loans made to local residents by the Jews, effectively cancelling their debts.

MARCH
17
1992

A referendum in South Africa resulted in white South Africans voting to end apartheid.

The policy of apartheid, which literally translates as 'apartness', was introduced to South Africa in 1948. Although the region had experienced racial segregation under the rule of a white minority for centuries, the adoption of apartheid made it more systematic by separating people into one of four racial groups.

Within the country, opposition to apartheid led to the Sharpeville massacre in 1960 and the Soweto uprising in 1976. By the late 1980s the government's policy had seen South Africa face severe criticism from the United Nations alongside international isolation that included an arms embargo and a wide-ranging cultural and sports boycott. Meanwhile, leading anti-apartheid activist Nelson Mandela had been imprisoned since 1962.

F. W. de Klerk of the National Party became President of South Africa after the resignation of P. W. Botha in 1989. In his address at the opening of Parliament the following February, de Klerk announced his intention to lift the ban on political parties such as the African National Congress and release Nelson Mandela. This was followed by a series of negotiations between the government and the ANC that gradually lifted the laws of apartheid.

In the face of hostility from the white Conservative Party who began to defeat the National Party in by-elections, de Klerk called for a whites-only referendum to determine whether to continue his negotiations. Eighty-five percent of the electorate turned out, of whom more than two-thirds voted in favour of de Klerk and the dismantling of apartheid. The country's first multi-racial elections were held two years later, on 27 April 1994.

MARCH

18

1834

The Tolpuddle Martyrs were sentenced to transportation to Australia for swearing a secret oath as members of a 'friendly society'.

The Industrial Revolution, combined with the first of the Enclosure Acts, had seen the earnings of poor farmers plummet. With the radicalism of the French Revolution still fresh in people's minds, the Swing Riots of the early 1830s had seen agricultural workers turn to violent protest. Adding to tensions between land owners and workers, the repeal of the Combination Acts in 1825 effectively legalised the creation of trade unions.

By 1834, farm workers in the Dorset village of Tolpuddle were being paid just 7 shillings per week. This was three shillings less than the average agricultural labourer's wage. Six men consequently formed the Friendly Society of Agricultural Labourers under the leadership of George Loveless, in protest at the reduction in pay.

Part of the society's initiation ceremony involved swearing a secret oath, something that was illegal under the Unlawful Oaths Act of 1797. Local magistrate and landowner James Frampton was consequently able to take the six men to court, where they were convicted by a jury of 12 landowners and sentenced to seven years transportation by Judge Sir John Williams on 18 March 1834.

The sentence was greeted with uproar from the British public who collected 800,000 signatures calling for their release. 100,000 people took part in a march calling for the same and two years after their conviction the new Home Secretary, Lord John Russell, granted them pardons. The Tolpuddle Martyrs eventually returned home, but five of six soon left England and emigrated to Canada while the sixth, James Hammet, stayed in Dorset until his death in 1891.

MARCH

19

1882

The first stone of Barcelona's iconic Sagrada Familia basilica was laid.

The *Basílica i Temple Expiatori de la Sagrada Família*, better known as the Sagrada Familia, was conceived by Josep Maria Bocabella. Having established the Spiritual Association of Devotees of St. Joseph, Bocabella undertook a journey to Rome, after which he was inspired to construct a church in the style of the Basilica della Santa Casa in the Italian town of Loreto.

The Association used a number of donations from supporters to purchase a plot of land in Barcelona, and subsequently accepted an offer by architect Francisco de Paula del Villar to draw up the plans for free. Construction of his design for a neo-Gothic church began on 19 March 1882, the Feast of Saint Joseph, at a ceremony presided over by the Bishop of Barcelona.

Del Villar's design included explicit instructions for all the columns to be built of finely-dressed stone, known as ashlar. This would have had serious consequences for the cost of the project, so the Association attempted to persuade the architect to use cheaper stone for the interior of the columns and to only cover the outside with ashlar. Unwilling to compromise, Del Villar resigned his post shortly after the crypt below the apse was completed the following year.

In his absence the 31-year-old Antoni Gaudí was appointed to oversee the construction. The young architect dramatically changed the original design and, when he died 40 years later, the church was still less than 25% complete. The structure is estimated to be finished in 2026, 144 years after construction began, though Gaudi himself is said to have commented that 'My client is not in a hurry.'

MARCH

20

1602

The United East India Company, better known in Britain as the Dutch East India Company, was established.

By the start of the 17th century merchants from the Dutch Republic had begun to undertake voyages to the 'Spice Islands' of the Indian Ocean. This put them in direct competition with established traders from other European nations including Portugal and Britain, both of whom had previously dominated the market.

Due to the high risks for individual investors who mounted these individual voyages, the Dutch government supported the creation of a new umbrella company two years after the establishment of the competing English East India Company. The United East India Company combined the various individual business interests into a single entity that was granted a 21-year monopoly on the Dutch spice trade. Consequently the risk to investors was reduced as their individual funds were invested in the entire company's voyages, meaning that if some ships failed to return they were not completely wiped out. In return investors received an annual dividend of 18%.

Known in the Netherlands as the *Vereenigde Oostindische Compagnie*, or VOC, the company grew to become arguably the first transnational corporation. Yet by the middle of the 17th century it had begun to function as a state within a state that possessed its own army and political authority. Having usurped both the British and Portuguese competitors in the East Indies, the VOC dominated trade in the Indian and South Pacific Oceans for almost two centuries. During this time it sent almost a million European people to work in the region in almost 5,000 ships, more than the rest of the continent combined.

MARCH
21
1921

Vladimir Lenin introduced the New Economic Policy at the 10th Communist Party Congress.

In the aftermath of the Bolshevik Revolution that saw the Communist party under Lenin seize control of Russia, the country was plunged into Civil War. Counter-revolutionary forces under the banner of the Whites attempted to wrest back control while the Bolsheviks implemented the policy of War Communism that saw the strict centralisation of all parts of the national economy.

The forced nationalisation of industry and requisition of grain to provide materials and food for the Red Army succeeded in its military objectives, but proved enormously unpopular with the general population. With no incentive to produce surplus food the farmers simply stopped growing, leading to serious shortages in the cities that led large numbers of workers to leave the industrial centres for the countryside. With production already low, by 1921 those who stayed had begun a series of strikes and protests that eventually led to the Kronstadt Rebellion on 7 March 1921.

This uprising by the very sailors who had helped propel the Bolsheviks to power in 1917 forced Lenin to reconsider his approach. On 21 March, at the 10th Party Congress, the formal decree that introduced the New Economic Policy was announced. Grain requisitioning was replaced with a fixed tax, while private enterprise and profit were permitted. This provided an incentive for farmers to produce more, since they could now sell any surplus. Meanwhile some industries were denationalised, and the relationship between the countryside and the cities was strengthened. However, while the NEP revived the economy it also saw the re-emergence of capitalist inequalities that prompted Stalin to abandon the policy in 1929.

The brothers Auguste and Louis Lumière staged their first film screening in Paris.

Put on for an audience of 200 invited attendees at the 'Society for the Development of the National Industry', the reaction to the moving black-and-white pictures caught the brothers by surprise. They had attended the conference to share Louis' recent work on colour photography and only showed the 45-second film *La Sortie des Usines Lumière (Workers Leaving the Lumière Factory)*, as a novelty after Louis' lecture.

The machine used to project the film had been patented by the brothers the previous month. Their father owned a photographic materials factory in Lyon and told his sons about the Edison kinetoscope that he had seen in Paris in 1894. Inspired by their father's enthusiasm they invented the Cinématographe which combined a camera, developer and projector into a single unit. Its drive mechanism was based on the 'presser foot' used in sewing machines, and used a clawed gear to engage with perforations in the side of a roll of film. As the gear rotated, individual frames moved in front of the lens to capture the moving image at a rate of 12 frames every second. The same mechanism could later be used to project the captured images.

The positive reception to the first film screening led the brothers to refine their invention and, on 28 December 1895, they staged their first public show at the Grand Café in Paris. Within less than a decade, however, the brothers withdrew from the motion picture industry and instead turned their attention to the development of colour photography, a technology that they went on to dominate for a number of years with their Autochrome process.

MARCH

23

1806

The Lewis and Clark Expedition began its journey home, having crossed the western United States.

Thomas Jefferson completed the Louisiana Purchase in 1803, adding 828,000 square miles of territory to the United States. Keen to explore and establish a presence in the western territory, the President soon appointed his personal secretary Captain Meriwether Lewis to lead the specially-established Corps of Discovery.

Lewis selected his former superior officer, William Clark, as second in command. As far as the government was concerned Lewis was in charge of the expedition, but in practice the two men shared equal responsibility and even addressed each other as 'captain' throughout their two-year journey to the Pacific Ocean.

The expedition departed on 14 May 1804 and the 31 members made their way westward along the Missouri River. During the journey they made contact with more than twenty different native groups and identified dozens of previously unknown botanical specimens.

Having crossed the Rocky Mountains and reached the Columbia River, the Pacific Ocean was sighted on 7 November 1805. After reaching its shores two weeks later, the expedition constructed Fort Clatsop to establish an American presence at the mouth of the Columbia River and provide shelter during the bitter winter.

After enduring a difficult few months characterised by illness and hunger, the expedition began the return journey on 23 March 1806. They arrived back in St Louis on 23 September having lost just one member of the party. Lewis and Clark later travelled to Washington D.C. where they reported their findings to Jefferson who gave them double pay and comfortable government jobs.

The oil tanker *Exxon Valdez* struck Bligh Reef in Alaska's Prince William Sound and began spilling approximately 11 million gallons of crude oil into the water.

Exxon Valdez had only recently departed the Valdez Marine Terminal when the captain, Joseph Hazelwood, left Third Mate Gregory Cousins in charge of steering the vessel while he retired to his quarters. Having moved outside the usual shipping lanes to avoid small icebergs that had been sighted earlier, the ship struck the reef at 12:04am.

Described by famed naturalist John Muir as a 'bright and spacious wonderland', Prince William Sound is one of the world's most remote locations. This made the clean-up operation both challenging and expensive. Exxon and the Alyeska Pipeline Company were later criticised for their response to the spill, which initially used chemical dispersants on the oil. They later attempted a mechanical clean-up but, despite their attempts to control the situation, the oil eventually spread over more than 1,000 miles of coastline and 11,000 square miles of water. High pressure hot water that was sprayed over the beaches to displace the oil was later found to have destroyed organisms in the environment. These not only formed a vital part of the food chain but could also have helped to biodegrade the oil.

Millions of fish and hundreds of thousands of seabirds died in the immediate aftermath of the disaster, while hundreds of otters and seals – as well as more than a dozen orcas – also perished as a result of the oil spill. In total, only 10% of the lost oil was completely retrieved. This means that, even decades after the spill, hundreds of miles of Alaskan beaches are still polluted with crude oil lying just below the sandy surface.

MARCH

25

1306

Robert I, better known as Robert the Bruce, was crowned King of Scots.

Born to a noble family, Robert was a distant descendant of David I who had ruled Scotland in the first half of the twelfth century. In 1296 Robert supported the invasion by Edward I of England that forced John Balliol, who had been declared King of Scots following a succession dispute with Robert the Bruce's grandfather, from the throne. Edward subsequently began a period of direct rule over Scotland, during which time Bruce turned on the English king and joined William Wallace's uprising. However, he later made peace with Edward and was able to retain control of his lands after the Scottish defeat at the Battle of Falkirk the following year.

By submitting to Edward's authority Robert the Bruce demonstrated enormous political astuteness that led to him becoming joint Guardian of Scotland alongside John Comyn, a nephew of the ousted John Balliol and a competitor for the throne of Scotland. Their rivalry divided the Scottish nobility and set the stage for Comyn's murder at the hands of Bruce or one of his followers in the Chapel of Greyfriars Monastery in Dumfries on 10 February 1306.

With his greatest rival dead, Bruce quickly proclaimed his right to the throne of Scotland. He was outlawed by Edward for treason and excommunicated by the Pope but, despite such clear opposition, he was crowned King of Scots by Bishop William de Lamberton at Scone just six weeks later on 25 March. The months immediately following his coronation saw Robert the Bruce struggle against the English forces, but over time he developed his military skill and built a broad base of support that led to his victory at the Battle of Bannockburn and later Scottish independence.

The Book of Mormon first went on sale at the bookstore belonging to E. B. Grandin in Palmyra, New York.

The Book of Mormon is a key sacred text of the Latter Day Saint movement that was published by Joseph Smith, the founder of the movement, when he was twenty-four years old. He claimed to have been visited by the angel Moroni who showed him the location of a buried book etched on golden plates in a previously unknown language referred to as 'reformed Egyptian'. He translated the plates into English with the help of special spectacles or seer stones, and dictated the resulting text to a scribe.

Smith approached the printer and publisher Egbert B. Grandin after work on the book was completed in 1829. He was eventually persuaded to print 5,000 copies, but only went through with the full task after prosperous local farmer and early Mormon convert Martin Harris mortgaged his farm to cover the $3,000 security payment. It took Grandin's staff of eight men and boys under chief compositor John H. Gilbert almost eight months of working 12-hour, six day weeks to complete the job.

Concerned that the book might undermine existing Christian beliefs, and could even be blasphemous, local people in Palmyra organised a boycott. With thousands of original copies remaining unsold, the financier Martin Harris was later forced to sell his farm to cover to outstanding debt.

The original building in which Grandin printed and sold the first edition of the Book of Mormon was bought by The Church of Jesus Christ of Latter-day Saints in October 1978. It was subsequently restored to its original layout and appearance, albeit with the addition of a visitors' centre.

Mary Mallon, better known as Typhoid Mary, was confined to permanent quarantine on North Brother Island in New York.

Mary Mallon was born in 1869 in what is now Northern Ireland and, by 1884, had emigrated to New York where she began working as a domestic servant and cook. Having been employed by a variety of wealthy families, the early 1900s saw outbreaks of typhoid fever in houses where Mallon had worked, although she never suffered herself. This link to the woman that would later be dubbed 'Typhoid Mary' was only identified in 1907 after New York City Health Department official George Soper began investigating the outbreaks.

One key piece of evidence linking typhoid to Mary Mallon was the sudden appearance of the disease in Long Island's Oyster Bay in 1906. Local doctors described the disease as 'unusual' in the area, but it was later found that New York banker Charles Henry Warren had rented a house there while Mallon was the family cook. 6 of the 11 household members caught typhoid fever in a single week. It was later noted that she didn't follow basic hygiene practices.

Mallon refused to cooperate with Soper's investigation, even after being linked to typhoid outbreaks in seven of the eight households she had worked for. She was eventually arrested, and tests confirmed she carried the pathogen that caused typhoid fever. Mallon was eventually released from quarantine in 1910 on the promise that she would not endanger the public by working as a cook, but eventually returned to the profession under an assumed name and caused a major outbreak of the disease in 1915.

Mallon was swiftly located and arrested. She was quarantined against her will on North Brother Island on 27 March, where she was held until her death from pneumonia 23 years later.

Operation Chariot successfully put the Normandie dry dock in the Nazi-occupied French town of St Nazaire out of action.

The raid by the Royal Navy and British Commandos was overseen by Combined Operations Headquarters. Their task was to disable the only dry dock on the Atlantic seaboard that was big enough to accommodate the terrifying German battleship *Tirpitz*. This was vital to British attempts to weaken the German presence in the Atlantic. If the St Nazaire facility could be put out of action, the Germans would have to send *Tirpitz* home for any repairs and would ultimately keep the dangerous ship out of the Atlantic.

265 commandos and 346 Royal Navy personnel arrived at the French docks in a convoy led by the old British destroyer HMS *Campbeltown* in the early hours of 28 March. The convoy was spotted before reaching the enormous gates of the dry dock but, despite intense fire from the German batteries on the shore, *Campeltown* ploughed into the dock gates at 1.34am. Commandos surged ashore to destroy key dock facilities with explosives while assault teams tried to draw away German defenders. Meanwhile, time fuses attached to explosives hidden in the bow of *Campbeltown* were set.

With almost all the British evacuation ships destroyed or unable to reach the docks, it became clear that the Commandos left on shore would be unable to leave by sea. They consequently fought on until they ran out of ammunition, after which all but five were taken prisoner. At around noon the explosives inside *Campbeltown* detonated, destroying the dry dock.

Only 228 men returned to England. 169 had been killed and 205 became prisoners of war, but the raid itself was a success as the dock remained inoperative for the rest of the war.

MARCH

29

1974

The Terracotta Army was discovered in Shaanxi province, China.

A group of farmers discovered the site of the ancient sculptures while digging a well outside Xiyang Village near the city of Xi'an. On the fifth day of excavation team-member Yang Zhifa uncovered pieces of a life-sized terracotta warrior beneath a layer of hard red earth, and soon found other fragments of clay models alongside artefacts including bronze arrowheads. Realising that they had stumbled upon a potentially important cultural site the farmers notified the local authorities who in turn called for a team of archaeologists to investigate.

One of the archaeologists, Zhao Kangmin, later revealed how 'we were so excited, we rode on our bicycles so fast it felt as if we were flying'. After retrieving a number of fragments he spent time at the local museum piecing together two 1.78m terracotta statues, confirming his suspicions that the site dated back to the reign of Qin Shi Huang, the first Emperor of China, who reigned in the third century BCE.

The find was initially kept secret for fear of the statues being destroyed by Red Guards caught up in the Cultural Revolution that had already destroyed other archaeological sites. However, it was later exposed by a journalist in a story that attracted the attention of officials in Beijing who initiated a full-scale excavation.

Thousands of sculptures have so far been uncovered, buried in an elaborate funerary complex spread of many square miles. The Terracotta Army was found in battle formation in a series of deep pits, guarding the nearby tomb mound of their Emperor that remains tantalisingly unexcavated.

MARCH

30

1856

The Crimean War officially ended with the signing of the Treaty of Paris.

The Crimean War began in October 1853, having been triggered by disagreements between Russia and the Ottoman Empire regarding Russia's right to protect the Orthodox Christian minority in the Ottoman-controlled Holy Land. Against a background of declining Ottoman power, Britain and France later joined the war to stop Russia gaining dominance around the Black Sea.

Having raged for two and a half years, with fighting mostly taking place around the Crimean Peninsula, the 'notoriously incompetent international butchery' ended when Russia accepted preliminary peace terms after Austria-Hungary mobilised with the opposing forces. The subsequent peace conference in Paris featured Russia on one side of the table and the alliance of Britain, France, the Ottoman Empire, and Sardinia-Piedmont on the other.

The treaty guaranteed the independence and territorial integrity of the Ottoman Empire, and sought to achieve that with the 'neutralisation' of the Black Sea. This denied military access to the waters and also restricted Russia and Turkey from building military fortifications on the coast. Furthermore, the Treaty of Paris restored the territory that each nation controlled to that which had existed before the war, while Russia was forced to abandon its attempts to protect the Ottoman Empire's Christian subjects.

In reality the treaty only returned temporary stability to Europe. The Ottoman Empire failed to reform and so continued to crumble as nationalist sentiment grew. The larger 'Eastern Question' itself remained unsettled and, in 1877, Russia and the Ottoman Empire again went to war.

The Bosnian Crisis came to end with Serbia's acceptance of the annexation of Bosnia and Herzegovina by Austria-Hungary.

The Bosnian Crisis, also known as the Annexation Crisis, was triggered on 6 October 1908 when Austria-Hungary announced the annexation of the former Ottoman territories of Bosnia and Herzegovina. While the Habsburg Empire had been permitted to occupy and administer the territories under the terms of the Treaty of Berlin in 1878, the unilateral annexation was greeted with diplomatic protests from the European powers. Serbia was particularly angered by the Austro-Hungarian action and mobilised its army the next day.

The annexation itself came just a day after Bulgaria declared independence from the Ottoman Empire, which had been plunged into chaos following the Young Turk Revolution earlier that year. With the Ottomans unable to respond to the Bosnian annexation beyond a trade embargo, it was left to the other Great Powers to resolve the crisis. They called for a conference to settle the matter but, with the support of Germany, Austria-Hungary refused to cooperate and the plan was abandoned.

Austria-Hungary therefore began separate negotiations to recognise the annexation by amending the Treaty of Berlin. The Russian public had pressured the government to come down firmly on the side of Serbia, but over the course of the next few months the other powers gradually acquiesced. With none of the other powers willing to go to war to preserve the Treaty of Berlin, Russia and Serbia were eventually forced to back down. On 31 March 1909 the Serbian government formally accepted the situation. This left both Serbia and Russia humiliated, and increased the tensions between themselves and Austria-Hungary.

APRIL

APRIL
1
1933

Francisco Franco announced the end of the Spanish Civil War, four days after Nationalist forces entered Madrid.

The Spanish Civil War began in July 1936 after a military coup by Spanish forces in North Africa failed to secure complete control over the country. Their unsuccessful attempt to overthrow the government of the Second Spanish Republic left the country divided between the generally left-leaning and urban Republicans and the conservative Nationalist rebels.

Having unified the Nationalist forces in 1937, Franco secured assistance from Hitler in Germany and Mussolini in Italy who provided both military equipment and personnel. Meanwhile the USSR provided assistance to the Republicans, even though all three countries had previously signed a non-intervention agreement.

By the end of 1938 the Nationalists had split the Republican-controlled areas in two, allowing them to focus on capturing Catalonia while keeping Madrid under siege. The fall of Catalonia in February 1939 triggered the resignation of the President of the Republic and the decision by both Britain and France to recognise the Nationalist government.

With Republican forces fleeing across the border into France, a coup was launched against the Prime Minister Juan Negrín with the intention of negotiating a peace deal with the Nationalists. However, Franco refused to accept anything other than unconditional surrender. By 27 March the Nationalists were facing virtually no resistance as they marched into previously Republican-held territory. Madrid surrendered the next day, and Nationalist troops seized the remaining Republican areas by the end of the month. On 1 April, Franco went on the radio to proclaim victory.

APRIL

2

1977

The racehorse Red Rum won an historic third Grand National at Aintree Racecourse in Liverpool.

The Grand National is an annual steeplechase that has been run since 1839, except for a brief interruption during the Second World War when Aintree Racecourse was commandeered for use by the army. Regarded as one of the hardest horse races in the world, the Grand National has been known to tempt even the most reluctant of Britain's gamblers.

The thoroughbred horse Red Rum had secured several wins in his early career before being bought by trainer Ginger McCain on behalf of Noel le Mare. Discovering that the horse had a hoof condition that threatened his ability to run, McCain took to training Red Rum on the beach at the seaside town of Southport where it is alleged the salt water helped to resolve the problem.

Red Rum ran his first Grand National in 1973, ridden by jockey Brian Fletcher. Having trailed the Australian horse Crisp for most of the race, Red Rum gained ground on the final straight and secured the win by three-quarters of a length. Red Rum returned to Aintree the following year where he again won the Grand National.

The next two years saw Red Rum beaten to second place but, on 2 April 1977, the horse once again secured the winning position in Britain's most famous horse race. At twelve years old many people had doubted whether Red Rum was capable of even finishing the race, let alone win it.

Red Rum's third and final Grand National victory secured his place as the most successful horse in the race's history. He was retired from racing the following year, but remains the most famous name in British horse racing.

The first Pony Express service left the American city of St Joseph in Missouri destined for Sacramento in California.

Established shortly before the first transcontinental telegraph, the mail service used mounted riders and was, for its short operational lifetime, the fastest way to send messages from one coast to the other. Operated by the Central Overland California and Pikes Peak Express Company, the first pouches of mail – known as a mochila – arrived at both their East and West destinations on the 14th April, ten days after they departed.

The joint founders of the company were already established businessmen in the American freight and drayage industry. William H. Russell, Alexander Majors, and William B. Waddell had each developed significant experience of transporting goods and equipment to the Pacific Coast as the population grew rapidly in the aftermath of the gold rush that began after 1848.

The partners established the Pony Express with the hope of winning a lucrative government mail contract, which in the end they did not secure. Adding to their financial pressures, just a few weeks after operations began the outbreak of the Paiute War resulted in around $75,000 worth of damage to Pony Express property. Despite its place in frontier lore, therefore, the business was a financial failure.

Sources indicate that despite grossing up to $90,000 the Pony Express lost in the region of $200,000 during its short 19-month operation. Unable to recoup its losses through the long-sought after government contract, it was made obsolete as soon as the transcontinental telegraph began operating on October 24, 1861. The closure of the Pony Express was announced just two days later on October 26, 1861.

APRIL
4
1925

The Nazi Party founded a paramilitary organisation that became the *Schutzstaffel*, better known as the SS.

The organisation was established on the orders of Adolf Hitler to act as his personal bodyguard. He had been released from prison the previous December, having been found guilty of treason following the failed Munich Putsch, and was keen to ensure his safety when attending party functions and events.

The SS was technically a division of the longer-established SA, but the group's loyalty to Hitler meant that over time it grew to be the dominant organisation. This came about under the leadership of Heinrich Himmler, who was appointed *Reichsführer-SS* in January 1929. He transformed the SS from a small bodyguard of less than 300 members into a private army containing over 50,000 men by the time Hitler became Chancellor of Germany in January 1933.

Membership of the SS was reserved for those men who would loyally and unquestioningly serve Hitler and the Nazi Party, and who met the SS's strict racial policy. Through racial selection of both SS members and their spouses, the Nazis hoped to create an 'elite' community of people with an 'Aryan-Nordic bloodline'.

The Night of the Long Knives in June 1934 removed any remaining authority the SA once had over the SS. A month later Hitler formally separated the two organisations, meaning that the SS became answerable to him alone. As the organisation grew even further under the Nazi dictatorship, separate SS subdivisions were established within a sprawling bureaucracy.

By the end of the Second World War the SS had responsibilities that stretched from policing and the collection of intelligence to running Nazi concentration and death camps.

Julius and Ethel Rosenberg were sentenced to death in the United States for conspiracy to commit espionage.

Julius and Ethel Rosenberg met when they were members of the Young Communist League in New York. It was only after his previous membership of the organisation was discovered that Julius was dismissed from his position at the Army Signal Corps Engineering Laboratories at Fort Monmouth, New Jersey. He had worked as an engineer-inspector for nearly 5 years during the Second World War, and it was during this time that he was recruited to spy for Russia.

Rosenberg went on to recruit a number of other people who were able to supply secret information, including Ethel's brother David Greenglass who worked on the Manhattan Project at the Los Alamos National Laboratory. He was arrested following a tip-off in May 1950, and named Julius Rosenberg as his contact.

During both a secret grand jury testimony and their subsequent trial the Rosenbergs refused to divulge information about their connections to the Communist Party. Despite this, they were found guilty of espionage and sentenced to death for their role in passing information about the US nuclear programme to the Soviet Union.

Although there have been subsequent attempts to clear their names, the publication of decrypted messages from the United States' VERONA project in 1995 clearly showed that Julius Rosenberg was guilty of espionage and that Ethel was fully aware of her husband's activities and actively assisted him. The general consensus among historians, therefore, is that the couple were guilty of the charge. However, debate still rages over whether or not their crime justified their executions.

APRIL

6

1917

The United States entered the First World War after Congress declared war on the German Empire.

American President Woodrow Wilson had made his case for war before a special joint session of Congress four days earlier. During his address he claimed that, 'we have no selfish ends to serve' since the war would 'make the world safe for democracy'. American involvement was, therefore, a moral obligation.

Wilson's decision to request a declaration of war came in the wake of two significant developments against the United States. Firstly, Germany's decision to resume unrestricted submarine warfare meant that all ships, including those from neutral countries, which traded with Germany's enemies were now a target for sinking. Secondly, the British passed on the intercepted contents of a secret telegram from the German Foreign Secretary, Arthur Zimmermann, to the Mexican government. The telegram sought a German alliance with Mexico in the event of the United States declaring war. Significantly, it promised that Arizona, Texas and New Mexico would return to Mexican control once victory had been achieved.

Wilson had initially been reluctant to declare war due to his belief that public opinion in the United States was against it. But with civilian merchant and passenger ships once again under threat, and with the Zimmermann telegram's indication of German intentions to attack the United States itself, the President felt that the American public were ready to change their minds.

Following Wilson's address to the joint session, the Senate and the House met separately to debate and vote on the resolution. The Senate passed it by 82 votes to 6, while the House of Representatives did so by 373 to 50.

APRIL

7

1141

Matilda, the daughter of King Henry I of England, was declared the 'Lady of England and Normandy' in advance of a coronation that never took place.

Matilda had married the future Holy Roman Emperor, Henry V, in 1114 after which she ruled Italy as Empress Matilda. Her father had intended for his only legitimate son, Matilda's younger brother William Adeline, to inherit the English throne after he died but he himself had died in the *White Ship* disaster in November 1120.

King Henry was desperate to ensure his family's succession. Consequently, following the death of Matilda's husband in 1125, she returned to her father's court. Henry nominated her as his heir in the event that he had no sons, and required his barons and court to swear an oath of loyalty to her. Three years later she was married to Prince Geoffrey of Anjou to whom she bore three sons, including the future Henry II.

Despite the oaths sworn to recognise Matilda's claim, the death of her father in 1135 prompted a succession crisis. Matilda was in Anjou at the time and her cousin, Stephen de Blois, quickly moved to secure the crown for himself. Matilda's subsequent invasion of England prompted a Civil War that became known as the Anarchy.

During the Battle of Lincoln in 1141 Matilda captured Stephen and imprisoned him, opening the door for her coronation. However, despite being proclaimed 'Lady of England' in Winchester by senior clergymen, Matilda was unpopular in London and was forced to retreat before her coronation took place. The war dragged on for a number of years, but Matilda returned to Normandy in 1148. Her son later ascended to the English throne as Henry II, the first Angevin king.

APRIL

8

1904

Times Square in New York was given its name shortly after the offices of *The New York Times* moved to the area.

Having once belonged to the prominent real estate investor John Jacob Astor, the second half of the 19th century saw the area around the modern Times Square become the centre of the New York carriage business. The establishment of the American Horse Exchange by the prominent businessman William Henry Vanderbilt fuelled this development which led to the area being named Longacre Square after London's carriage district which centred on Long Acre.

While the late 1800s saw the area develop a reputation as a red light district, the arrival of electricity attracted the impresario Oscar Hammerstein I who opened a huge theatre complex called the Olympia in 1895. Although the nearby Empire Theatre had opened two years earlier, the imposing Olympia contributed to a change in the economic makeup of Longacre that coincided with the arrival of New York's first rapid transit system.

Easy access to middle- and upper-class restaurant and theatre goers, alongside the fast distribution network provided by the new Interborough Rapid Transit line, persuaded Adolph S. Ochs of *The New York Times* to move his newspaper's headquarters to the area at the start of the 20th century. Having chosen a prime piece of land he built the Times Tower, the second tallest building in the city at the time, with its basement containing the printing presses right next door to the new subway line. To coincide with the arrival of the newspaper, Mayor George B. McClellan Jr. approved a resolution to change the name from Longacre Square to Times Square. Even after the newspaper moved offices the name stayed, as did the neon lights and millions of visitors.

APRIL

9

1767

John Hancock, one of Boston's wealthiest merchants, and a leading figure in Boston politics, forcibly removed customs officials from his ship *Lydia*.

Despite emerging victorious from the Seven Years' War that had ended in 1763, Britain was desperate to recoup the costs. Attempts to raise money by imposing the Sugar Act and the Stamp Act on its colonies had met significant opposition for both economic and constitutional reasons. Despite these tensions, the British government introduced the Townshead Acts in 1767 which sought to challenge the extensive smuggling that went on in the colonies, and thus generate tax revenue for Britain.

Lydia arrived in port on the afternoon of 8 April, and was closely watched by British customs officials known as tidesmen. They were under orders to ensure that the cargo was properly declared and landed, rather than smuggled away.

Despite only being there to observe, at least one of the tidesmen went below deck the next evening and entered the ship's hold. Hancock himself challenged the officials and demanded to see the documents that gave them permission to search his ship. Having found that they did not have the necessary writ of assistance, Hancock ordered members of the ship's crew to eject them.

The commissioners wanted to press charges but the Attorney General, Jonathan Sewall, ruled that no crime had been committed by the crew. However, the British customs commissioners continued to target Hancock. Their next opportunity came during the *Liberty* affair the following year, so it has since been argued that Hancock's actions on board *Lydia* represented the first act of physical resistance to British authority that developed into the American Revolution.

APRIL

10

1971

The United States table tennis team heralded the era of 'ping pong diplomacy' by becoming the first official American delegation to visit China in 20 years.

Relations between America and China had soured in the aftermath of the Communist Revolution, and grew worse as a result of the Korean War in which the countries fought on opposing sides. Relations were so poor that, by the time the two countries travelled to Nagoya in Japan for the 31st World Table Tennis Championships in 1971, they had no diplomatic or economic relationship.

Richard Nixon intended to bring China in from the cold when he took up the presidency in 1969. Meanwhile, increasing tensions between China and the USSR had similarly led Chairman Mao to consider rebuilding relations with the United States. Both table tennis teams being in Nagoya offered the perfect opportunity.

Having missed the US bus after practice one evening, American player Glenn Cowan travelled back to his room with the Chinese team. Although the Chinese claim that Cowan 'stumbled up the steps' of their bus, he claimed in an interview that he was invited to travel with them. Whatever the reality, during the short bus journey Cowan was given a silk-screen picture of the Huangshan mountains by the Chinese player Zhuang Zedong.

Favourable press coverage, which led Mao to comment on Zhuang Zedong's positive actions as a diplomat, resulted in the entire American team being invited to China after the tournament ended. Having arrived in the country on 10 April, they spent ten days touring Guangzhou, Beijing and Shanghai. Their visit heralded a new period in Sino-American relations that culminated in President Nixon himself travelling to China the following year.

APRIL
11
1950

The Stone of Scone was found on the site of the High Altar at Arbroath Abbey, nearly four months after it disappeared from Westminster Abbey.

The Stone of Scone is a block of red sandstone that was used in the coronation of the monarchs of Scotland and, later, the monarchs of England and the Kingdom of Great Britain. It was captured by King Edward I of England in 1296 and taken from Scone Abbey in Scotland to Westminster Abbey in London.

Since it was a powerful symbol of Scottish nationhood, a plot to remove the Stone from Westminster Abbey and return it to Scotland was hatched by University of Glasgow student Ian Hamilton and a number of accomplices. Having secured funding from Scottish businessman Robert Gray, Hamilton and three other students drove to London on Christmas Eve 1950 and put their plan into action.

The three men from the group entered the Abbey through a side door that night, and made their way to the Coronation Chair. They managed to remove the Stone, but damaged the chair itself in the process. The Stone also fell to the floor and broke into two unequal parts. The smaller was quickly taken to a waiting car driven by the one female accomplice, Kay Matheson, while Hamilton returned to load the larger half into a second car.

The two halves were reunited in Scotland a few weeks later, and the Stone was repaired by a stonemason. The conspirators met two Arbroath councillors at the ruined Abbey on 11 April, and laid the Stone on the site of the High Altar. The councillors later informed the police, and the Stone was recovered and returned to Westminster Abbey. It now resides in Edinburgh Castle, having been formally returned to Scotland by the British government in 1996.

APRIL
12
1917

The Canadian Corps successfully captured Vimy Ridge in the First World War.

Vimy Ridge was a 7km ridge that had been held by the Germans since the Race to the Sea in 1914. French forces had made numerous attempts to seize the ridge over the next two years at the cost of approximately 150,000 casualties. However, due to the need to move French troops to Verdun, in October 1916 the position was taken over by the four divisions of the Canadian Corps.

By early 1917 the war had become one of attrition. Desperate to break the stalemate, French and British commanders planned a major offensive near the city of Arras to divert German forces from the main French offensive further south. The Canadians were tasked with seizing Vimy Ridge, which the Germans had heavily fortified.

The Canadian Corps under the command of Lieutenant-General Sir Julian Byng, and with the assistance of numerous British support units, carefully rehearsed their attack in the preceding weeks. They studied detailed maps and aerial photographs of the enemy lines, laid communication cables, dug a series of tunnels leading directly to the front lines, and stockpiled shells for the enormous artillery barrage that was to precede the assault.

Over 1 million shells were fired at the German lines for a week before the attack. Referred to by German troops as 'the week of suffering', the bombardment destroyed many of their defences and left them exhausted. At 5:30 am on 9 April the first wave of Canadian troops advanced behind a creeping artillery barrage through sleet and snow. They captured most of their objectives on the first day, and took control of the final target – a heavily fortified mound known as the Pimple – by nightfall on 12 April.

Troops from the British Indian Army committed the Amritsar Massacre when they opened fire on nonviolent protesters and pilgrims at Jallianwala Bagh.

The First World War had seen the introduction of a series of emergency powers by the ruling British government that sought to suppress the emerging Indian nationalist movement. The Rowlett Act that came into effect in March 1919 extended these powers and was greeted with significant political unrest, especially in the Punjab region. On 10 April violence erupted in Amritsar and troops killed several nationalist protesters while the crowd killed at least five Europeans. The following day they beat a female English missionary.

In response to the volatile situation, the British government placed Amritsar under martial law and passed control to Brigadier General Reginald Dyer. Dyer immediately banned gatherings of more than four people, although it is likely that many Punjabis from outside the city were unaware of the ban when they arrived at Amritsar for the annual Baisakhi celebrations on 13 April. An estimated ten thousand people gathered at Jallianwala Bagh, a large walled park in the city, although it is unclear how many were there to celebrate the festival and how many were nationalist protesters attending a demonstration.

Dyer arrived at the Bagh with armed soldiers in the late afternoon and blocked the exits. Without warning, he then gave the order for his troops to open fire in an attack that only stopped after most of the ammunition had been used. According to the British inquiry 379 people were killed, although Indian estimates place the figure at more than a thousand. Winston Churchill, the Secretary of State for War at the time, condemned the attack as 'monstrous'.

APRIL

14

70

The future Roman Emperor Titus began the Siege of Jerusalem, during which the Second Temple was burned and destroyed.

The Roman attack on Jerusalem came four years into the First Jewish–Roman War. Triggered by ethnic tensions between Romans and Jews in Judea, the Great Revolt quickly spread throughout the province. Emperor Nero sent four legions, approximately 80,000 soldiers, under the command of his trusted general Vespasian and his son Titus to crush the uprising. By the time Vespasian was recalled to Rome in 69 CE to be appointed Emperor, the Roman forces had driven most of the rebels back to the fortified city of Jerusalem.

Titus moved to besiege the city in early 70 CE, coinciding with Passover. Assisted by the experienced general and former governor of Judea, Tiberius Julius Alexander, he positioned three legions on the western side and a fourth to the east on the Mount of Olives. Pilgrims were permitted to enter the city to celebrate Passover, but the Romans refused to allow them out again. The increase in population placed additional strain on the already-depleted food and water supplies in the city.

Many of the details of the siege were recorded by the Jewish historian Josephus, who had defected to the Roman side after his surrender earlier in the war. Having failed to negotiate with the defenders of the city, but having breached the Third and Second walls, the Romans sought to force the Jews into starvation by erecting a wooden palisade that used every tree in a 10 mile radius.

When the Romans breached the final defences in August the remaining defenders were massacred and the Temple was destroyed, leaving the Western Wall as the only surviving feature.

APRIL

15

1989

Ninety-six Liverpool Football Club fans died and hundreds more were injured in a crush at Hillsborough Stadium in Sheffield.

Liverpool were facing Nottingham Forrest in a sold out 1988-89 FA Cup semi-final. The match was scheduled to be played at the neutral home of Sheffield Wednesday, and fans of the two teams were allocated segregated areas based on their approach routes. This led to Liverpool being assigned to the smaller Leppings Lane stands, despite the team having more supporters.

Many English football stadiums at the time featured standing-only 'pens' that were surrounded by high steel fences to keep fans separated from each other and from the pitch. Although Hillsborough had experienced non-fatal crushes previously, no changes were made to the layout of the terrace.

As Liverpool fans began to arrive at the stadium, a bottleneck began to form due to the small number of turnstiles. Over 5,000 fans were still outside the ground fifteen minutes before kick-off, so police opened a large exit gate in order to relieve pressure. This led to thousands of Liverpool supporters entering pens 3 and 4, exerting enormous pressure on those fans already inside who began to be crushed against the fencing. Some managed to escape by climbing the fences while others were pulled to safety by fans in the upper stand, but 96 people died and 766 were injured.

Numerous inquests followed the disaster, with the authorities initially diverting blame to the Liverpool fans themselves. In April 2016 the Goldring inquest returned the verdict that the police failed in their duty of care and that the fans were unlawfully killed due to gross negligence.

Vladimir Lenin arrived in Russia after a decade of self-imposed exile.

Lenin, the leader of the Bolshevik Party, had left Russia in 1907 after Tsar Nicholas II cancelled many of the reforms he had promised following the 1905 revolution. While abroad he remained busy organising Bolshevik groups and publishing Marxist works, but following the February Revolution and the abdication of the Tsar in 1917 he began making plans to return to Russia.

The country had been weakened by the exhausting toll of the First World War and this, combined with disastrous food shortages, had prompted the popular revolt that overthrew the Tsar. In his place the Provisional Government ruled the country, and they opted to continue the war effort despite strong opposition from the Russian people.

German officials were keen to further destabilise the situation. Despite being at war, Lenin and other Bolshevik exiles were granted permission to return to Russia from Switzerland through Germany in a 'sealed train'. This meant that Lenin and his companions were never legally recognised as being in Germany.

The group then took a ferry to Sweden followed by a second train to Finland, arriving at Finland Station in Petrograd on 16 April. The next day Lenin published the April Theses in which he denounced both the Provisional Government and the First World War, and claimed that Russia was 'passing from the first stage of the revolution…to its second stage, which must place power in the hands of the proletariat and the poorest sections of the peasants'. Less than seven months later the Bolsheviks overthrew the Provisional Government in the October Revolution.

APRIL

17

1961

The Bay of Pigs Invasion was launched by the CIA-sponsored paramilitary group Brigade 2506.

The invasion saw over 1,400 American-trained Cuban exiles attempt to overthrow Fidel Castro. Castro had come to power in 1959 during the Cuban Revolution which toppled the previous president, General Fulgencio Batista. The new government quickly began introducing agrarian reforms and nationalising US-owned interests. These actions led to the USA imposing a trade embargo against Cuba from late 1960, after which Castro began to further develop his relationship with the USSR.

As concerns grew over these developments, US President Dwight D. Eisenhower authorised the CIA to begin devising a way to overthrow Castro. He allocated $13.1 million for them to begin training counter-revolutionary Cuban exiles and, on 4 April 1961, his successor John F. Kennedy authorised the final invasion plan.

While the seaborne invasion force gathered in Guatemala, a smaller group of Cuban exiles attacked Cuban airfields on 15 April using CIA-obtained B-26 bombers painted to appear like they were captured Cuban planes. That evening the Cuban government tabled a motion to the United Nations, accusing the United States of being behind the attacks. Consequently a series of airfield attacks planned for the early hours of the 17 April were cancelled by Kennedy.

The amphibious assault went ahead as planned but quickly began to go wrong. The exiles from Brigade 2506 were pinned on the beach by a counterattack from the Cuban Army and assorted militiamen, leading to 114 exile deaths and the capture of over a thousand others. In the aftermath, Cuba developed even closer links with the USSR that led to the Cuban Missile Crisis the following year.

Pope Julius II laid the cornerstone of the current St Peter's Basilica, one of Catholicism's most sacred buildings.

St Peter's Basilica, whose enormous Michelangelo-designed dome makes it one of the most dominant features on the Rome skyline, is located on what Catholics believe is the burial site of Saint Peter, one of the Twelve Apostles of Jesus Christ.

Emperor Constantine the Great had built an earlier basilica on the site of a shrine that was reputed to mark St Peter's burial place in the 4th century. However, this building had fallen into a poor state of repair by the 15th century and in 1505 Pope Julius II made the decision to demolish the 1,100-year-old basilica and build an entirely new one.

Such an undertaking would prove to be incredibly costly but, with funds partially provided by the selling of indulgences, construction began on a design by architect Donato Bramante in 1506. A number of adaptations were made to the plans over the next few decades, although a large part of the current building was designed by Michelangelo after he took over the project in 1547.

It took over a century to complete St Peter's Basilica, which was consecrated by Pope Urban VIII on 18 November 1626. Judged by many as the greatest example of Renaissance architecture, the basilica is the largest church in the world. Even more than 500 years after its construction, the dome still remains one of the largest in the world and continues to tower over lavish decorations and unmatched pieces of religious art. Yet, despite its position as perhaps the most famous Catholic building in the world, St Peter's Basilica is not the mother church. This is rather St John Lateran, the cathedral church of Rome and the official seat of the Pope.

APRIL

19

1839

The Treaty of London was signed, which recognised and guaranteed the independence and neutrality of Belgium.

In 1813 Napoléon's rule of the Netherlands was ended by the combined armies of Russia and Prussia, and control was given to William Frederik of Orange-Nassau. Two years later, as a result of the Congress of Vienna, modern Belgium became part of the United Kingdom of the Netherlands.

These southern provinces were predominantly Catholic, and a sizeable number of the inhabitants spoke French. However, William clearly favoured Protestantism and had tried to impose Dutch as the official language. This led to tensions which were exacerbated by economic problems that included high unemployment and arguments over the effect of free trade on the less developed south. A revolution erupted in 1830 that led to the states declaring independence on 4 October, although William refused to recognise the independent Belgium for over nine years.

In signing the treaty that formally recognised the existence of the independent Kingdom of Belgium, the Netherlands were joined by Britain, Austria, France, Russia, and the German Confederation. Furthermore, Britain insisted that the signatories also recognise Belgium's perpetual neutrality.

The neutrality clause was of central importance in the outbreak of the First World War, since Germany violated Belgium's neutrality when its forces crossed the border in the Schlieffen Plan. Britain thus claimed to be upholding the Treaty of London when it declared war on 4 August 1914 – much to the anger of German Chancellor Theobald von Bethmann-Hollweg who couldn't believe Britain would go to war over a 'mere a scrap of paper'.

APRIL

20

1902

Marie and Pierre Curie proved the existence of the new element radium when they chemically isolated one-tenth of a gram of pure radium chloride.

Marie and Pierre Curie were both pioneering scientists in their own right, but as a research partnership they are most famous for their work on radioactivity. Inspired by the work of the French physicist Henri Becquerel who had been the first person to discover radioactivity, the Curies' work won them the 1903 Nobel Prize in Physics which they shared with Becquerel himself.

Marie had been born and raised in Poland but, since women were not permitted to attend university there, she moved to France to take up a place to study at the Sorbonne in Paris. Having secured degrees in both physical sciences and mathematics by 1894 she married Pierre, an established physicist, whom she had met through a mutual friend. Marie subsequently began to pursue a Ph.D. for which she studied the recently-discovered rays emitted by uranium.

Having coined the term radioactivity to describe the radiation she observed, Curie focused on the minerals pitchblende and torbernite in her search for materials that emitted more radiation than uranium itself. Inspired by his wife's discovery that the element thorium was radioactive, Pierre dropped his own research in 1898 to work with her. In July they published a joint paper announcing the existence of an element they named polonium, and in December they did the same for radium.

To unequivocally prove their existence, the Curies sought to isolate them from pitchblende. Having processed tons of the mineral, they eventually obtained one-tenth of a gram of radium chloride on 20 April 1902, for which they shared the 1903 Nobel Prize in Physics.

APRIL

21

1918

The German fighter pilot Baron Manfred Albrecht Freiherr von Richthofen, better known as the Red Baron, was shot down and killed.

Richthofen was born into the German aristocracy in 1892. He began military training when he was 11 years old, and served as a cavalry reconnaissance officer in the early months of the First World War. However, the advent of trench warfare made the cavalry virtually obsolete and his unit was disbanded.

Frustrated at being reassigned to non-combative roles, Richthofen applied to the Imperial German Army Air Service and was granted permission to join in May 1915. Having begun as an observer on reconnaissance missions, he began to train as a pilot in October and joined one of the first German fighter squadrons the following year.

Richthofen quickly gained a reputation as a formidable fighter pilot. Having scored his first confirmed victory on 17 September 1916, Richthofen went on to shoot down a total of 80 enemy aircraft although only 19 of these were made in the red Fokker Dr.I triplane that is commonly associated with him. As a squadron leader Richthofen ensured that his squadron followed the *Dicta Boelcke*, a series of formalised tactical rules for air combat that had been developed by his mentor, Oswald Boelcke.

Richthofen was fatally wounded over Morlancourt Ridge near the village of Vaux-sur-Somme. Despite the single bullet severely damaging his heart and lungs he managed to land his aircraft in a field before he died. He was buried with full military honours by No. 3 Squadron of the Australian Flying Corps in France, although his remains now lie in Richthofen family grave.

APRIL

22

1884

Thomas Stevens departed San Francisco on a large-wheeled Ordinary, also known as a penny-farthing, to become the first person to cycle around the world.

Stevens was born in England and emigrated to the USA when he was seventeen years old. A contemporary magazine describes him as having worked a railroad mill in Wyoming before securing a job at a Colorado mine where he had the idea of cycling across the United States. Having already developed a love of cycling, Stevens bought a 50-inch Columbia penny-farthing in 1884. Built by the Pope Manufacturing Company of Chicago, it was on this bicycle that he departed San Francisco at 8am on 22 April 1884.

The first leg of Stevens' journey took him 3,700 miles east to Boston, which he reached after more than three months' travelling along everything from wagon trails to canal towpaths. Determined to travel light, his handlebar bag contained only a change of socks and shirt, a raincoat that doubled as a tent, and a revolver.

Stevens arrived in Boston on 4 August, making him the first person to cycle across North America. He then chose to wait until the following year to cross the Atlantic to Liverpool and begin the next part of his journey. Crossing the Channel to France, he cycled across Europe to Constantinople before crossing into Asia.

Stevens made it to Iran before being forced to turn back to Turkey, having been denied passage through both Siberia and Afghanistan. He resorted to taking a steamship to Karachi from where he cycled to Calcutta and another ship to Hong Kong. More cycling to China's east coast got him to a ship bound for Japan where his incredible ride finished on 17 December 1886. His journal records 'DISTANCE ACTUALLY WHEELED, ABOUT 13,500 MILES'.

Duke Wilhelm IV of Bavaria signed the *Reinheitsgebot*, a law to ensure the purity of beer that specified a limited number of ingredients.

The early 1500s experienced economic and agricultural tensions which saw brewers and bakers competing to purchase grain to produce their goods. In an effort to avoid price inflation, the *Reinheitsgebot* consequently limited brewers to only use barley while wheat and rye were exclusively made available to bakers for bread.

The original purity law was signed in Ingolstadt and stated that beer brewed in Bavaria could only contain barley, hops and water. As the political situation in Germany changed over the subsequent centuries the *Reinheitsgebot* continued to be a central piece of legislation. Its pan-German implementation was even a prerequisite for Bavaria joining the German Empire in 1871. The strict nature of the law meant that it has often met opposition from some German brewers leading to some adaptations. These include recognising that yeast is required for fermentation, and permitting malted 'grains' rather than just barley to be used.

Despite the subsequent changes, some people have blamed the *Reinheitsgebot* for the lack of diversity in German beers. As recently as 2016 the German daily newspaper Der Spiegel criticised the law for denying brewers the opportunity to experiment with new ingredients and styles. Consequently some breweries have begun to create brews that don't follow the law, but they are not allowed to call them 'beer'.

Meanwhile the *Reinheitsgebot* continues to have a number of supporters, and German beers brewed to its specifications have the status of a protected traditional foodstuff under European Union law.

APRIL

24

1916

The Easter Rising began in Dublin, with the aim of securing an independent Irish Republic.

The armed insurrection by Irish Republicans began on Easter Monday 1916, meaning that the date of the annual commemoration changes each year due to Easter being based on the lunar calendar. Organised by the seven members of the Military Council of the Irish Republican Brotherhood, the Rising brought together over 1,200 men and women from the Irish Volunteers and other organisations to overthrow British rule.

After their initial success of taking control of key defensible locations in Dublin, the rebels issued the Proclamation of the Irish Republic and established the Provisional Government. The Proclamation was read by Patrick Pearse outside the rebels' newly-established headquarters at the General Post Office, and it took the British and many Dubliners completely by surprise.

When the British did act, however, they did so decisively. Martial law was declared on Tuesday evening, and within just a few days more than 16,000 British troops had been brought in to the city. When the Provisional Government surrendered on the 29th April, at least 485 people had lost their lives and 2,600 were injured. The vast majority of those both killed and wounded were civilians.

Of the more than 3,000 people arrested in the aftermath, 15 of the most prominent were executed within two weeks of the end of the uprising. A further 1,400 were imprisoned in England, many without having stood trial. While the Rising itself had won little support from most Dubliners, the British reaction to it helped to build support for Irish independence. The Sinn Féin republican party went on to win a landslide victory in the General Election of 1918.

APRIL

25

404 BCE

The Peloponnesian League, led by Sparta, defeated Athens in the Peloponnesian War.

The conflict formerly began in 431 BCE following the collapse of the previous Thirty Years' peace between Athens and Sparta. As the two dominant powers in Greece, the city-states each led alliances of other independent territories in the area. The Athenian empire had the stronger navy due its location on the Aegean Sea, while the Peloponnesian League under Sparta had the stronger land army.

The contemporary historian Thucydides wrote an extensive account of the tensions between the two powers, and claimed that the war began due to Sparta's concern at the growing power of Athens. In 431 BCE Sparta launched the first of many invasions of Attica under the command of the Spartan king Archidamos. This signalled the start of the first of three phases of the Peloponnesian War that engulfed much of the Greek world and left the Athenian empire in tatters.

During the first phase of the war, known as the Archidamian War, Sparta benefitted from an outbreak of the plague in Athens. This killed the leading Athenian general, Pericles, along with up to two-thirds of the population of the city. Although Athens went on to mount some successful offensives the two sides agreed to the uneasy Peace of Nicias in 421 BCE.

The war resumed in 415 BCE, after which Athens launched a disastrous attack on Syracuse in Sicily. Subsequent years saw Sparta build its own naval fleet with financial support from Persia, and it was with this that they were able to destroy Athens' fleet at Aegospotami in 405 BCE. Athens surrendered the following year, dramatically altering the balance of power in Greece.

APRIL

26

1478

The Pazzi family in Florence launched their unsuccessful plot to overthrow the Medici family with an assassination attempt against the brothers Lorenzo and Giuliano de' Medici.

The Pazzis had been a powerful and influential family since the 13th century. Yet by the early 1400s their successful banking network, and the status that came with it, had been overshadowed by that of the Medici family who had grown to dominate Florentine political and economic life. The Pazzi Conspiracy saw family members conspire with other opponents of the Medicis including the Pope's nephew, Girolamo Riario, and the archbishop of Pisa, Francesco Salviati. Although Pope Sixtus IV lent his support to the plot, he was very careful not to sanction killing.

The assassins struck during High Mass on the morning of 26 April 1478. Having gathered with a crowd of up to 10,000 other worshippers at the Duomo, Bernardo Bandini dei Baroncelli and Francesco de' Pazzi stabbed Giuliano de' Medici 19 times. His brother Lorenzo was wounded but managed to escape with the help of his friend Angelo Poliziano.

Over the next few months the people of Florence pursued the conspirators and killed at least 80 people associated with the plot by 20 October. Francesco de' Pazzi and Salviati were hanged from the windows of the Palazzo della Signoria while other plotters were thrown from windows to be set upon by the angry crowds below.

The failure of the conspiracy resulted in the opposite situation to what had been intended. Lorenzo de' Medici was able to strengthen his hold on Florentine politics despite Pope Sixtus IV placing the city under interdict, while the Pazzi family were banished and their lands and property confiscated.

APRIL

27

1906

The Russian Empire's State Duma met for the first time at the Taurida Palace in St Petersburg.

The Duma was to form the lower house of a new legislative assembly. It was proposed by Sergei Witte, the Chairman of the Russian Council of Ministers, in response to the wave of violence that culminated in the Russian Revolution of 1905. Tsar Nicholas II formally declared the creation of the Duma when he issued the October Manifesto later that year.

Elections for the Duma took place in March 1906 and permitted men over the age of 25 to vote. Having been boycotted by a number of parties on the left, the election resulted in a centre-left parliament of which the moderate Constitutional Democrats held the most seats.

Witte, the architect of the October Manifesto, was forced to resign on 22 April and the following day the Tsar issued the Russian Constitution of 1906, otherwise known as the Fundamental Laws. Under the terms, the authority of the Duma was severely restricted while the Tsar was given the title 'supreme autocrat'. He had the power to dismiss the Duma and call elections, while Article 87 permitted him to impose laws as emergency legislation.

Despite possessing such limited powers, the Duma adopted a broadly anti-autocratic agenda and pushed for further reforms after the liberal deputy Professor Sergey Muromtsev was elected as the Duma's President. Their calls for increased liberties were ignored by the government. The first two bills sent to the Duma for approval were for the construction of a greenhouse and a new laundry.

Just 72 days after it convened, the Tsar dissolved the assembly on 21 July. He appointed the more repressive Peter Stolypin to the position of Prime Minister the same day.

APRIL

28

1789

23-year-old Acting Lieutenant Fletcher Christian led a mutiny on the Royal Navy vessel HMS *Bounty*.

Bounty had departed England in late 1787 to collect and transport saplings of the breadfruit tree from Tahiti to various British colonies in the West Indies as a cheap source of food for slaves on the plantations. The ship, a three-masted cutter, was commanded by Lieutenant William Bligh who had previously accompanied Captain James Cook on his third and final voyage.

Bounty arrived in Tahiti on 26 October 1788, but the outward voyage had seen relations between Bligh and his crew gradually deteriorate. Having arrived at their destination many crewmen began relationships with the local women, while Bligh began to impose increasingly harsh discipline that only served to worsen relations between him and his men.

The ship and her crew departed Tahiti on 5 April 1789 and, according to later testimonies, it was Bligh's increasingly angry outbursts that led to the mutiny. Christian was a particular target and by the evening of 27 April he was considering desertion. Instead, after encouragement from other members of the crew, he led a mutiny. Bligh was frogmarched to the upper deck at musket point shortly after 5am on 28 April. Together with 18 crewmen who refused to join the mutineers, Bligh was forced onto an overloaded launch with enough food and water to last around five days.

Some of the mutineers were returned to Tahiti while Christian and the others established a settlement on the remote Pitcairn Island. Meanwhile Bligh's crew sailed their open boat approximately 4,000 miles to the Dutch settlement of Coupang in Timor where the survivors boarded a ship to England, arriving on 14 March 1790.

Sir Francis Drake entered the Bay of Cádiz and attacked the Spanish naval fleet in an event known as 'Singeing the King of Spain's Beard'.

Tensions between Protestant England and Catholic Spain had steadily increased due to a combination of religious, economic and political factors. Alongside ongoing religious conflicts that saw the excommunication of the English ruler Elizabeth I in 1570, the Spanish were frustrated by repeated raids from English privateers against their territories in the West Indies and of English support for the Dutch Revolt against Spain.

These tensions led to the outbreak of the Anglo-Spanish War in 1585. The first months of the conflict saw Drake lead a series of attacks against Spanish possessions in the West Indies and the Americas, which prompted King Philip II of Spain to begin planning the invasion England and the restoration of Catholicism.

The Spanish king began to assemble his fleet, which was later to become known as the Armada, in the Spanish port of Cádiz and the Portuguese port of Lisbon. Meanwhile, in England, Queen Elizabeth put Drake in charge of a fleet that was to inspect and disrupt the Spanish preparations. He set sail on 12 April with four Royal Navy galleons and twenty smaller ships.

Drake's fleet arrived at the Spanish port on 29 April and began to attack that evening. Having destroyed or captured numerous naval and merchant vessels Drake spent the next few weeks patrolling the coast between Cádiz and Lisbon and destroying every ship he encountered. Over one hundred ships in total were destroyed or captured, and Spanish plans for the invasion of England had to be put back for over a year.

APRIL

30

1963

A boycott against the Bristol Omnibus Company in England was launched due to their racist employment policy.

Around 3,000 people of West Indian origin lived in the city of Bristol in 1963, predominantly around the St Pauls area. There was not yet any legislation against discriminating on racial grounds so it was common in both housing and employment, while so-called 'coloureds' often suffered violence at the hands of gangs of white Teddy Boys.

In 1955, the same year as the Montgomery Bus Boycott took place on the other side of the Atlantic, the Transport and General Workers Union had reportedly passed a resolution that 'coloured' workers should not be employed on buses in Britain. The management of the Bristol Omnibus Company shared this attitude. Consequently, despite an acute labour shortage in the early 1960s, it was impossible to get a job on a bus crew unless you were white.

A group of West Indian men formed an action group to challenge the situation. In April 1963 the London-accented Paul Stephenson telephoned the bus company and set up an interview for Guy Bailey, a young man of West Indian heritage. He was turned away from the interview because he was black. At a press conference in his flat on 29 April, Stephenson called for people to boycott the bus company until the 'colour bar' was abolished.

The boycott, which was supported by people across the city as well as the press, succeeded. On 28 August, the same day that Martin Luther King made his 'I Have a Dream' speech, the company's management announced the end of its discriminatory employment policy. The city's first non-white bus conductor began work the following month.

MAY

MAY

1

1776

The Covenant of Perfectibility, the forerunner of the original Bavarian Illuminati, was founded by Adam Weishaupt in Ingolstadt.

Weishaupt became a professor of Canon Law at the University of Ingolstadt in 1773, having graduated with a doctorate of law five years earlier. The university was controlled by the Jesuits but, not being a cleric himself, Weishaupt found himself increasingly frustrated by the religious authorities.

Having been inspired by the Enlightenment, Weishaupt set up his own secret society to spread its ideas. Beginning with just five members, the early years of the society saw it expand so slowly that by the summer of 1778 there were still only 27 members. In an attempt to develop his own organisation, in 1777 Weishaupt was initiated into a lodge of the Freemasons and the following year he formally renamed his society the Order of Illuminati.

Despite the order's humble beginnings, the early 1780s saw the Illuminati began to establish bases in other Bavarian cities. The library contained books and other literature that were banned in Bavaria due to their 'liberal' content, and this formed the basis of the society's beliefs and goals.

As recruitment increased throughout the early 1780s, the Illuminati attracted the attention of the government. The exposure of a number of members who held powerful civic and governmental positions fuelled criticisms that the society was undermining Bavaria.

In response the state's ruler Charles Theodore, who had suppressed liberal thought since his succession in 1777, issued an edict in 1784 that banned the Bavarian Illuminati. After the collapse of the society, Weishaupt fled Bavaria and never returned.

MAY

2

1945

The Battle of Berlin ended after German General Helmuth Weidling surrendered to Soviet General Vasily Chuikov.

Determined to capture Berlin before the Western Allies, Stalin's generals began their assault on the defensive line of the Oder and Neisse rivers on the morning of 16 April. Two million German civilians and no more than 200,000 German soldiers were in and around Berlin when the USSR broke through the defences having suffered casualties in the tens of thousands.

Travelling at up to 30-40km a day, the first Red Army troops reached Berlin in time for Hitler's 56th birthday on 20 April. Artillery began bombarding the city and didn't cease until the surrender almost two weeks later. Meanwhile other Soviet units encircled the city leading to Hitler, who was based in the *Führerbunker*, angrily declaring that the war was lost. Nevertheless he appointed General Weidling to command the Berlin Defence Area with a force of 45,000 soldiers supported by police officers, members of the Hitler Youth, and the *Volkssturm* militia.

By 30 April, Soviet troops had reached the Reichstag and, late that evening, successfully placed a flag on top that was removed the following morning by German defenders. The building was finally taken over on 2 May and a new flag was raised, of which an iconic photograph was taken. General Weidling and his staff surrendered the same morning having failed to negotiate a conditional surrender.

Following the surrender the Soviets sought to restore essential services and provide food to the German survivors. However, some troops who reached the city lacked the discipline of the first echelon and committed shocking crimes against Berliners including rape, pillage and murder.

MAY

3

1915

Lieutenant-Colonel John McCrae, a Canadian doctor, wrote the war poem 'In Flanders Fields', which inspired the symbol of the poppy to commemorate members of the military killed in war.

McCrae had published his first poems while studying medicine at the University of Toronto, after which he served in the Canadian Field Artillery during the Boer War. Returning to Canada after the war, he embarked on a successful career as a pathologist and was made a member of the Royal College of Physicians prior to the outbreak of the First World War.

McCrae was appointed to the 1st Brigade CFA (Canadian Field Artillery) where he assumed the position of Medical Officer and Major. While serving in Belgium he fought at the Second Battle of Ypres that began on 22 April 1915, an experience he described in a letter to his mother as a 'nightmare'. During this battle his close friend Alexis Helmer was killed, and McCrae himself performed the burial service on 2 May.

The next day, while apparently sitting in the back of an ambulance, McCrae composed 'In Flanders Fields'. Cyril Allinson, a Sergeant Major in McCrae's unit, later recounted watching McCrae write the poem. He was apparently unhappy with the final piece and threw it away, but it was retrieved by another member of the unit.

McCrae edited the poem and submitted it to *The Spectator* for publication, but following that paper's rejection succeeded in getting it published in *Punch* on 8 December 1915. It was met with universal acclaim at the time, and its imagery of red poppies led to the flower's associated with remembrance in the years following the war. McCrae continued to serve in the army, but died of a pneumonia-related illness on 28 January 1918. He is buried in France.

MAY

4

1970

Ohio National Guardsmen shot and killed four Kent State University students.

President Richard Nixon had promised to end American involvement in Vietnam following his election in 1968. Opposition to the war increased when the My Lai Massacre became public knowledge the following year and the draft lottery was reintroduced for the first time since the Second World War. By the time news broke that Nixon had authorised military action against Cambodia to eliminate suspected Viet Cong forces on 30 April 1970, protests against the war had spread around the country.

On 1 May 1970 around 500 students at Kent State University in Ohio attended a protest on the campus where they agreed to stage another rally three days later. Later that evening violence broke out in the town. The police used tear gas to drive students back to the university, and the next day the local mayor called the Ohio Governor and asked him to send the Ohio National Guard to take control of the situation. That evening there were further clashes.

The planned demonstration on 4 May attracted 3,000 protestors and spectators, despite the university's attempts to ban the event. With approximately 100 Ohio Guardsmen stationed nearby, the protesters were ordered to disperse. Having refused to do so the guardsmen fired tear gas into the crowd after which seventy-seven of them began to march on the crowd who had begun throwing rocks. After finding themselves blocked by a fence around an athletic field the guardsmen eventually turned back in the direction they had come. With little warning 29 of the guardsmen then fired on the crowd or into the air, unleashing almost 70 rounds in thirteen seconds. Four students were killed and another nine were injured.

MAY

5

1912

***Pravda*, the official newspaper of what became the Communist Party of the Soviet Union, was first published.**

Prior to the foundation of the CPSU many revolutionary socialists belonged to the Russian Social Democratic Labour Party. It was the RSDLP that had originally split into Bolshevik (majority) and Menshevik (minority) factions in 1903.

An early version of *Pravda* appeared that year, although at the time it was a journal without political affiliation. Its editorial board gradually began to include active members of the RSDLP and, by 1909 when its headquarters moved to Vienna, the board was dominated by Bolsheviks under the editorship of Leon Trotsky.

The Central Committee of the RSDLP had first suggested making *Pravda* its official mouthpiece in 1910, but it wasn't until the Mensheviks were expelled from the party in January 1912 that this happened. The Bolshevik leader Vladimir Lenin moved the paper to St Petersburg and the first edition was published on 5 May, the anniversary of Karl Marx's birth.

The first edition of the newspaper consisted of just four pages, and focused on workers' issues. As its circulation increased to as many as 60,000 copies by July 1914, *Pravda* was shut down by the tsarist government censors.

Despite this suppression, *Pravda* continued to be printed under a serious of pseudonyms. The newspaper formally reopened following the February Revolution of 1917 and by 15 March it was being co-edited by Joseph Stalin following his return from exile.

Pravda remained the official newspaper of the Soviet Communist Party until it was abolished in 1991. The newspaper continues to exist, albeit not as a daily publication.

MAY

6

1983

West Germany's Federal Archives revealed that forensic tests proved the Hitler Diaries were forgeries.

In the final days of the Second World War, an aeroplane carrying some of Hitler's closest staff members crashed near the German border with Czechoslovakia. Hitler's personal valet, Sergeant Wilhelm Arndt, was killed and the personal effects he was carrying on behalf of the Fuhrer were lost. On hearing of the crash, Hitler allegedly exclaimed that, 'In that plane were all my private archives that I had intended as a testament to posterity. It is a catastrophe!' Journalist Robert Harris later described this possibility of lost documents belong to Hitler as providing 'the perfect scenario for forgery'.

A series of diaries purporting to be the lost journals of Adolf Hitler were later forged by Konrad Kujau. Posing as a Stuttgart antiques dealer, he successfully struck a deal with journalist Gerd Heidemann who had convinced his bosses at the newspaper *Stern* to buy the diaries. They eventually handed over 9.9 million Deutsche marks for 62 volumes, and sold the serial rights to other publications.

Authenticity of the diaries was originally confirmed by historians including Hugh Trevor-Roper and Gerhard Weinberg, but they grew more sceptical as the April 1983 publication date approached. The newspaper subsequently submitted three volumes to the *Bundesarchiv* for forensic examination. Initial tests highlighted both textual inconsistencies and the presence of materials that didn't exist until a decade after their alleged creation. More volumes were submitted for further tests and, on 6 May, the government formally announced that they were forgeries. Kujau was later arrested and imprisoned while the journalist, Heidemann, was found to have skimmed money from *Stern*'s payments for which he too was sent to jail.

MAY

7

1915

The British ship RMS *Lusitania* sank after being attacked by the German U-boat *U-20* off the coast of Ireland.

The *Lusitania* was launched by the Cunard Line in 1906 and was one of the largest ocean liners of its time. It undertook its first voyage in 1907 and went on to win the Blue Riband, the unofficial award for the fastest transatlantic crossing.

The outbreak of the First World War saw Britain impose a blockade on German ports, which prompted the German Navy to attempt the same on the British Isles. However, the Royal Navy limited the impact of Germany's blockade so the *Lusitania* was able to continue its journeys between Liverpool and New York City.

On 4 February 1915 the commander of the German High Seas Fleet announced that German submarines would begin unrestricted warfare and sink allied ships in the waters around the British Isles. Prior to the *Lusitania*'s scheduled voyage from the USA on 1 May, the German Embassy in Washington took out newspaper adverts warning that passengers undertook the voyage at their own risk.

1,962 people and around 173 tons of war munitions were on board the *Lusitania* when it left New York under Captain William Thomas Turner. Having crossed the Atlantic, the ship was hit on its starboard side at 2.10pm by a torpedo fired by *U-20*. The *Lusitania* sank in just 18 minutes and 1,198 people lost their lives.

The German government attempted to justify the sinking, but it was met with outrage in the Allied countries. Despite the deaths of American civilians, President Wilson chose to remain neutral in the war. Germany abandoned unrestricted submarine warfare in August, but resumed it in early 1917. This, and the discovery of the Zimmermann Telegram, led to Wilson's decision to declare war.

MAY

8

1942

The Battle of the Coral Sea, the first naval battle in which the participating ships never came in sight of each other, ended.

The Coral Sea is situated off the northeast coast of Australia. Following Japan's entry into the Second World War, the Imperial Japanese Navy sought to establish perimeter defences in the region to protect the Japanese empire and isolate Australia and New Zealand from their ally the United States.

Japanese forces launched Operation *Mo*, in which they planned to seize Port Moresby in New Guinea and Tulagi in the Solomon Islands, on 3 May 1942. However, the Allies had intercepted messages about the impending attack and launched a series of surprise airstrikes against the Japanese from the US fleet carrier *Yorktown*.

The Allied attack failed to stop the Japanese landings on Tulagi, but caused significant damage to the fleet that reduced its effectiveness in the second stage of the plan. Clearly aware of the presence of enemy aircraft carriers in the area, the Japanese consequently sought to locate and destroy the allied naval forces.

On the morning of 7 May, Japanese carrier-based planes located and sank a US destroyer and an oiler while American planes sank the light Japanese carrier *Shōhō* and a cruiser. The following day Japanese aircraft damaged the US carriers *Yorktown* and *Lexington*, which was later scuttled. Meanwhile the Japanese carrier *Shōkaku* was heavily damaged and had to withdraw, while *Zuikaku* suffered large aircraft losses that excluded it from the Battle of Midway the following month. Consequently while Japan experienced a tactical victory in terms of the number of ships sunk, the Allies gained a strategic advantage as Japan was forced to abandon Operation *Mo*.

MAY

9

1671

Colonel Thomas Blood attempted to steal the Crown Jewels from the Tower of London.

Blood was born in Ireland but travelled to England in 1642 following the outbreak of the English Civil War. Having originally fought on the side of Charles I, he switched to join the Roundheads midway through the war. Oliver Cromwell later made him a justice of the peace and granted him land as a reward.

Following the restoration of the monarchy under Charles II, Blood lost the land he had been granted by Cromwell and fled to Ireland. After two failed attempts to kidnap and later kill the Duke of Ormonde, he staged his bid to steal the Crown Jewels.

Blood initially visited the Tower dressed as a parson and was accompanied by a woman pretending to be his wife who feigned a violent stomach ache that won sympathy from the family of Talbot Edwards, the Master of the Jewel House. They struck up a friendly relationship, and soon Blood proposed that his imaginary nephew should marry their daughter.

Blood, his 'nephew' and two other companions visited the Tower on 9 May. Edwards was persuaded to show them the Crown Jewels but, on unlocking the door, was hit with a mallet and stabbed. The thieves removed the metal grille from in front of the jewels and used the mallet to flatten the crown while the sceptre was cut into two. One of the thieves hid the orb in his trousers.

Edwards regained consciousness and raised the alarm. The thieves were apprehended as they ran to their horses, but Blood refused to answer questions for anyone except the King who not only pardoned Blood but also gave him land in Ireland worth £500 a year. Edwards, meanwhile, received a reward of £300.

MAY

10

1857

The Indian Mutiny, also known as the First War of Indian Independence, began in Meerut.

By the middle of the 19th century, the British East India Company ruled two thirds of the Indian subcontinent on behalf of the government. The remainder paid tribute to the British, but there was increasing discontent among native rulers about their rapidly declining position. For ordinary Indians there were also concerns about the pace of Westernisation that threatened local traditions and ignored religious practices.

Against these undercurrents of hostility the East India Company relied on its sizeable army to maintain order. Although figures vary between sources, by 1857 up to 300,000 Indian sepoys had been recruited to the army alongside approximately 50,000 European troops. While this meant the Company relied on local troops to maintain control, this presented few problems until the introduction of the Enfield P53 rifle in 1856.

The new rifle required soldiers to bite the end of a pre-greased cartridge to release the powder and load the weapon, but rumours began circulating that the grease was made from cow and pig fat. The former was offensive to Hindus, while the latter was offensive to Muslims. On 9 May 1857, 85 sepoys of the 3rd Bengal Light Cavalry were court marshalled in the garrison town of Meerut, 40 miles northeast of Delhi, for refusing to use the new cartridges. Sentenced to up to ten years' imprisonment, their comrades broke them out of jail the next day. They killed a number of Europeans, as well as up to 50 Indian civilians, before marching to Delhi from where the uprising spread throughout northern India. The response from the British was brutal, but it still took them more than 18 months to regain control.

MAY

11

868

The world's earliest dated printed book, a copy of the *Diamond Sutra*, was created in China.

The book itself is actually a scroll measuring just over 5 meters, and which was made from seven separate strips of yellow-stained paper pasted together. The printing itself was done using large wooden blocks and, although earlier printed books have survived, this copy of the *Diamond Sutra* is the oldest that bears a specific date.

This date is given in the colophon, the short statement at the end of the manuscript that provides publishing details. This states that it was 'Reverently made for universal free distribution by Wang Jie on behalf of his two parents on the 13th of the 4th moon of the 9th year of Xiantong'. This makes it nearly 600 years older than the Gutenberg Bible, the first book to be printed with moveable type.

Although the *Diamond Sutra* itself is a Buddhist sacred text that originated in India, this particular scroll was printed in Chinese. This dissemination of the religion is explained by some historians as being due to the Silk Road trade route. Sutras were sermons given by the Buddha, and the text of the *Diamond Sutra* is a record of the address he gave to a disciple called Subhuti. It gets its name from the Buddha himself, who said that it would enable followers to cut through worldly illusions of reality like a diamond blade.

This particular manuscript was sealed-up in what is known as the 'Library Cave' near the city of Dunhuang in north-west China during the 11th century. The cave, containing numerous documents and artefacts, was rediscovered by Taoist abbot Wang Yuanlu in 1900. Seven years later Hungarian archaeologist Aurel Stein bought a number of the manuscripts, including the *Diamond Sutra*, from Wang. It is now kept in the British Library in London.

MAY

12

1846

The Donner Party departed Independence, Missouri on their ill-fated journey to California.

The 1840s had seen a dramatic increase in the number of pioneers undertaking the long and dangerous journey to settle in the western United States. The California Trail shared its initial stages with the 2,170-mile (3,490 km) Oregon Trail but, after reading about a short cut in a guidebook by Lansford Hastings, a party led by George Donner and James F. Reed decided to take the new route.

The group of 20 wagons carrying almost 90 people found the Hastings Cutoff to be considerably rougher terrain than they had been led to believe. Slowed by steep inclines and the need fell trees and move rocks to provide a path for the wagons, the group struggled to move more than one and a half miles a day compared to the fifteen they might have expected to cover on the established trail.

By the time the party had crossed the Wasatch Mountains and reached the Great Salt Lake Desert they were running out of food and water. Families were forced to abandon their animals and, in some cases, even their wagons on the inhospitable plain. When they eventually re-joined the main trail route it is estimated that the Hastings Cutoff had cost them a month's travel time.

This was to have catastrophic consequences as, by the time they reached the Sierra Nevada Mountains, the trail was blocked with snow. Forced to spend winter in the mountains, by January some families were so short of food that they had to eat the ox hides that acted as roofs for their cabins. A snowshoe party consequently set out to find help on a 33-day journey that saw them resorting to cannibalism to survive. Although the survivors were rescued, almost half the people who originally set out from Missouri had died.

The first Formula One World Championship Grand Prix race took place at the Silverstone circuit in England.

Formula One racing can trace its origins back to the European Grand Prix championships that took place in the 1920s and 1930s. Racing was put on hold following the outbreak of the Second World War, but restarted again at its conclusion. 1946 saw the development of a set of standardised rules for cars and drivers that were collectively referred to as Formula One, and plans began to be made for a drivers' championship.

Although numerous races took place throughout the year, the Championship would only record the results of the British, Swiss, Monaco, Belgium, French and Italian Grand Prix alongside the Indianapolis 500 in the United States of America. Points were to be awarded to the top five finishers of each race, and each driver's best four results were used to determine their overall championship position.

The first race of the World Championship took place at the Silverstone circuit on the border of Northamptonshire and Buckinghamshire. An estimated 200,000 spectators travelled to the circuit to watch eleven out of the 21 qualifying competitors finish the inaugural Championship race, which was dominated by Alfa Romeo's drivers who secured the top three finishing positions. King George VI, his wife Queen Elizabeth, and their daughter Princess Margaret were also in attendance.

The race winner was Italian driver Giuseppe Farina, who finished 2.6 seconds ahead of his teammate Luigi Fagioli. Farina went on to finish the year as the first official Formula One World Champion with a total of 30 points.

MAY

14

1955

The USSR and seven other European countries signed the Treaty of Friendship, Cooperation, and Mutual Assistance better known as the Warsaw Pact.

The Warsaw Pact was established shortly after West Germany was admitted to NATO. The USSR was concerned by the remilitarisation of West Germany, something it had tried to avoid when it proposed a new European Security Treaty that failed to gain support from the Western powers in November 1954.

Just five days after West Germany joined NATO, representatives of the Soviet Union, Albania, Poland, Romania, Hungary, East Germany, Czechoslovakia, and Bulgaria met in Warsaw where they signed the treaty. While the agreement established a system of collective security between the member states it also set up a unified military command under the leadership of the Soviet Union. The Pact permitted Soviet troops to be garrisoned on satellite territory, consequently strengthening Soviet control over the Eastern Bloc and acting as a military counterpart to Comecon, the socialist economic organisation that had been established in 1949.

The presence of Soviet troops was a contributing factor to the 1956 uprisings in both Hungary and Poland. Both these countries did, however, take part in the Warsaw Pact invasion of Czechoslovakia in 1968 that ended the Prague Spring. Only Romania and Albania refused to join the invasion, the latter subsequently withdrawing completely from the pact.

The Warsaw Pact was formally declared 'nonexistent' on 1 July 1991, although in practice it had been in decline for two years as a result of the overthrow of communist governments in the member states that had begun in 1989.

Richard and Maurice McDonald opened the first McDonald's restaurant in San Bernardino, California.

The McDonald brothers had successfully operated the 'Airdrome' hotdog stand in Arcadia, California, for three years before they began their first McDonald's Bar-B-Que restaurant in San Bernardino. The restaurant had twenty-five items on the menu, and was typical of restaurants of its time where customers arrived by car and were served by waiting staff known as car hops.

In 1948 the brothers streamlined their entire restaurant experience when they temporarily closed the restaurant for remodelling. It reopened in October 1948 with a new design where customers ordered food directly at the counter. The brothers also reduced the number of items on the menu and introduced their Speedee Service System that adopted an assembly line approach to simplify food preparation.

Many of these design innovations had first been introduced by the White Castle hamburger chain in the 1920s, but the success of the McDonald brothers' restaurant saw them seek opportunities to expand their business. In 1953 they began to offer franchise opportunities, firstly of the serving system and then of the entire brand including the name and the architectural design.

The aggressive expansion of the McDonald's brand was overseen by Ray Kroc, originally a provider of milkshake machines, who persuaded the McDonald brothers to franchise the restaurants throughout the country. The brothers agreed, and received 0.5% of gross sales in franchised restaurants. Kroc completely bought the brothers out in 1961. He paid them $2.7 million for the business, and went on to create the global chain we know today.

MAY
16
1916

The secret Sykes-Picot Agreement between Britain and France, formally known as the Asia Minor Agreement, was ratified.

The agreement was designed to deal with the future of the Ottoman Empire, which had been known as 'the sick man of Europe' in the preceding years due to its declining power. After the Ottomans joined the First World War on the side of the Central Powers, the Allies began discussing policy towards their territory.

Britain and France had already agreed to Russia's claim to Constantinople and the Straits of Dardanelles by the time representatives from the two countries began discussing further questions of territorial control in November 1915. The British diplomat Mark Sykes concluded negotiations with his French counterpart François Georges-Picot in March 1916 and the agreement was ratified in May, having secured Russian assent at the end of April.

The Sykes-Picot Agreement carved up the Ottoman Empire into spheres of influence that conflicted directly with the promises Britain had made to Hussein bin Ali, Sharif of Mecca, to secure Arab support against the Ottomans. When the secret agreement was published in November 1917 following the Bolshevik Revolution, Sir Henry McMahon who had negotiated the Arab deal with Hussein resigned.

Over a century after its creation, the Sykes-Picot Agreement continues to be the focus of significant debate due to its lasting impact on the Middle East. It is often criticised for establishing 'artificial' borders in the region that ignored ethnic and sectarian characteristics, and which have caused almost continuous conflict ever since.

Royal Air Force No. 617 Squadron attacked German dams in Operation Chastise, otherwise known as the Dambuster Raids.

617 Squadron was formed specifically to attack three major dams that provided hydro-electric power and water to the Ruhr Valley, an area of enormous industrial significance to Germany. Operation Chastise was developed with the intention of destroying the dams and depriving the German war effort of the Ruhr's potential output.

The operation was developed in such secrecy that, with just two nights to go until the night of the attack, only Wing Commander Guy Gibson and a small number of key officers knew the intended targets. Despite being just 24 years old, Gibson had already flown over 170 missions and had been specifically chosen to lead 617 Squadron.

The destruction of the dams depended on the correct deployment of a new explosive that had been invented by Barnes Wallis, the Assistant Chief Designer at Vickers aircraft factory. Nicknamed the 'bouncing bomb', he created a cylindrical bomb that would be spun backwards at a speed of 500rpm before being dropped onto water from a precise height at a precise speed. The bomb would then bounce over the torpedo nets installed in the dams' reservoirs before spinning down the dam wall and exploding.

The squadron began their mission from RAF Scampton on the evening of 16 May. Arriving at their targets in the early hours of the 17 May, they breached two of the dams and lightly damaged the third. Eight of the aircraft were shot down during the mission and 53 airmen were killed. The flood waters from the breached dams killed up to 1,600 civilians in the Ruhr Valley, and slowed German industrial production for a number of months while repairs were carried out.

MAY
18
1830

British inventor Edwin Budding went into partnership with foundry owner John Ferrabee to manufacture the world's first lawn mower.

Edwin Budding grew up near the Gloucestershire town of Stroud, where he often saw teams of labourers using scythes to manually cut the lawns of the landed gentry. The labour-intensive nature of this work would later inspire him to create the ubiquitous machine.

Having begun work in an iron foundry as a pattern maker, Budding came across a mechanical napping machine created by John Lewis in 1815 that was used to trim fibres from the surface of woven cloth to produce an even finish. Later developments to this machine used a cylindrical cutting blade that directly influenced Budding's lawn mower design.

Powered by a large iron roller and a series of gears that span the cutting cylinder close to a knife plate, Budding's mower was pushed from behind. A second roller could be adjusted to alter the cutting height, while the clippings were flung into a collection box at the front.

On 18 May Budding signed an agreement with John Ferrabee, owner of the Phoenix Iron Works at the nearby town of Thrupp, to manufacture the machine. One of the first models was sold to Regent's Park Zoological Gardens in London where the head gardener reported that the new lawn mower allowed two men to do as much work as six or eight men with scythes. Ferrabee subsequently licensed other manufacturers to produce Budding mowers, while Budding returned to inventing. He went on to create the first adjustable spanner in 1842.

MAY

19

1919

The Turkish War of Independence began when General Mustafa Kemal Pasha, the Inspector of the Ottoman 9th Army and later known as Atatürk, arrived at the town of Samsun on the Black Sea coast.

The city of Constantinople had been occupied by Entente forces since 13 November 1918, less than two weeks after they had signed the Armistice of Mudros with the Ottoman Empire. In addition to occupying Constantinople, the Allies also seized various other areas of the Ottoman Empire over the following months. This occupation by foreign troops was described by Mustafa Kemal as 'humiliating'.

On 15 May 1919 Greek forces, with the permission of the Entente powers, landed in Smyrna, now known as Izmir. Ethnic tensions were already high in the Anatolia region, and the wave of violence that ensued helped to consolidate a range of Turkish resistance groups into a unified force. The Sultan in Constantinople was under the influence of the occupying powers and was asked to send a member of the armed forces to quell the unrest.

Mustafa Kemal secured this assignment and departed Constantinople for Samsun on board the cargo ship SS *Bandirma*. After a difficult three-day voyage in poor weather, and without a functioning compass, he and his staff landed on 19 May. Instead of disbanding the army they began to organise a more formalised resistance movement, and for this reason 19 May is considered the start of the Turkish War of Independence. A month later, Mustafa Kemal issued the Amasya Circular declaring that the independence of the country was in danger. This document was a direct criticism of the government in Constantinople, and is often seen as the first formal written evidence of Mustafa Kemal's nationalist intentions.

MAY

20

1882

Germany, Austria-Hungary and Italy formed the Triple Alliance.

Germany and Austria-Hungary had formed the defensive Dual Alliance in 1879 in which both countries agreed to assist each other if they were attacked by Russia and promised benevolent neutrality to the other in case of war with another nation.

Two years later Italy, which had North African imperial ambitions, was frustrated by France's seizure of Tunisia. Wishing to secure a foreign alliance in case of future aggression from France, Italy consequently turned to Germany and Austria-Hungary, expanding their established relationship to form the Triple Alliance in 1882.

The alliance provided Italy with German and Austro-Hungarian assistance in case France chose to attack, in return for which Italy would assist Germany if they were attacked. Meanwhile Austria-Hungary benefited from a guarantee that Italy would remain neutral in case of a war with Russia, removing the risk of a war on two fronts and providing some security amidst the rising tensions in the Balkans.

The alliance was renewed in 1887, 1907 and 1912. Meanwhile, in October 1883, Romania had secretly joined the Triple Alliance. This move was so secret that only King Carol I and a few senior politicians even knew. However, similar to Italy's involvement in the agreement, this did not result in Romania joining the Central Powers when war broke out in 1914. Having based their decisions on the fact that the first country to take offensive action was Austria-Hungary when it attacked Serbia, both Italy and Romania initially opted for neutrality. They claimed that, since the Triple Alliance was defensive, they were not duty bound to support the aggressor.

MAY

21

1972

Hungarian-born geologist Laszlo Toth attacked and seriously damaged Michelangelo's *Pietà* statue with a hammer.

The *Pietà* is a marble sculpture that was created by Michelangelo between 1498 and 1499. It depicts the body of Jesus lying on his mother Mary's lap shortly after he was taken down from the cross, and is celebrated as one of the greatest pieces of Renaissance sculpture due to its balance of classical beauty and naturalism. Notably the *Pietà* is also the only piece that Michelangelo ever signed.

Laszlo Toth graduated from a Hungarian university with a degree in geology, after which he spent a number of years in Australia. He moved to Italy in June 1971 where wrote a number of letters to Pope Paul VI in an attempt to meet him. A man who shared a room in a hostel with Toth later claimed that he had found his constant reading of the Bible unusual.

Toth unleashed his act of vandalism on the Pietà on Pentecost Sunday. He entered St Peter's Basilica in the Vatican City as part of the crowd attending mass, where he jumped over an altar railing in the chapel that housed the statue. He then set about attacking the huge marble sculpture with a geologist's hammer while shouting, 'I am Jesus Christ; I have risen from the dead!'

Toth struck the statue fifteen times before he was wrestled to the ground by bystanders, but his attack severed Mary's arm at the elbow, removed part of her nose, and damaged one of her eyelids. The attack caused over 100 marble fragments to be strewn over the floor, some of which were taken by the crowd and never returned.

The statue was later successfully repaired, while Toth was found to be insane and was committed to an Italian psychiatric hospital for two years. Following his release he was deported back to Australia.

MAY

22

1849

Abraham Lincoln was issued a patent for his invention to lift boats over shoals and other obstructions in a river.

As a teenager the future President had taken a flatboat along the Ohio and Mississippi Rivers. After moving to Illinois he was employed by Denton Offutt, a merchant and owner of a general store, to ferry goods along the Mississippi and its tributaries. During these river trips Lincoln's boats had run aground on more than one occasion, leading to the exhausting process of freeing the boat before it sank or the cargo went overboard. These experiences were to provide the inspiration for his invention.

Lincoln is believed to have begun work on his device in 1848, in which 'adjustable buoyant air chambers' attached to the boat could be forced under the water and inflated to float the boat free of the obstruction without the need to unload any of the cargo. He filed an application to the Patent Office on 10 March 1849, and Patent No. 6469 was awarded two months later on 22 May.

A model of the device is said to have been produced with the assistance of Walter Davis, a mechanic from Springfield, although Paul Johnston from the National Museum of American History believes it may instead have been made in Washington. Whatever the truth behind the creation of the model, this is the furthest that Lincoln's invention ever got since nobody ever tried to install the system on a full-size boat. The model itself can be seen on display at the Smithsonian Institute, and is claimed by the curator of the Marine Collection to be 'one of the half dozen or so most valuable things in our collection'. The invention is also significant in that it makes Abraham Lincoln the only President in the history of the United States to have been awarded a patent.

MAY
23
1618

Two Catholic imperial officials and their secretary were thrown out of the window of the Bohemian Chancellery in the Second Defenestration of Prague.

Prague had witnessed its first defenestration (literally 'the act of throwing someone or something out of a window') in 1419, but it is the second event that is perhaps better known since it acted as a catalyst for the Thirty Years War.

Both defenestrations were rooted in religious conflict. The latter came after the newly elected Catholic king, Ferdinand II, encouraged his cousin Matthias, the Holy Roman Emperor, to order the construction of two new Protestant chapels in the Bohemian towns of Broumov and Hrob to stop. The largely Protestant population in Bohemia argued against the order as they believed that it violated the 1609 Letter of Majesty, issued by the earlier Holy Roman Emperor Rudolf II, which allowed them to freely practise their religion.

In the face of the Protestant opposition, Ferdinand dissolved the assembly of the Bohemian estates. However, this did not stop the Protestant leaders from gathering on the morning of 23 May. They made their way to the Bohemian Chancellery where they put the Catholic imperial regents on trial for disobeying the Letter of Majesty.

Two regents – Count Vilem Slavata of Chlum and Count Jaroslav Borzita of Martinice – were found guilty of violating the Right of Freedom of Religion. The two men, along with the regents' secretary, were then thrown from the third-floor window. They all survived the fall with only minor injuries. Catholics claimed that they were saved thanks to divine intervention, while Protestants maintained that they fell into a dung heap. In the aftermath, both Catholic and Protestant forces began gathering for war.

MAY
24
1943

Josef Mengele, the Nazi 'Angel Of Death', was transferred to begin work at Auschwitz concentration camp.

Menegele had been a member of a right-wing paramilitary group that was absorbed into the Nazi SA in 1934. In 1937 he formally joined the Nazi Party and, the following year, began serving in the SS. By the start of 1943 Mengele had proved himself as both an effective medical officer in the field and a dedicated member of the Race and Resettlement Office.

Having developed an interest in the study of twins as part of his earlier genetics research, Mengele applied for a transfer to the concentration camp service. He was posted to Auschwitz-Birkenau on 24 May 1943 where he initially served as the chief physician in the Romani family camp. As he moved up the ranks numerous sources record his delight in taking part in the 'selections' that determined which prisoners were to be killed in the gas chambers and which were to be spared, as these often provided him with new subjects.

Mengele's experiments involved such gruesome actions as injecting live subjects with chemicals, purposefully infecting people with diseases and, in one well-evidenced case, sewing two twins together in an attempt to create conjoined twins. Mengele was consequently responsible for the deaths of numerous victims thanks to his sadistic and barbaric actions.

Mengele was evacuated from Auschwitz in January 1945 and gradually moved west, escaping capture by the USSR. He was eventually taken as a prisoner of war by the Americans in June but, due a combination of factors, was later able to obtain false papers and flee to South America where he died, having evaded capture for war crimes, in 1979.

MAY

25

1977

The first instalment of the *Star Wars* film series was released in cinemas in the United States of America.

The iconic space opera was written and directed by the American filmmaker George Lucas. His directional debut, the dystopian science fiction film *THX 1138* was not received well by critics or filmgoers. However his second release, *American Graffiti*, was much more successful and was a key factor in securing financial support for *Star Wars* from 20th Century Fox President Alan Ladd, Jr.

Lucas himself has often presented conflicting accounts of the film's development, but what is clear is that it took him over three years to write the screenplay. Yet despite the significant time spent crafting both the script and the universe in which it was set, Lucas continued to rewrite the script while shooting.

External scenes for the film were filmed in Tunisia, Guatemala and Death Valley while the internal shots were completed on sets based at the massive sound stages of Elstree and Shepperton Studios near London. Within a week of the start of filming, the production had already begun to run behind schedule, and *Star Wars* ended up going nearly a third over its original $8 million budget.

Demand for the finished film from theatres was initially so low that 20th Century Fox forced them to show it in return for copies of the more eagerly anticipated *The Other Side of Midnight*. Despite this difficult start, when adjusted for inflation the science fiction epic went on to become the third highest-grossing film in the world.

Star Wars was nominated for ten Academy Awards of which it won six, alongside a Special Achievement for Sound Effects Editing. However, the film's impact on both popular culture and the development of cinema is immeasurable.

Operation Dynamo, better known as the evacuation of Dunkirk, began.

Applauded by the British press as a heroic and miraculous rescue, Operation Dynamo saw an armada under the command of the Royal Navy successfully evacuate over 338,000 Allied troops from the beaches around the French port of Dunkirk.

The German army had invaded France on 10 May, and within just two weeks had cut off and surrounded a combined force of British, French and Belgian troops. Referred to by the recently-appointed British Prime Minister Winston Churchill as 'a colossal military disaster' the only hope was to retreat to the port of Dunkirk and evacuate as many soldiers as possible.

Operation Dynamo was overseen by Vice Admiral Bertram Ramsay who reputedly worked in a room within the cliffs of Dover that once housed an electrical dynamo, though there is no reliable evidence for this claim. The order to begin the operation was received at 18:57 on 26 May, less than a week after planning began.

The operation is famous for the flotilla of 'little ships' that sailed from Britain to assist the evacuation. Most of these were used to ferry soldiers from the beaches to the large navy ships that would sail across the Channel, although the majority of soldiers boarded ships directly from the stone and concrete mole that protected the harbour.

The evacuation took place amidst ferocious attacks from German aircraft and artillery. In response, the Royal Air Force sent all available aircraft to protect the operation. Churchill later praised the fact that hundreds of thousands of soldiers had been evacuated from Dunkirk, but in a speech on 4 June needed to warn the public that 'wars are not won by evacuations'.

MAY
27
1703

Tsar Peter the Great of Russia founded the city of St Petersburg.

Peter the Great had become Tsar in 1682 and his rule is characterised by immense cultural and political changes in Russia that saw the country transformed into a modern world power. Keen to replace Sweden as the leading power in the Baltic, Peter began the Great Northern War that was fought from 1700 to 1721.

In 1703 Peter's forces captured Swedish possessions at the mouth of the Neva river, and it was here that he laid the foundation stone for the Peter and Paul Fortress on Zayachy Island. This marked the beginning of the construction of St Petersburg, although the first residential building to be completed was a small log cabin built for the Tsar that stands today inside a protective pavilion. Peter wanted his new city to be built entirely of stone and brick, so he ordered this first house to be painted red with white detailing to appear like brick.

The construction of St Petersburg at the mouth of the Neva was an enormous undertaking. The Tsar had to hire large numbers of European engineers and architects to drain the marshland and develop the city. He banned the creation of other stone buildings in Russia so that all the country's stonemasons and artisans could be used to construct its buildings, and he ordered the conscription of 40,000 serfs a year to work as labourers in the harsh conditions.

St Petersburg went on to become the capital of Russia for two centuries, and was the location for numerous notable events that helped to shape world history. Its historic centre is now a UNESCO World Heritage site, and it houses one of the world's largest art collections in the Hermitage Museum that was founded by Catherine the Great in 1754.

A solar eclipse during the Battle of Halys led to a truce between the kingdoms of Media and Lydia, making it the earliest historical event that can be dated with absolute certainty.

The Eclipse of Thales was recorded in *The Histories* of the Greek historian Herodotus. He claims that the philosopher Thales of Miletus accurately predicted the eclipse in advance, marking what science writer Isaac Asimov later described as 'the birth of science'.

Herodotus writes that the Lydians under King Alyattes II and the Medes under Cyaxares had been at war for five years over their competing interests in Anatolia. The spark had been a desire for revenge over the killing of one of Cyaxares' sons by nomadic hunters who were subsequently given protection by the Lydians. Having fought a series of indecisive battles in the preceding years, the two armies met again in 585 BCE during which a solar eclipse took place.

There is some doubt over Herodotus' claim that Thales predicted the eclipse in advance, especially as no records survive regarding exactly how he made his calculations. However, the eclipse was also recorded in other accounts. Herodotus describes how 'suddenly the day became night' and that the warring armies interpreted this as an omen to stop fighting. The peace was sealed by Alyattes' daughter marrying one of Cyaxares' surviving sons.

Later astronomers were able to pinpoint the exact date of historical eclipses, using the same calculations that help to predict future ones. By combining data of these ancient events with contextual knowledge of the Battle of Halys, 28 May 585 BCE was consequently identified as the most likely date. This makes the day of the battle a cardinal date, meaning it provides a waypoint from which numerous other dates in the ancient world can be calculated.

MAY
29
1953

Edmund Hillary and Tenzing Norgay became the first people to reach the summit of Mount Everest.

The two mountaineering pioneers were part of the ninth British Mount Everest expedition that had sought to reach the summit of the world's highest mountain. At the time, only the Nepalese approach to Everest was open to climbers, but the government in Kathmandu only granted permission to one expedition a year.

With a British team unlikely to be granted another attempt until at least 1956, the Joint Himalayan Committee who oversaw British expeditions believed it was vital that the 1953 expedition was a success. They made the decision to appoint British Army Colonel John Hunt as the leader of the expedition, although his appointment was opposed by some other members of the team. Hillary himself was initially unhappy as he was fiercely loyal to Eric Shipton, the climber who had previously led expeditions for the Committee.

The 400-strong team of British climbers, Sherpa guides and porters set up base camp in March 1953, and established advanced camps further up the mountain throughout April and early May. A first attempt was made on the summit by Tom Bourdillon and Charles Evans on 26 May, but they were defeated by problems with their oxygen equipment.

Hillary and Norgay were directed to begin their attempt the next day. Poor weather meant that they began their final ascent on the morning of 29 May, reaching the summit at 11:30am where Hillary took a photo of Norgay, alongside a series of other shots looking down the mountain as proof that they had reached the summit. News of their achievement reached Britain on the morning of 2 June, the day of Queen Elizabeth II's coronation.

MAY

30

1381

The Peasants' Revolt was triggered when John Bampton arrived in Essex to investigate non-payment of the poll tax.

Although sparked by the introduction of a new poll tax, the roots of the Peasants' Revolt lay in the dramatic social and economic upheaval that had emerged after the devastation of the Black Death. The plague had reached England in 1348 and soon wiped out up to half of the entire population. In the aftermath the surviving peasantry had demanded better wages and conditions, so grew increasingly angry at the government's attempts to limit such changes.

This resentment was aggravated by the introduction of taxes to fund the English campaign against France in the Hundred Years' War. Richard II was only ten years old when he inherited the throne in 1377 and his government forged ahead with the introduction of a new poll tax. By the time Parliament passed a third poll tax in 1380 the situation was incredibly volatile.

Many people, especially those in the south-east of the country, refused to pay. This prompted the government to begin investigating those who had not paid. John Bampton and his clerks were greeted by a crowd of villagers determined not to pay any further taxes and, after the officials attempted to arrest their leader, violence broke out.

The revolt quickly spread from Essex to Kent and beyond. Tax collectors and landlords were attacked, while tax records and registers were destroyed. By the time the crowds reached London in mid-June, Wat Tyler had emerged as leader of the Kentish rebels. After rejecting a series of royal charters granted at Mile End the previous day, Tyler presented a comprehensive set of demands to Richard on 15th June at Smithfield. Tyler was later attacked and killed by members of the royal party, heralding the collapse of the revolt.

The Jaffna Public Library in Sri Lanka was burnt down during a violent rampage by an organised mob of ethnic Sinhalese.

The Jaffna Public Library was built in 1933 to serve the capital city of the Northern Province of Sri Lanka. By the 1980s it had become one of the largest libraries in Asia, and the foremost repository of Tamil literature and culture. The attack on the library resulted in the burning of over 97,000 books and manuscripts of enormous cultural and historical value. The attack was racially motivated, and was a major cause of the Sri Lankan Civil War that broke out two years later.

Ethnic tensions had been developing between Sri Lanka's minority Tamils and majority Sinhalese for much of the 20th century. Official discrimination against the Tamils by the government led to young Tamils increasingly turning to militant groups such as the Liberation Tigers of Tamil Eelam, otherwise known as the Tamil Tigers, who sought the creation of a separate Tamil state.

The burning of the Jaffna Public Library came after three Sinhalese policemen were shot and killed during a political rally by the Tamil United Liberation Front who sought an independent state for the Tamils. This triggered three days of violence by the police that saw the indiscriminate killing of four civilians and the destruction of Tamil-owned businesses and property. The library was attacked in an aggressive act of biblioclasm, the deliberate destruction of books.

The government's failure to respond to the attack and to protect the Tamils and their cultural heritage helped to consolidate opposition. The burning of the library therefore acted as a rallying call for militant Tamils, and helped to bring about the Sri Lankan Civil War that erupted in 1983 and lasted for almost 26 years.

JUNE

JUNE 1 1495

The royal Exchequer Rolls from Scotland recorded the first known written reference to Scotch whisky.

The Scottish Exchequer was responsible for recording royal income and expenditure in Scotland. The well-preserved calfskin parchment, better known as vellum, bears an entry on 1 June 1495 that records 'To Friar John Cor, by order of the King, to make *aqua vitae* VIII bolls of malt'.

The Latin term *aqua vitae* means 'water of life'. In Scottish Gaelic this same phrase translates as *uisge-beatha*, the first word being pronounced 'ush-kee'. English language transcriptions subsequently recorded the word as 'whisky'. In terms of the quantity, the boll was a form of measurement in Scotland at the time. Consequently the record indicates that King James IV provided enough malt to distil approximately 1,500 bottles of alcohol in the last accounting year. Such a quantity suggests that the distillation process was well-established by this time, but no earlier reference to the production of what we now call Scotch whisky have ever been found.

Friar John Cor, the recipient of the malt, was a monk from the Tironensian order based at Lindores Abbey in Fife. Little is known about the monk himself, with historians even being unsure of the extent of his role in the distillation process. Later records do however show him receiving money from the king at Christmas and being given black cloth for clothing as a clerk in royal service.

The records are therefore a key part of the story of Scotch whisky. However, subsequent writers have been unable to confirm whether the exchequer rolls' exclusive reference to 'malt' meant it was a single or blended malt whisky. It's also unknown how much of the estimated 800 gallons were drunk.

JUNE

2

1962

Chile and Italy met in the 1962 FIFA World Cup, which resulted in 'the most stupid, appalling, disgusting and disgraceful exhibition of football possibly in the history of the game'.

Nicknamed the Battle of Santiago, the match between the Chilean host nation and the Italians was preceded by provocative articles in the Italian press. Chile had suffered devastating damage in the 1960 Valvida earthquake, which was the largest ever recorded and caused at least $3.24 billion of damage when adjusted for inflation. In the wake of the disaster, Italian journalists criticised the decision to allow Chile to continue to host the competition as 'pure madness'. Shortly before the competition was due to begin, Italian newspapers published further inflammatory comments about the country's infrastructure, people and capital city.

These tensions came to a head at the Group 2 match between Chile and Italy at the Estadio Nacional in Santiago. In front of over 66,000 people, the players unleashed such violence that the Mirror, a British newspaper, described the pitch as 'a battlefield'. The match was refereed by experienced Englishman Ken Aston who sent off an Italian player within the first few minutes, but later failed to reprimand Chilean Leonel Sánchez for throwing punches at two separate Italian players, breaking the nose of one of them.

Despite armed police needing to be called three times during the match, the game finished with Chile winning 2-0 against a 9-man Italian team. Aston was heavily criticised by both sides, but defended himself by saying that he was more like 'an umpire in military manoeuvres'. He was later appointed to the FIFA Referees' Committee, where he introduced red and yellow cards as a visual sign of a caution or sending off.

JUNE

3

1956

Authorities in the Californian city of Santa Cruz banned rock and roll music at public gatherings.

The previous evening had seen around 200 teenagers attend a concert at the Santa Cruz Civic Auditorium by the Los Angeles-based Chuck Higgins and his Orchestra. Higgins and an earlier band, the Mellotones, had scored a West Coast hit four years earlier with the saxophone instrumental 'Pachuko Hop'. This jump blues single has since been described as one of the key releases that bridged the upbeat jazz styles of the 1940s to the frenetic rhythm and blues that was to emerge the following decade.

Shortly after midnight members of the Santa Cruz police, under the command of Lieutenant Richard Overton, entered the venue and shut down the concert. He later described the predominantly teenage crowd inside the auditorium as being 'engaged in suggestive, stimulating and tantalizing motions induced by the provocative rhythms of an all-negro band'.

The next day the Santa Cruz authorities announced an outright ban on rock and roll music, with the justification that 'rock and roll and other forms of frenzied music [were] detrimental to both the health and morals of our youth and community'.

According to a report in a local newspaper from the time, the Chief of Police had said that, 'we have nothing against rock and roll music…it's just what some people do while listening to it.' Within days, however, Santa Cruz's teenagers had begun to protest against the ban. In response, City Manager Robert Klein announced that the music, 'along with other harmless types of swing music, enjoyable to young and old' was welcome. Despite this, a scheduled concert by another rock and roll artist was cancelled by the auditorium manager.

JUNE

4

1920

The Treaty of Trianon was signed between Hungary and most of the Allies of the First World War.

The Austro-Hungarian Empire had begun to collapse by the autumn of 1918, and the Hungarian Prime Minister declared the termination of the joint state on 31 October. Austria signed the Treaty of St Germain on 10 September 1919 in which it recognised Hungary's independence.

The Treaty of Trianon went on to strip Hungary of nearly three-quarters of its territory. Romania, Czechoslovakia, and Yugoslavia received the vast majority of this land and population. The border changes meant that over 3 million ethnic Hungarians found themselves living in a different country. Furthermore, the Treaty specified that one year after the date of signing these people would also lose their Hungarian nationality.

The territorial changes had a dramatic effect on Hungary's economy. Large parts of the country's former infrastructure and industry lay outside the new borders, while the loss of the coastline meant that it was both difficult and expensive to engage in international trade. Unemployment skyrocketed, while industrial output declined.

The treaty also placed severe limits on Hungary's military which was forbidden from possessing an air force, tanks, and heavy artillery. The army was limited to 35,000 soldiers and conscription was banned, exacerbating the already mounting unemployment.

The social, economic and political effects of the treaty later led the historian and former British Ambassador to Hungary, Bryan Cartledge, to describe it as 'the greatest catastrophe to have befallen Hungary since the Battle of Mohacs in 1526'.

JUNE
5
1883

The first Orient Express train, known at the time as *Express d'Orient*, departed Paris.

The Orient Express was created by Georges Nagelmackers, a wealthy Belgian and the founder of the Compagnie Internationale des Wagons-Lits that specialised in luxury travel. A number of biographers refer to him being inspired to create the transcontinental route after seeing George Pullman's lavish sleeper cars in the United States.

Having returned to Belgium where he began work on his vision, Nagelmackers' first successful long-distance railway journey saw him transport guests on a 2,000km return trip aboard the first 'Train Eclair de luxe' – the luxury lightning train – from Paris to Vienna in 1882. The success of this trip, on which passengers were served an array of extravagant foods including oysters and game in the sumptuous surroundings of the purpose-built carriages, led to the creation of a more regular timetable that operated as *Express d'Orient* from June the following year.

Although the first train only went as far as Vienna, by 1889 the route had been extended to Constantinople in Turkey. This direct route across the continent, combined with the train's opulent furnishings, soon made it popular with royalty, diplomats and spies. It also provided the perfect backdrop for numerous creative works.

Although service was interrupted by both the First and Second World Wars, the Orient Express continued to operate for more than thirty years during the Communist period of eastern European history. However the train was eventually retired as a result of declining demand, with the last direct Paris–Istanbul service running on 19 May 1977.

JUNE

6

1822

Alexis St Martin, who had been shot in the stomach, was first treated by US Army surgeon William Beaumont who became known as the 'Father of Gastric Physiology'.

St Martin was a French-Canadian voyageur who was employed by the American Fur Company to transport furs in large cargo canoes. While visiting the company's store on Mackinac Island in Michigan, he was accidentally shot at close range with a shotgun that had been loaded with lead pellets for hunting ducks.

The surgeon from the local US Army fort was called to treat the injured man, whom it was assumed would die of the horrific effects of the gunshot. A large cavity had been opened in his side, his ribs were fractured, and there was a hole in his stomach. However, despite the dire diagnosis St Martin slowly recovered. The one key reminder of the accident was that the hole in his stomach had attached itself to the hole in his body, leaving a direct route into his stomach from the outside.

Known as a permanent gastric fistula, the direct access to St Martin's stomach led Dr Beaumont to contract the illiterate voyageur as his servant and medical test subject. Beaumont's experiments, which often involved the observation of pieces of food that had been tied to string and inserted directly into his subject's stomach, led to enormous advances in the scientific understanding of digestion.

Beaumont's decision to keep the hole open, rather than perform surgery to close it, raised very few ethical questions at the time. The doctor actually gained enormous prestige from his research, which he published in his book *Experiments and Observations on the Gastric Juice and the Physiology of Digestion*. His subject, St Martin, later returned to Canada where he died naturally in 1880.

JUNE

7

1520

Henry VIII of England and Francis I of France met at the Field of Cloth of Gold.

In 1518 the English Cardinal Wolsey had negotiated the Treaty of London, a non-aggression pact that was signed by the twenty major European powers of the time. However, peace held for barely a year before two of the signatories went to war and Wolsey began to arrange meetings between Henry VIII and the other monarchs to salvage the agreement.

Francis I of France was barely three years younger than Henry and, like his English counterpart, was keen to display the grandeur of his court. Consequently both men approached their forthcoming meeting as an opportunity to outshine the other, resulting in a more than two week-long festival of riches and entertainment.

The meeting took place between the communes of Ardres in France and Guîne, which at the time was under English rule. Both rulers erected lavish temporary palaces and pavilions due to the castles in the nearby communes being in a poor state of repair. The extensive use of cloth of gold, which was woven with real gold thread and silk, would later give the site of the meeting its name. The extravagance of the two kings knew no bounds, with Henry's encampment featuring a gilt fountain that ran with wine and claret.

The event also featured such competitions as jousting and wrestling, with Henry being defeated by Francis in the latter. Yet despite the joviality provided by these games and other entertainment including banquets and exotic animals, the meeting ended on 24 June with little political progress. Less than three weeks later Henry signed an alliance with the Holy Roman Emperor Charles V, Francis' main rival on the continent.

JUNE

8

793

Norse raiders attacked the holy island of Lindisfarne off the Northumbrian coast in an event that is generally accepted as the start of the 'Viking' period of British history.

The monastery on Lindisfarne had been established by Saint Aiden in the early 7th century, and grew to be an important centre of Christianity in Anglo-Saxon Britain. Although the attack on the Holy Island was not the first time that Vikings had targeted Britain, it is notable due to being an assault on the holiest site in the kingdom of Northumbria and, arguably, Anglo-Saxon Britain. The raiders laid waste to the island, slaughtering the monks that lived there, and stealing vast quantities of treasure.

The island was probably targeted due to being both remote and wealthy, although Christian commentators at the time proposed other explanations. Alcuin, a Northumbrian scholar who was working as a tutor in the Frankish kingdom, wrote to both the bishop of Lindisfarne and the Northumbrian king. His letters expressed upset at the attack but also questioned whether it was 'the outcome of the sins of those who live there'.

Although the religious community on Lindisfarne survived the attack of 793, Viking raids on monasteries and other religious sites in Britain continued for many years. Consequently some of the best examples of early medieval religious metalwork have been found in Scandinavian graves from the time.

From the middle of the 9th century the Norsemen began to see Britain as a place for colonisation rather than plunder. Within a few decades they had established an area of independent rule known as the Danelaw, the legacy of which can be seen in many place names in the North of England and the East Midlands.

JUNE

9

68

Nero, the last Roman emperor of the Julio-Claudian dynasty, committed suicide.

Nero was Augustus' great-great grandson and was adopted by his great-uncle, Claudius, after he married his mother Agrippina the Younger. Following Claudius' death in 54 CE, the sixteen-year-old Nero became emperor with the support of the Praetorian Guard whose leaders were loyal to his mother.

There are few surviving sources relating to Nero's reign, with the majority of what we know being drawn from Tacitus, Suetonius, and Cassius Dio. Consequently historians have to exercise caution when drawing conclusions about his rule, but the contemporary accounts suggest that he acted with moderation and respect for the Senate during the early years of his reign.

By 62 CE, however, Nero had ordered the murder of both his mother and his wife while his rule became increasingly brutal and unpredictable. He immersed himself in artistic pursuits at the expense of government, and approved vicious punishments for the Christians he blamed for starting the Great Fire in 64 CE.

Nero's extravagant orders for the reconstruction of Rome, alongside his other expensive pursuits, had a devastating effect on the economy. Dissent turned into revolt throughout the provinces and, in response to his failure to respond to the growing insurrections, the Spanish governor Galba came out in opposition to Nero. Galba soon won the support of the legions while Nero, having fled Rome, was tried *in absentia* and condemned to death as an enemy of the people. Hearing the news, Nero prepared to commit suicide but only did so with the help of a servant. His death led to the catastrophic Year of the Four Emperors in which the empire descended into civil war.

JUNE

10

1924

Giacomo Matteotti, an Italian socialist politician, was kidnapped and then murdered by members of the Fascist party.

Matteotti had been a leading member of the Italian Socialist Party but, following divisions in the party, he co-founded the Unitary Socialist Party in 1922. Matteotti became an outspoken critic of Mussolini and the Fascists, and publicly criticised the new political organisation's use of violence in a pamphlet published in 1921.

Three years later, in 1924, Matteotti published a book that was highly critical of the new government called *The Fascisti Exposed: A Year of Fascist Domination*. On 30 May that year he made a particularly zealous speech in the Chamber of Deputies in which he criticised Mussolini and accused the Fascists of only winning the recent election due to their use of violence to intimidate the public.

Less than two weeks later, on June 10, Matteotti disappeared. His neighbours reported an unknown car's registration plate to the police who quickly found the car with blood on the back seat. Although this didn't directly link the car to Matteotti's disappearance, Mussolini ordered the arrest of Amerigo Dumini and other members of his recently-created Ceka secret police. Opposition deputies showed their opposition to the Fascists by moving from the Chamber in an event known as the Aventine secession. Matteotti's body was later found following an extensive search, showing that he had been stabbed in the chest with a carpenter's file.

Despite a significant loss of political support, and the suggestion that he was involved in ordering the murder, Mussolini successfully turned events to his advantage. A speech in January 1925 saw him begin the transition to dictatorship when he stated that he would bring stability to Italy, even if that meant using force.

JUNE
11
1963

Vietnamese Buddhist monk Thich Quang Duc burned himself to death at a busy crossroads in Saigon.

Quang Duc's self-immolation came in response to the persecution of Buddhists by the government under Diem, who belonged to the Catholic minority and was supported by the USA. Buddhists were regularly subjected to discriminatory policies that ranged from limited access to United States aid to the availability of employment. Even the military saw some Buddhists convert in order to improve their chances of promotion.

In early May 1963 the government banned the Buddhist flag. This coincided with Phat Dan, otherwise known as Vesak, the birthday of Gautama Buddha. Buddhists were incensed by the ban and, on 8 May, a number of Buddhists in the city flew the flag and later marched on the government-controlled radio station where government troops repelled the protesters with live ammunition. Nine people were killed, but Diem blamed the violence on the Viet Cong. His refusal to hold the local authorities to account or to grant religious equality triggered more protests around the country.

On the morning of 11 June, 350 Buddhist monks and nuns processed along the road outside the Cambodian embassy in Saigon. Thich Quang Duc calmly emerged from a car and adopted the lotus position on a cushion in the intersection where he was doused in petrol from a five-gallon can. After chanting a prayer he struck a match and his body was engulfed in flames.

Photographs of the act shocked the world, and increased international pressure on Diem who failed to implement the reforms that he promised in the aftermath. On 1 November he was overthrown in a coup and assassinated the following day.

JUNE

12

1987

US President Ronald Reagan made a speech in front of the Brandenburg Gate in Berlin in which he called on the USSR's leader, Mikhail Gorbachev, to 'Tear down this wall!'

Reagan was in Berlin to celebrate the city's 750th anniversary, and was scheduled to make a speech in front of 20,000 people to mark the occasion. His presence in the city was not universally popular, however, and there are reports of up to 50,000 people taking to the streets the previous day in anti-Reagan protests.

Tensions were also running high in the American President's administration. There was considerable disagreement over whether the phrase 'tear down this wall' should even be included in the speech. The National Security Council and the State Department were particularly concerned that such a direct challenge to the Soviet Union would increase tensions between the two countries, and could damage the positive relationship that Reagan had begun to forge with Gorbachev. The President's deputy chief of staff, Kenneth Duberstein, later reported that Reagan said he would include the phrase because 'it's the right thing to do'.

The President began his speech at 2pm, protected by two panes of bulletproof glass that were erected to shield him from potential East German snipers. TASS, the Soviet press agency, remarked that the speech was 'openly provocative…war-mongering'.

Despite the highly emotive atmosphere in front of the Brandenburg Gate on the day, Time magazine later claimed that the speech received 'relatively little coverage from the media'. Even John Kornblum, a senior US diplomat who was based in Berlin at the time, stated on the twentieth anniversary of the speech that it 'wasn't really elevated to its current status until 1989, after the wall came down'.

JUNE
13
1966

The US Supreme Court ruled in *Miranda* v. *Arizona* that all criminal suspects must be informed of their Fifth and Sixth Amendment rights before questioning.

Any suspect arrested in the USA must be informed of four key rights. 'You have the right to remain silent. Anything you say can, and will, be used against you in court of law. You have the right to an attorney. If you cannot afford one, one will be appointed for you.'

Known as the *Miranda* warning, the requirement for the police to inform all criminal suspects of these rights came about as the result of Arizona labourer Ernesto Miranda's 1963 conviction for kidnapping and rape. A confession made to the Phoenix Police Department was entered as evidence yet, despite the form being printed with the statement that he had 'full knowledge of my legal rights', it later emerged that he had not been informed of either his right to an attorney or his right to remain silent.

Although Alvin Moore, Miranda's court-appointed lawyer for his trial, objected to the use of the confession this was overruled by Judge Yale McFate and Miranda was sentenced for 20-30 years imprisonment. Having failed to win an appeal to the Arizona Supreme Court, the case eventually made it to the US Supreme Court where Miranda was represented by attorney John Paul Frank.

The Supreme Court ruled in a 5-4 majority that, in order for evidence from questioning to be used in court, the police must have first informed the suspect of their rights. Since Miranda's conviction was based on a confession before which he had not been informed of his rights, his conviction was overturned. However, he was later retried and again found guilty thanks to the testimony of the woman he had been living with at the time.

JUNE

14

1645

The Battle of Naseby, a decisive engagement of the English Civil War, was fought between the Royalist army of King Charles I and the Parliamentarian New Model Army.

The New Model Army was formed as a result of concerns over the effectiveness of the existing Parliamentarian army that was based on local volunteers, many of whom were reluctant to fight away from home. The new army would be made up of full-time professional soldiers whose loyalty would be national rather than regional. The introduction of the Self-Denying Ordinance further strengthened the new force, since it resulted in a more effective military leadership.

The New Model Army, under the command of Sir Thomas Fairfax, was besieging the King's former capital in Oxford when news arrived that the Royalist army had captured the Parliamentarian town of Leicester. Fairfax abandoned the siege on Oxford and marched north to engage the Royalists, whom he found on the border between Northamptonshire and Leicestershire. Fairfax's army was joined by Oliver Cromwell's cavalry on 13 June. Faced with the choice of either fighting or retreating, the King accepted battle.

Fairfax had positioned the Parliamentarian army on a ridge, but was persuaded by Cromwell to move it to a weaker position to encourage the Royalists to attack. Prince Rupert of the Rhine soon broke through the Parliamentary left flank, but rode on to pursue fleeing Parliamentarians rather than turn and outflank the infantry. This weakened the Royalists, and Cromwell's cavalry were able to break the remaining cavalry before turning against the infantry in the centre. Before long the Royalists began to surrender, while Charles fled. The Royalist army was virtually destroyed in the battle, with around 6,000 of its 8,000 men either killed or captured.

JUNE

15

1859

The Pig War border confrontation began when Lyman Cutlar shot a British-owned pig on San Juan Island.

The archipelago of which San Juan Island is part lies between Washington State on the United States mainland and Vancouver, in what was then British North America. The 1846 Oregon Treaty had established a boundary along the 49th parallel along 'the middle of the channel which separates the continent from Vancouver's Island'. The problem was that San Juan Island itself lies in the middle of the channel, leading both countries to claim sovereignty over it.

By 1859 the British Hudson's Bay Company had established a sheep ranch on the island. A small number of American settlers had also arrived under the terms of the Donation Land Claim Act, even though the ownership of the land was disputed.

On 15 June 1859 a free-roaming black pig owned by the Hudson Bay employee Charles Griffin began rooting through American settler Lyman Cutlar's potato patch. Cutlar shot the pig. Although the exact details of what happened next are unclear, a number of sources claim that Cutlar offered $10 compensation while Griffin demanded $100. Whatever the truth, Griffin reported Cutlar to the British authorities who threatened to arrest him. In response the US General William S. Harney sent 66 soldiers from the 9th Infantry, which the British governor responded to by sending three British warships.

By 10 August a force of 461 Americans and five British ships with over 2,000 men were caught in a tense standoff. However, the arrival of British Rear Admiral Robert L. Baynes heralded a de-escalation of tensions after he refused to 'involve two great nations in a war over a squabble about a pig'. An international commission eventually ruled in 1872 that America should control the island.

JUNE

16

1846

Pope Pius IX began what is still the longest reign of a Catholic Pope.

Born Giovanni Maria Mastai-Ferretti, Pius IX's election by the Papal conclave of 1846 came at a time of significant political unrest across Europe. A particular issue facing the 50 members of the College of Cardinals who attended the conclave regarded the future governance of the Papal States, which the new Pope would rule. A conservative faction wished to see the continuation of a policy of papal absolutism, while more moderate cardinals hoped for some liberal reforms.

Going against the general mood of the rulers of Europe who wished to see a conservative Pope, the moderate Cardinal Bernetti successfully persuaded other like-minded cardinals to vote for Mastai-Ferretti. The papal historian Valérie Pirie wrote that, as one of the scrutineers responsible for recording the votes of the conclave, Mastai-Ferretti therefore proclaimed his own election.

His appointment was met with enthusiasm from European liberals, and he was celebrated by English Protestants as a 'friend of light'. Having named himself Pius after Pope Pius VII, the first years of the new Pope's rule saw a number of liberal actions including the release of political prisoners and the beginnings of a constitution for the Papal States. However, the revolutions of 1848-49 and a number of nationalist terrorist attacks began to turn him away from this initially liberal agenda.

By the 1850s Pius IX had become more conservative, and he began to consolidate the power of the Church. The capture of the Papal States by the Italian Army in 1870, however, led to him declaring himself the 'Prisoner of the Vatican'.

JUNE

17

1631

The death of Mumtaz Mahal, the chief consort of the Mughal emperor Shah Jahan, prompted her husband to construct the Taj Mahal.

Mumtaz Mahal, whose name means 'the Exalted One of the palace', was originally known as Arjumand Banu Begum. Born into a prominent Persian noble family, she married the future Mughal emperor Shah Jahan in 1612. She is widely recorded as being the favourite of his three wives with whom he shared a genuine love, and who was a valued confidant and trusted advisor.

The birth of the couple's fourteenth child resulted in Mumtaz Mahal's death on 17 June 1631 from postpartum haemorrhage as a result of excessive blood-loss during a thirty hour labour. The couple were supervising a military campaign in the Deccan Plateau, and so the empress' remains were temporarily buried at Burhanpur. Her husband entered a long period of mourning, after which he commissioned the construction of the magnificent Taj Mahal as a mausoleum.

Work on the Taj Mahal began in 1632 and, although the majority of the mausoleum's construction was completed by 1643, the rest of the elaborate complex was not finished for another decade. The mausoleum itself is built of white marble that is inlaid with 28 different types of precious and semi-precious stones brought from all over India and Asia.

In 1658 Shah Jahan was deposed by his third son, Aurangzeb, who put him under house arrest in Agra Fort from where he could see the Taj Mahal in the distance. When he died eight years later, Shah Jahan's body was taken there by river and laid to rest next to his beloved Mumtaz Mahal.

JUNE

18

1887

Germany and Russia signed the secret Reinsurance Treaty that ensured they would each remain neutral if the other went to war with a third European power.

Germany, Russia and Austria-Hungary had entered into a second *Dreikaierbund* in 1881. Like the one before it, the agreement was designed by the German Chancellor, Otto von Bismarck, to isolate France from potential allies and avoid rivalry between his two neighbours over territory in the Balkans. Continuing tensions between Austria-Hungary and Russia over this region led to the agreement's collapse in 1887 and forced Bismarck to find another way to maintain French diplomatic isolation.

Germany had already formed the Dual Alliance with Austria-Hungary in 1879, so the Reinsurance Treaty was created to ensure Russia continued to side with Germany. In return Germany agreed to a Russian sphere of influence in Bulgaria and the Black Sea.

By the time the treaty came up for renewal in 1890, Wilhelm II had become Kaiser of Germany. He insisted that Bismarck resign the Chancellorship in March that year, and argued that his personal relationship with Tsar Alexander III would be enough to avoid any future problems with Russia. Bismarck's successor Leo von Caprivi was also unwilling to seek a renewal of the Reinsurance Treaty, meaning that it lapsed.

Without the treaty to tie St Petersburg to Berlin, the Russian government began to forge closer relations with France. France's improving diplomatic situation was formalised in the Franco-Russian Alliance of 1892. This opened up Germany to the possibility of a war on two fronts, making the failure of the Reinsurance Treaty a contributing factor to the outbreak of the First World War.

JUNE 19 1949

The first NASCAR race took place at the Charlotte Speedway in North Carolina.

Stock car racing had its origins in the era of Prohibition, when illegal alcohol was distributed by fast cars across the United States. In order to outrun the police, many bootleggers modified their otherwise ordinary or 'stock' cars and over time began to organise events and compete against one another.

Mechanic Bill France Sr. moved to the spiritual home of automobile racing at Daytona Beach in Florida in 1935. He later began to organise his own events but, by the late 1940s, had become frustrated with inconsistent rules and unscrupulous promoters. In response he called a meeting of influential members of the racing community at the Streamline Hotel and, on 21 February 1948, the National Association for Stock Car Auto Racing was formed.

Forced to delay the inaugural season due to a shortage of new cars following a rise in demand after the war, the first Strictly Stock race took place on 19 June 1949. Around 13,000 spectators turned up to the Charlotte Speedway to see 33 drivers, one of whom was female driver Sara Christian, complete 200 laps of the 3/4 mile circuit.

Glenn Dunnaway finished the race three laps ahead of his nearest rival, Jim Roper. However, a post-race inspection found that the rear springs of Dunnaway's car had been illegally modified. Since this broke the fundamental rule of only racing 'strictly stock' cars, he was disqualified and the $2,000 prize was handed to Roper.

The season featured a further seven races as well as two exhibition races. Red Byron, who had finished third in the first race, went on to win the Drivers' Championship. Jim Roper only started one other NASCAR race.

JUNE

20

1756

British prisoners of war were imprisoned in the 'Black Hole of Calcutta' after the Bengali army captured Fort William from the East India Company.

The East India Company had built Fort William to guard their trading base at Calcutta at a time when the provincial governors of the Mogul empire, known as nawabs, wielded significant power. The Nawab of Bengal, Siraj-ud-daula, was concerned that the Company had begun to strengthen the fort in response to French interests in the area. Fearing that a stronger fortress would undermine his own political power in the province, he ordered the work to stop. When the British refused to comply he sent an army of a reported 50,000 soldiers, 500 elephants and 50 cannon to lay siege to the fortress.

The nawab's army met very little resistance as it advanced through Calcutta towards the fort, so the majority of British residents fled to the ships in the harbour. A small garrison remained in the fort under the command of John Zephaniah Holwell, an inexperienced military commander whose primary role was as a tax collector.

Unable to defend the fortress, Holwell was forced to surrender on the afternoon of 20 June. He later reported that at 8pm 146 people were imprisoned in the fort's tiny 4.30m x 5.50m lock-up, of whom only 23 survived the night due to heat exhaustion and suffocation. Reports of the incident prompted a mixture of British anger and patriotism, and led to a violent retaliation by Robert Clive the following year.

It is now known that Holwell's figures were exaggerated, but a comprehensive study of the incident undertaken by Professor Brijen Gupta in the late 1950s concluded that of the lower number of around 64 prisoners, only 21 came out alive the next morning.

JUNE
21
1791

King Louis XVI of France and his family were caught attempting to escape Paris during the Flight to Varennes.

By the summer of 1791 the royal family had been living in the Tuileries in the heart of Paris for almost two years. They had been forced to move there from the lavish Palace of Versailles after the October Days of 1789, and felt as if they were prisoners as a result of their rapidly declining power.

The startling pace of change was viewed with alarm by the other monarchies of Europe, and this led to fear in France that the king himself was conspiring with foreign powers to topple the fledgling revolutionary government. Yet, convinced that he would find support for his rule in the countryside, on the night of the 20-21 June 1791 the king reinforced the people's lack of trust in him.

In what became known as the Flight to Varennes, Louis and the rest of the immediate royal family fled the Tuileries under cover of darkness. The plan had been largely formulated by the Swedish Count Axel von Fersen, who was rumoured to be Marie Antoinette's lover.

Disguised to avoid being noticed by the palace guards, the family travelled in a large heavy coach pulled by six horses. Their slow progress meant the journey to the eastern frontier took considerably longer than had been anticipated and soon word of their escape had spread. In Sainte-Menehould they were recognised by the local postmaster who checked the king's likeness against an assignat.

While the royal party continued their slow progress the postmaster rode ahead to the next town, Varennes, which lay just 30 miles from the Austrian border. Here the escapees were arrested and returned to Paris, the royal reputation in tatters.

JUNE

22

1948

The ship *Empire Windrush* arrived at Tilbury Docks in London carrying 492 West Indian immigrants.

The ship, originally known as MV *Monte Rosa*, was a German cruise ship that had been used as a troop transporter during the Second World War. She was seized by Britain at the end of the war, when she was renamed.

In 1948 the British government passed the Nationality Act, which gave British citizenship to people who lived in Commonwealth countries and allowed them the right to settle in Britain. Britain desperately needed workers in the aftermath of the Second World War, so Commonwealth citizens were encouraged to immigrate and help to rebuild the 'Mother Country'. A series of advertisements in and around Jamaica advertised tickets for the journey on board *Empire Windrush* for £28, which equates to around £600 today.

Many of the passengers who bought this first wave of tickets had been members of the Royal Air Force during the war. A number of them sought to rejoin the armed forces, while others undertook the voyage to see what opportunities Britain would present.

Although the press generally greeted them warmly as 'sons of Empire', some members of parliament opposed the arrival of the immigrants. Their presence was needed to staff a number of industries but, although Britain was short of workers, there was also a shortage of housing. This led to the new arrivals being temporarily housed in the deep level air-raid shelter in South Clapham, approximately two miles away from Brixton town centre, while they searched for accommodation. The majority permanently settled in Britain, but the Afro-Caribbean community experienced significant prejudice, intolerance and racism in subsequent years.

JUNE

23

1894

The International Olympic Committee was founded at the Sorbonne in Paris.

Prior to the IOC's establishment by Pierre de Coubertin, the British physician Dr William Penny Brookes had established the Wenlock Olympian Games in the English market town of Much Wenlock. Although he always maintained that he had the idea of reviving the ancient Olympic Games for amateur athletes himself, Coubertin entered correspondence with Brookes and benefited from his connections with the Greek government.

Coubertin was the secretary general of the Union of French Sports Associations and first proposed establishing the modern games at its meeting on 25 November 1892. Although his enthusiasm was met with little more than general applause, Coubertin was not deterred and began to lay the groundwork for what was to become the first Olympic Congress at the Sorbonne in Paris in 1894.

Having initially invited participants to a meeting entitled 'Reflections on and Propagation of the Principles of Amateurism', Coubertin later changed the name to a 'Congress on the Revival of the Olympic Games'. 79 delegates from 9 countries subsequently met at the Sorbonne, although Coubertin himself recognised that there still little enthusiasm for reviving the games.

Despite this, a vote was held at the final meeting of the congress on 23 June that established the International Olympic Committee. Coubertin was elected to the role of general secretary with the Greek businessman and writer Demetrios Vikelas as the first president. It was further agreed that the first modern Olympic Games would take place in Athens in 1896 with the second in Paris four years later. The IOC has remained responsible for the Olympic Games ever since.

JUNE
24
1812

Napoléon's Grande Armée began its failed invasion of Russia when it crossed the Neman River in what Russians refer to as the Patriotic War of 1812.

Russia had upset Napoléon by withdrawing from the Continental System, a French-led embargo against trade with Britain, in 1810. Meanwhile the Russian Tsar, Alexander I, was concerned by the formation of the Grand Duchy of Warsaw to the south. Napoléon consequently led his army across the Neman River in an attempt to secure Poland from the threat of a Russian invasion, and to force the Tsar to once again cease trading with Britain.

Up to 650,000 French soldiers invaded Russian Poland on 24 June for what Napoléon hoped would be a quick victory. The Grande Armée made significant progress into the Russian interior, forcing the Tsar's vastly outnumbered forces back into Lithuania, but erratic weather conditions made the advance difficult. Supply wagons struggled on muddy tracks caused by thunderstorms while the troops were affected by sunstroke and disease in the hot and humid swamp-like conditions.

The retreating Russians also adopted scorched-earth tactics that destroyed farmland and villages, making it increasingly difficult for Napoléon to feed his army. Despite the problems this caused, the French successfully advanced for almost three months before reaching Moscow. The city had been evacuated, and Napoléon's hopes of agreeing a peace treaty with Alexander were not realised.

Realising that his troops could not survive the winter, Napoléon led his army out of Moscow at the end of October. However, his numbers were seriously depleted and by December an estimated 380,000 men had died while another 100,000 had been captured.

JUNE

25

1678

Elena Cornaro Piscopia became the first woman to receive a Doctorate of Philosophy, otherwise known as a Ph.D.

Elena Cornaro was the daughter of Giovanni Battista Cornaro Piscopia, a member of an influential Venetian noble family. When she was seven years old her father was persuaded to start her on a classical education at which she excelled. By the time Giovanni was appointed to the powerful position of *Procuratore di San Marco de supra* in 1664, his daughter had already become fluent in numerous languages as well as showing an impressive ability in subjects ranging from music and mathematics to philosophy and theology.

In 1669 Cornaro translated the Spanish volume the *Colloquy of Christ* by the Carthusian monk Giovanni Lanspergio into Italian. This accomplishment led to her becoming president of the Venetian society Accademia dei Pacifici in 1670. Just two years later at the University of Padua, Cornaro's tutor in philosophy persuaded his colleague in theology to petition the university to grant her the highest level of degree.

Gregorio Cardinal Barbarigo, the bishop of Padua, initially supported her pursuit of a degree but later withdrew this when he learned that the female savant wished to earn it in theology. He instead offered the compromise that she could pursue a degree in philosophy.

Due to the number of people who wished to see her intellect in person, her examination was held in Padua's Cathedral of the Blessed Virgin on 25 June 1678. Cornaro's defence saw her explain two passages chosen at random from Aristotle. She spoke confidently and fluently in classical Latin for over an hour, and was subsequently awarded the doctoral degree in front of the rapturous audience.

JUNE

26

1974

Sharon Buchanan, a cashier at the Marsh supermarket in Troy, Ohio, scanned the world's first Universal Product Code (better known as a barcode) on a 10-pack of Wrigley's Juicy Fruit gum.

Bernard Silver and Norman Joseph Woodland had patented a bullseye shaped machine-readable code in 1949, but the UPC that was adopted by the Ad Hoc Committee of the Universal Product Identification Code was developed by a team of IBM engineers under George Laurer. The standard rectangular design measures approximately 1.5" x 0.9" and is made up of black bars and white spaces that represent a sequence of numbers unique to the item it is printed on.

The code was to be read by a scanner using a laser beam as a source of light. The black bars would absorb light, while the white space reflected it back to the scanner. The intensity of the reflected light would then be read, and the unique pattern would be deciphered by a computer that would provide pricing information and adjust the stock database to reflect the sale. Such equipment was costly, however, and this meant that the UPC was not widely used by retailers until the 1980s.

The checkout equipment used for the first reading of a UPC was built and installed by National Cash Register, a company that was based in Ohio. The selection of a packet of Wrigley's gum by the first customer, Clyde Dawson from the research and development department of Marsh Supermarket, was not a coincidence. Despite having many other items in his basket he picked the chewing gum to demonstrate that it was possible to print a barcode on small items. One of the Juicy Fruit packets from the supermarket is now held by the Smithsonian Institute.

JUNE

27

1950

US President Harry S. Truman ordered air and naval forces to assist South Korea against an invasion by North Korea.

Towards the end of the Second World War in 1945 the 'Big Three' powers of the USA, the USSR and Great Britain met at the Yalta Conference. As part of a wide-ranging series of agreements, Korea was divided along the 38th parallel with a Soviet occupied zone in the north and Americans in the south.

In May 1948 the north, led by Kim Il-sung, declared itself the communist Korean Democratic People's Republic. The democratic Republic of Korea soon followed in the south, and within a year both the USSR and the USA had withdrawn the majority of their troops. Meanwhile, the two Korean nations claimed the right to rule the other.

In the early morning of 25 June, North Korean troops crossed the 38th parallel and invaded South Korea. The action was condemned later that afternoon by the United Nations Security Council, who issued UN Security Council Resolution 82. This called for the North to immediately draw back to the 38th parallel. Two days later, on 27 June, the Security Council approved Resolution 83 which recommended providing military assistance to South Korea. The USSR could have been expected to veto both of these resolutions, but at the time was boycotting the Security Council over its refusal to admit the newly-proclaimed People's Republic of China.

Truman announced American intervention shortly after Resolution 83 to broad approval from both Congress and the public. Fighting continued until 27 July 1953 when an armistice was signed that established the Korean Demilitarized Zone along the 38th parallel. A peace treaty was never concluded.

JUNE

28

1880

The Australian outlaw Ned Kelly was arrested following a violent shoot-out with police at Glenrowan in Victoria.

Edward 'Ned' Kelly's father, John 'Red' Kelly had arrived in Australia after serving a sentence in Van Diemen's Land for stealing two pigs in his hometown in Ireland. He later married and started a family but was sentenced to hard labour for cattle theft, after which he unexpectedly died. His eldest son, Ned, soon found himself in trouble with the law for assisting the bushranger Harry Power in a number of robberies. He was later sentenced to three years' imprisonment for stealing horses.

In April 1878, Kelly allegedly shot police constable Alexander Fitzpatrick. Ned and his brother Dan fled into the bush and a reward of £100 was offered for their capture. In October three policemen who had located the brothers and their associates, Joe Byrne and Steve Hart, were shot and killed. The government soon declared the gang outlaws, but they evaded capture and turned to robbing banks.

On the night of 26 June 1880 the Kelly Gang killed a police informant, and then rode to the town of Glenrowan where they held dozens of hostages in the town's hotel. A police train was alerted to the situation, and the hotel was soon surrounded.

The gang engaged in a raging gunfight wearing homemade metal armour. Early the next morning Ned left the hotel and emerged from the bush to make one final stand. He was soon shot in his unprotected legs and arrested. Almost all the hostages were released by 10am, and in the early afternoon the hotel was set on fire. Steve Hart, Joseph Byrne and Dan Kelly were killed. Ned was later found guilty of the murder of Constable Lonigan in 1878 and was sentenced to death. He was executed by hanging on 11 November 1880.

JUNE
29
1613

The Globe Theatre in London burned to the ground during a performance of *Henry VIII.*

The Globe Theatre was situated on the southern side of the River Thames near today's Southwark Bridge. It was owned by shareholders who were actors in the Lord Chamberlain's Men whose lease had expired on their previous venue. On 28th December 1598, while the landowner was celebrating Christmas, they dismantled the old building and transported its timbers across the river to construct the Globe. Completed in 1599, the three-storey amphitheatre had an open-air standing space at its centre while the surrounding galleries were roofed with inexpensive but highly flammable thatch.

The play *All is True*, which was later referred to as *Henry VIII*, was staged at the Globe in 1613. In the play the king attends a ball at Cardinal Wolsey's house, and his arrival was heralded on stage with the firing of a cannon. A number of contemporary accounts record that during a performance on 29 June the cannon situated close to the roof misfired and set fire to the thatching.

Sir Henry Wotton recorded how the blaze 'kindled inwardly, and ran round like a train, consuming within less than an hour the whole house to the very ground'. The account goes on to describe how one man whose breeches were set on fire extinguished the flames by pouring a bottle of ale over himself.

The Globe was rebuilt with a tile roof, and it continued operating until 1642 when it closed as a casualty of Parliament's ban on theatrical plays. The entire structure was demolished a few years later to make way for tenement housing yet, despite the Restoration overturning the theatrical ban in 1660, the Globe was never rebuilt. A modern reconstruction opened in 1997 near the original site.

JUNE

30

1937

The world's first emergency telephone number, 999, began operating in London.

On 10 November 1935 a resident of Wimpole Street called the local Welbeck telephone exchange to report a fire that had broken out in the house opposite. This was the established way of seeking the emergency services, but there was no way of prioritising such calls since they used the same exchange number as all other calls. Consequently the caller was unable to raise the alarm, and five women died in the fire.

A letter from the frustrated neighbour appeared in *The Times* shortly afterwards, and this brought the issue to national attention. On 10 December the Postmaster General, who was responsible for the telephone network, informed parliament that he was to launch an inquiry into what he referred to as 'urgency calls'.

The 999 service was launched in London on 30 June 1937, and initially covered a 12 mile radius from Oxford Street. The number was initially chosen because it was easy to modify existing payphones, which used rotary dials, to allow the number 9 to connect without money needing to be inserted. 111 was ruled out since the accidental touching of telephone wires could accidentally trigger the call.

The first verified 999 call that led to an arrest took place a week after the service began operating, when a burglar was apprehended following a call from a member of the public to the police. Within a short space of time the system consistently proved to be a success, and its popularity and effectiveness in London led to the introduction of a 999 service in Glasgow the following year. It reached other British cities after the Second World War, but only expanded to cover the whole of the UK in 1976.

JULY

JULY

1

1911

The German gunboat SMS *Panther* was sent to the Moroccan port of Agadir, sparking the Second Moroccan Crisis.

France had emerged from the First Moroccan Crisis of 1906 in a much stronger position than neighbouring Germany, whose Kaiser Wilhelm II sought to develop economic and commercial interests in the country. The two countries formalised their positions in an agreement two years later but, by 1911, the domestic situation in Morocco had declined. In early 1911 the Sultan, Abdelhafid, faced an uprising by native tribes who also attacked French forces stationed in the country.

In response, 20,000 French and colonial troops were sent to the city of Fez under the pretext of protecting European residents and their property. This was interpreted by some in Germany as an attempt to extend French control over Morocco, and in response the gunboat SMS *Panther* was dispatched to the port of Agadir.

While France was unwilling to take military action, the arrival of the German navy raised some concerns in Britain that Germany might seek to establish a naval base. An article in *The Times* newspaper on 20 July further raised public tensions, while David Lloyd George's Mansion House speech the following day stated that Britain would not tolerate German aggression in Africa.

In the midst of such a hostile atmosphere the situation was eventually resolved through negotiations between the German and French governments. In return for recognising France's position in Morocco, Germany received territory in the Congo. However, the damage that the naval dimension of the crisis caused to German relations with Britain was irreparable and only deepened the mistrust that was to contribute to the outbreak of the First World War.

JULY

2

1881

James A. Garfield, the 20th President of the United States, was shot by Charles J. Guiteau at the Baltimore and Potomac Railroad Station in Washington D.C.

Guiteau had attempted various types of employment before turning his hand to politics in the lead-up to the 1880 presidential election. He wrote a speech called 'Grant against Hancock' when Ulysses S. Grant was still the forerunner for the Republican nomination, but revised it to 'Garfield against Hancock' after the latter won the candidacy.

Although Guiteau passed copies of the speech to members of the Republican National Committee, he is only believed to have delivered the speech twice at the most. Despite this he became convinced that he was responsible for Garfield winning the election, and expected a diplomatic posting in return. He even moved to Washington the day after Garfield's inauguration and regularly visited the State Department and the White House to reiterate his demand.

Guiteau was formally banned from the White House, and on 14 May was told by Secretary of State James G. Blaine to 'never speak to me again of the Paris consulship as long as you live'. This dismissal led him to begin plotting the assassination of the President.

After buying a British Bull Dog revolver with money borrowed from a relative, Guiteau undertook target practice and began stalking Garfield. Having read about the President's vacation plans in the press, he waited at the Baltimore and Potomac Railroad Station where he shot him at close range. Guiteau later declared, 'I am a Stalwart of the Stalwarts! I did it and I want to be arrested! Arthur is President now!' Garfield died 11 weeks later, while Guiteau was found guilty of murder and was hanged on 30 June 1882.

JULY

3

1940

British naval ships attacked the French Navy at Mers-el-Kébir in Algeria during the Second World War.

On 22 June 1940, France and Nazi Germany signed the Second Armistice at Compiègne. This signalled the end of the Battle of France, and Britain was concerned that the significant naval force of the Marine Nationale would now pass to the pro-Nazi Vichy government. If these ships were used by the Axis powers, they would secure a significant advantage in the Battle of the Atlantic.

Winston Churchill received reassurances from Admiral François Darlan, commander of the French Navy, that the ships would remain under French control. However, Churchill and the War Cabinet were unwilling to risk the possibility that they might change hands.

Having decided that it was necessary to neutralise the French fleet, Operation Catapult was launched on 3 July. French ships in British ports were captured, while those at Mers-el-Kébir were offered an ultimatum by Force H under the command of Admiral Sir James Somerville. If the French didn't surrender their ships or move them away from the reach of the Axis, they would be sunk.

Negotiations continued for much of the day, but at 5:54pm Churchill ordered the British ships to open fire in the first Anglo-French naval exchange since the Napoleonic Wars. The French were anchored in a narrow harbour that made them an easy target for the British guns. 1,300 French sailors were killed in just a few minutes, while one battleship was sunk and five more seriously damaged.

Churchill later recalled the 'hateful decision, the most unnatural and painful in which I have ever been concerned' but, in the context of the war, the attack at Mers-el-Kébir proved to the world that Britain was determined to keep fighting.

JULY

4

1862

Charles Dodgson, better known as the author Lewis Carroll, told a story to the sisters Alice, Lorina and Edith Liddell that was to develop into *Alice's Adventures in Wonderland.*

Dodgson was a lecturer in mathematics at Christ Church College in Oxford University where, alongside his academic work, he also wrote poems and short stories that were published in national publications under his pseudonym. He became close friends with the family of Henry Liddell, the Dean of Christ Church, from 1856 and was known to take the children on rowing trips along the Thames.

On 4 July, the Reverend Robinson Duckworth joined Dodgson and the children for a trip along the river for a picnic in the village of Godstow. During the journey Dodgson entertained the three Liddell girls with a story about a girl called Alice who fell into a rabbit hole. It is said that Alice Liddell enjoyed the story so much that she asked him to write it down for her. Dodgson eventually gave her an expanded handwritten and illustrated copy of *Alice's Adventures Under Ground* two years later, on 26 November 1864.

In the meantime he had approached the publisher, Macmillan, with an early version of the manuscript. He tested his drafts on the children of his friend George MacDonald, who reportedly adored the story. Macmillan committed to publishing the novel on its completion, and so Dodgson approached the celebrated artist Sir John Tenniel to provide illustrations.

Tenniel rejected the first print as he was unhappy with the print quality so the first UK edition, published at the end of 1865, was actually the second print. The book was an immediate success, and brought Dodgson – or at least his Lewis Carroll – enormous attention. It has remained in print ever since.

JULY

5

1946

The bikini swimsuit was introduced for the first time, four days after an atomic test at the Bikini Atoll.

Although there is evidence of bikini-like clothing being worn by ancient civilisations, the modern 2-piece swimsuit only appeared in the aftermath of the Second World War. While swimming costumes for women had gradually become less conservative through the first half of the twentieth century, wartime fabric rationing had forced designers to remove excess material which resulted in more form-fitting garments that had fewer panels covering the wearer's body.

A minimalist two-piece swimsuit was introduced by French fashion designer Jacques Heim in May 1946. Named the 'Atome' after the smallest known particle of matter, the bottom part still covered the wearer's naval. Meanwhile Louis Réard was working on his own design which used even less material.

Réard hired exotic dancer Micheline Bernardini from the Casino de Paris to model his creation, since he couldn't persuade any of the usual models to wear it. He called a press conference at the Piscine Molitor in Paris on 5 July 1946, four days after an atomic test at the Bikini Atoll that inspired the swimsuit's name. Here he stated that, 'like the [atom] bomb, the bikini is small and devastating'.

Despite receiving enormous media interest, the public reaction to the bikini was initially one of shock. Even in the late 1950s some magazines were still writing disapprovingly of the fashion, with *Modern Girl Magazine* declaring 'it is inconceivable that any girl with tact and decency would ever wear such a thing'. Yet while there was a conservative reaction from some quarters, photographs of celebrities wearing bikinis soon brought mainstream acceptance that has turned the 2-piece swimsuit into an $800 million business.

JULY

6

1947

The Kalashnikov AK-47 assault rifle went into production in the Soviet Union.

The AK-47 was designed by Soviet tank commander-turned-inventor Mikhail Kalashnikov. Having been injured in the Battle of Bryansk in October 1941, he was recovering in hospital when he heard fellow-soldiers lamenting the poor quality of the Russian army's rifles.

Kalashnikov created a number of weapons from 1942 onwards, entering them into competitions organised by the Soviet military. Although he lost out to other designers, he built on his efforts to eventually create the *Avtomat Kalashnikova model 1947*, better known as the AK-47. Following a series of field trials it was adopted by the Soviet army in 1949 as their standard issue assault rifle.

The AK-47 soon spread around the world as the simple design meant it was cheap to manufacture. Throughout the Cold War the USSR helped communist movements to acquire the weapon. It proved particularly popular amongst these groups due to its incredible reliability, especially when pitted against weapons such as the American M16 that was prone to jamming in the difficult conditions of the Vietnam War.

Variations of the AK-47, alongside outright copies, continue to be produced meaning that an estimated 100 million AK-47 derivatives exist in the world today. According to the World Bank, this means that AK-47s make up over 15% of all guns in the world.

Throughout his life Kalashnikov blamed politicians for the violence that saw his gun in use, not the gun itself. However, shortly before his death he did express concern over whether he should bear responsibility for the deaths caused by the weapons he created.

JULY

7

1911

The North Pacific Fur Seal Convention, the first international treaty that dealt with wildlife conservation issues, was signed.

Archaeological evidence indicates that seals have been hunted for their pelts, their flesh and their fat for over 4,000 years. By the end of the 19th century, however, industrialisation of hunting had brought a rapid decline in the seal population of the Bering Sea.

The USA had purchased Alaska and the surrounding islands in 1867, leading the American government to claim authority over the sealing industry in the region. This led to an increase in offshore or pelagic sealing that further reduced the seal populations.

Through arbitration Great Britain and the USA agreed to jointly enforce a series of hunting regulations designed to preserve the seal herds. It soon became clear that the terms of the agreement were not stringent enough to allow the seal populations to recover. Fearing the possibility of extinction if the situation was not dealt with, a joint commission of scientists from Britain and the USA advised on the creation of a new treaty.

Having been heavily influenced by the efforts of the young artist and environmentalist Henry Wood Elliott, the North Pacific Fur Seal Convention banned all pelagic seal hunting north of the 30th parallel in the Pacific Ocean. Management of on-shore commercial seal hunting within the region was also placed under the jurisdiction of the United States. Having been signed by Britain, Japan, and Russia, the treaty guaranteed them payment or a minimum quota of seal furs in return.

The treaty stayed in place until the Second World War, but the restoration of peace saw the creation of new international agreements that regulated hunting in the interests of wildlife conservation.

JULY

8

1947

Walter Haut, the public information officer of the Roswell Army Air Field, issued a press release saying that the military had recovered the remains of a 'flying disc'.

On 14 June, J.B. Foster ranch foreman William Brazel found a 'large area of bright wreckage made up of rubber strips, tinfoil, a rather tough paper and sticks'. Thinking little of it, he didn't collect the debris until 4 July and only informed the local Sheriff on 7 July after hearing reports of 'flying discs'.

Sheriff Wilcox immediately contacted Major Jesse Marcel at the Roswell Army Air Field. An officer from the base soon visited the site from where the debris had been recovered and retrieved some other small pieces. Marcel took the fragments back to Roswell Army Air Field from where it was soon sent to Fort Worth Army Air Field.

In the meantime, the RAAF issued the press release detailing the recovery of the 'flying disc'. The local newspaper, the *Roswell Daily Record*, featured the story on their front page in what is believed to be the first use of the term 'flying saucer'. On the same day an FBI telex from Fort Worth stated that the object resembled 'a high altitude weather balloon with a radar reflector'. This led to less sensationalist newspaper reports the next day.

Interest in the Roswell discovery subsided until UFO researchers in the late 1970s began interviewing people who claimed to have connections with the 1947 events. Numerous books followed, to which the Air Force responded by releasing two reports beginning with *The Roswell Report: Fact vs. Fiction in the New Mexico Desert* in 1994. These concluded that the debris was from Project Mogul, a top secret project by the US Army Air Force, which was designed to detect Soviet atomic bomb tests.

JULY

9

1971

Henry Kissinger, Richard Nixon's National Security Advisor, made a secret trip to China to meet with Premier Zhou Enlai.

Even before Nixon became president in 1969 he had expressed a desire to improve American relations with China. The USA had been virtually isolated from China since the Communists came to power in 1949, and Nixon was keen to end these two decades of mutual hostility. While part of his motivation was to contain China's potential nuclear threat, he also sought to use China to find a way to end the Vietnam War while exploiting the increasingly poor relationship between China and the USSR.

Kissinger was given the delicate task of making contact with the Chinese government and, following the Chinese invitation to the American ping pong team in April 1971, it was clear that China was also interested in improving the relationship. However, without any direct channels of communication between the two countries, Kissinger was forced to use Pakistan as a third party through which the diplomatic visit would be organised.

Kissinger set out on a publicly announced trip to Vietnam, Thailand, India, and Pakistan in early July 1971. At the conclusion of his meetings in Pakistan, it was then announced that Kissinger was ill and would recuperate in a hill station. In reality the motorcade to the hill station was a decoy, since Kissinger and a small group of advisors had boarded a Pakistani plane to Beijing.

They landed at noon, and spent a total of 49 hours in China. During this time they held a series of talks with the Chinese government that set out the parameters for a visit by President Nixon himself. On 15 July Nixon appeared on television from the Oval Office to announce that he would visit China the following year.

The Vichy government was established in France after the National Assembly approved a new French Constitutional Law that granted full powers to Marshal Pétain.

France declared war against Germany on 3 September, two days after the Nazi invasion of Poland. Despite being at war, however, the two countries only experienced minor skirmishes in early September. This period of little military action, which became known as the Phoney War, was followed 8 months later by a full-scale German invasion of France that began on 10 May. The French were overwhelmed by the Nazi war machine, and were soon forced to decide whether to continue to fight while the government relocated to North Africa, or remain in France and seek an armistice.

Eventually the Cabinet agreed to seek an armistice, which was signed on 22 June in Compiègne Forest. This had been the location for the November 1918 armistice that Germany had signed to end the Great War, and was specifically chosen by Hitler as a form of revenge. The railway carriage in which the 1918 ceasefire had been agreed was even brought from a museum to host the discussions.

The French decision to sign an armistice led to the resignation of Prime Minister Paul Reynaud, who was replaced by First World War hero Marshal Philippe Pétain. Two-fifths of France had been designated 'unoccupied' under the terms of the armistice, and its administrative centre lay in the city of Vichy. However, the government nominally ruled the German-occupied areas as well.

The French State officially collaborated with Nazi Germany from 30 October, when Pétain announced the policy in a radio broadcast. The new Provisional Government of the French Republic was established on 3 June 1944 following the Allied liberation.

The Hollywood Bowl opened in Bolton Canyon near Los Angeles.

The natural amphitheatre that later became home to the Hollywood Bowl was originally a Cahuenga Indian ceremonial ground. Nestled in the Hollywood Hills, by 1919 it had become known as Daisy Dell and was a popular picnic spot with Los Angeles families. That year it was bought as part of a 59 acre purchase of land by the newly-formed Theatre Arts Alliance that was keen to find a location to stage outdoor productions.

Alliance members William and H. Ellis Reed identified the natural amphitheatre and, on their advice, the Alliance purchased the site for $47,000. A female pianist, believed to be local woman Carrie Jacobs Bond, subsequently tested the acoustics by playing a piano placed on a barn door in approximately the same location as the venue's iconic band shell.

Although the Alliance was restructured the following year, the site itself quickly became a popular venue for productions ranging from choral concerts to Shakespeare plays. The first Easter Sunrise Service was performed by the Los Angeles Philharmonic in March 1921 without any formal stage in place. Even after the venue officially opened as the Hollywood Bowl on 11 July 1922, the stage consisted of a simple wooden platform covered with a canvas awning. The audience sat on moveable wooden benches.

Within just four years, however, the Bowl had become so popular that permanent seating was installed along with a band shell that further helped to reflect sound towards the audience. It has since become one of the most iconic live music venues in the world, and continues to be the summer home of the Los Angeles Philharmonic.

JULY

12

1561

Moscow's Trinity Church, later renamed Cathedral of the Intercession of the Most Holy Theotokos on the Moat and better known as Saint Basil's Cathedral, was consecrated.

Ivan the Terrible had originally constructed a series of small wooden memorial chapels as a way to commemorate his numerous military successes against the Tatars. These were built next to the original Trinity Church in the centre of the marketplace near the Moscow Kremlin. Ivan ordered the construction of the new stone church in 1555 to commemorate his capture of Kazan and Astrakhan.

What later became Saint Basil's Cathedral is therefore a more lavish replacement of an earlier building. Little is known of its construction, with even the identity of the architect a mystery. Tradition dictates that two architects, Barma and Postnik, built the church although later writers have suggested that these are simply different names for the same person.

The building itself consists of eight outer churches arranged around a ninth central one, and is constructed on top of a white stone foundation that matches the nearby Kremlin. A series of later developments led to the nine separate structures becoming joined into a single building, and the bright colours that decorate the walls of the cathedral were added from the late 17th until the middle of the 19th century. These are said to reflect the colours of Heaven described in the Book of Revelation. Before they were repainted, the domes were uniformly decorated with gilded tin.

The Cathedral was confiscated from the Russian Orthodox Church as a result of the Bolshevik Revolution and introduction of state atheism. It continues to function as a public museum.

The radical French journalist Jean-Paul Marat was stabbed to death in his bathtub by Charlotte Corday.

Marat was a well-respected doctor who, despite his wealth and privilege, had a passion for social justice. In the late 1780s he put his career on hold and dedicated his time to writing in favour of political, economic and social reform in his own radical newspaper. This soon adopted the name *L'Ami du Peuple* (*'The People's Friend'*).

Marat's writings often called for violence against the upper class, members of the government, and enemies of the people. As a result he occasionally had to hide in Paris' extensive sewer network, where he may have developed the skin condition that saw him confined to a medicinal bath for hours on end.

On 13 July 1793, Marat granted an audience to the 24-year-old Charlotte Corday from Normandy while he soaked in his medicinal bath. Corday presented Marat with a list of names of supposed traitors, but she was actually a moderate Girondin sympathiser. After Marat told her that he would arrange for the execution of the traitors, she pulled out a five-inch kitchen knife and stabbed him once in the chest, severing a major artery and causing him to die almost immediately of massive blood loss.

Corday was guillotined in Paris just four days after killing Marat. She claimed in her trial to be a supporter of Republicanism, and said that she had 'killed one man to save 100,000'. However, the assassination raised fears of counter-revolution and contributed to the subsequent Terror in which thousands of Frenchmen and women were guillotined on charges of treason.

Marat's bathtub, and the knife that he was killed with, are now on display at the Musée Grévin waxworks in Paris.

JULY

14

1881

American outlaw Billy the Kid was shot and killed by Sheriff Pat Garrett in Fort Sumner, New Mexico.

Billy the Kid was born Henry McCarty and spent his early life in New York. By 1873 he had moved west to New Mexico as a result of his mother remarrying after the death of his father, but within a year she died and the 15-year-old McCarty moved into a boarding house where he was soon caught stealing food.

Within four years McCarty, who by now had adopted the name William H. Bonney, had moved to Lincoln County in New Mexico. He began working for John Tunstall, a rancher involved in a struggle for power in the county. After Tunstall was shot and killed by Sheriff William Brady's posse, in what became known as the Lincoln County War, Bonney committed revenge killings including that of the Sheriff.

Bonney was charged with murder but managed to evade capture and soon became the most wanted outlaw in the West. Almost a year later he agreed to provide a statement against the numerous people involved in the ongoing Lincoln County War in return for his own freedom. Despite providing his testimony as promised, he was placed in a jail from which he later escaped and became an outlaw once again.

By the end of 1880, New Mexico Governor Lew Wallis had posted a bounty of $500 on Bonney, and the search was taken up by Sheriff Pat Garrett. Garrett's posse captured Bonney and his gang on 23 December. Bonney was sentenced to death for the murder of Sheriff Brady but escaped jail two weeks before his scheduled execution. A number of months later Garrett mounted another posse and found Bonney at the Maxwell Ranch in Fort Sumner where he killed him, since the bounty permitted his capture alive or dead.

JULY

15

1815

Napoléon Bonaparte voluntarily surrendered to British Captain Maitland on board the Royal Navy ship HMS *Bellerophon*.

Napoléon's return from exile on the island of Elba in March 1815 heralded the start of the Hundred Days which saw Napoléon seek to re-establish his position as Emperor of the French. On 18 June, his army was defeated at the Battle of Waterloo by British and Prussian armies of the Seventh Coalition, prompting Napoléon to abdicate two days later.

Having been warned to leave Paris, Napoléon moved first to the Château de Malmaison and then to the southwestern port of Rochefort from where he hoped to escape to the United States. By this time, however, British Royal Navy warships had begun a blockade of French ports to prevent Napoléon leaving. Unable to either remain in France, or flee across the Atlantic, Napoléon was forced to surrender to the British.

On 14 July, Captain Maitland of HMS *Bellerophon* was informed that Napoléon would surrender on board his ship the next day. The former Emperor duly boarded the brig *Épervier* on the morning of 15 July and made his way to the *Bellerophon*. In order to avoid Napoléon being received by Vice-Admiral Henry Hotham on board HMS *Superb*, which was also off the coast of Rochefort, Maitland sent a barge to meet him.

Shortly before 7am, Napoléon and his General Henri Gatien Bertrand arrived at the *Bellerophon* and announced that 'I am come to throw myself on the protection of your Prince and your laws'. He was subsequently taken to England, from where he was exiled to the remote island of Saint Helena in the South Atlantic. He died there on 5 May 1821.

JULY

16

622

The Islamic calendar started with the first new moon after the Prophet Muhammad and his followers migrated to Medina.

The calendar begins with the Prophet's Flight as this is a key event in Islamic history for which all early followers could agree on the specific date. There was disagreement over the exact date of other events, such as the birth of the Prophet or when he first received the Divine message.

Known as the Hijra the Prophet Muhammad led his followers from Mecca to Medina, which at the time was called Yathrib, due to rumours of an assassination plot against him. Despite the migration taking place in 622, this year was only set as the start of the Islamic calendar by the Caliph Umar in 638 due to the pressing need to have a formalised dating system to improve administration. Until then the Muslim community had identified years according to a key event that took place within it – such as 'the year of permission'.

While the Islamic calendar is linked to the Hijra, the actual start date is based on the beginning of the month of Muharram in the year of the Prophet's arrival in Medina. This lunar month was already important to pre-Islamic Arabs and so served as a sensible demarcation, especially as it had been named by Allah in the Quran as one of the four sacred months.

16 July 622 was only identified on the Western Julian calendar during the medieval period. Muslim astronomers created a tabular Islamic calendar that they then projected backwards to identify the equivalent date on the Julian calendar. A tabular Islamic calendar relies on arithmetical rules to determine the length of the months, rather than astronomical calculations. Lunar observations are still used to specify the correct date of Islamic holidays and rituals.

JULY

17

1453

The Battle of Castillon, considered to be the last battle of the Hundred Years' War, was fought between France and England.

After more than a century of conflict, by the end of 1451 the French under King Charles VII had captured almost all the remaining English possessions in France. Charles' army had driven the English out of the remaining regions of Guyenne and Gascony but the locals, who had been English subjects for almost three centuries, requested liberation by Henry VI. The English king obliged in October 1452 by sending the military commander John Talbot, Earl of Shrewsbury, who seized the area around Bordeaux with little difficulty.

Frustrated by the loss of the territory, Charles spent the winter preparing a large army for a counter-attack. When the French forces advanced in the summer of 1453 the 6,000 English troops were outnumbered. The French were also supported by the powerful artillery of Jean Bureau who prepared a heavily fortified camp to besiege the English-held city of Castillon on the Dordogne River.

Keen to relieve Castillon, Shrewsbury left Bordeaux in early July and successfully routed a small detachment of French archers a few miles outside the city. Bolstered by this success, and having heard reports that the French in the main camp were retreating, Talbot ordered his troops to continue without waiting for reinforcements.

The French artillery inflicted huge losses on the ill-prepared English army, repeating the devastation as waves of reinforcements arrived. Shrewsbury himself was killed in the battle, and before long the remaining English troops began a desperate retreat to Bordeaux. Castillon surrendered to the French the next day and, although Bordeaux survived a siege until October, the Battle of Castillon was the last military engagement of the Hundred Years' War.

JULY

18

1976

Romanian gymnast Nadia Comăneci scored the first ever perfect 10 in Olympic history on the uneven bars at the Summer Games in Montreal.

The International Federation of Gymnastics introduced a code of points to regulate scores in 1949. This allowed judges to determine a competitor's overall score by taking into account such factors as the difficulty of the routine alongside deductions for poor form, execution, steps or other technical mistakes such as falls.

It had long been believed that a 'perfect 10' – a top score with no deductions – was impossible to achieve. Despite this, Czech gymnast Věra Čáslavská scored perfect 10s at the 1967 European Championships. It still seemed such an unlikely outcome, however, that the International Olympic Committee ordered a scoreboard for the Montreal Games that could only show up to 9.99.

This was a massive oversight. On 18 July, Nadia Comăneci achieved a score of 10.00 on the uneven bars. Unable to show this on the scoreboard, confusion resulted after a score of 1.00 was displayed. The announcer was consequently forced to inform the crowd and competitors that the 14-year-old Romanian gymnast had, in fact, achieved a perfect 10.

Comăneci achieved a further three 10s on the uneven bars and another three 10s on the balance beam in the 1976 Games. She won the gold medal for both the individual all-around competition and the balance beam, in addition to a silver and bronze for the team all-around and floor exercise. She still holds the record for being the youngest Olympic gymnastics all-around gold medallist, because current rules now require competitors to turn 16 in the same calendar year as the competition.

JULY

19

1870

The Franco-Prussian War began with a declaration of war by the French emperor, Napoléon III.

The Franco-Prussian War marked the culmination of a long period of declining relations between France and the German state of Prussia. The latter had defeated Austria in the Seven Weeks' War three years previously, and France was concerned that the established balance of power within Europe was at risk.

In June 1870, Prince Leopold of Hohenzollern-Sigmaringen, a relative of King Wilhelm I of Prussia, was offered the vacant Spanish throne. Leopold accepted the offer, but Napoléon III complained that the appointment would mean France was surrounded by Prussian influence. In the face of France's hostility, Wilhelm I persuaded Leopold to withdraw his candidacy.

Count Benedetti, the French Ambassador to Prussia, met Wilhelm shortly afterwards to demand a promise that the candidature would not be renewed. Wilhelm saw this as questioning his honour, and refused to give the promise. He informed Bismarck, the Minister President of Prussia, of the meeting by telegram and on 14 July an edited version – known as the Ems Telegram – was released to the press. Bismarck changed the tone of the conversation to give the impression that Wilhelm had offended the French Ambassador.

This pushed Napoléon, persuaded by the media and his wife, to declare war on Prussia on 19 July 1870. Prussia quickly secured the support of the South German states and, aided by superior military planning and rail links, mobilised quickly. France was defeated decisively within 4 weeks, and Emperor Napoléon III himself was taken prisoner. Although the Siege of Paris prolonged the conflict, the French government signed the Peace of Frankfurt in 1871.

JULY

20

1807

Regarded by some as the world's first internal combustion engine, Napoléon granted a patent for the Pyréolophore to Nicéphore Niépce and his brother Claude.

Nicéphore Niépce was the son of a wealthy lawyer, so had fled France during the Revolution as he who was suspected of having royalist sympathies. He later returned home and served in Napoléon's army before resigning on health grounds and becoming the Administrator of the district of Nice.

By 1801 Niépce and his older brother Claude had returned to manage the family's estate while conducting scientific research. It was here that they developed their internal combustion engine, which harnessed the power of hot air expanding during an explosion. Their first fuel was lycopodium powder, made of dried plant spores, which was ignited inside the airtight copper machine.

The brothers presented their internal combustion engine in a paper to the French National Commission of the Academy of Science in 1806. However, the engine's major test came in 1807 when it was installed on a boat on the river Saône. Small amounts of fuel were released into a jet of air provided by mechanical bellows inside the machine. The pressure of the explosion forced water out of an exhaust pipe protruding from the boat's rear. This in turn propelled the boat forward in short bursts, and successfully moved it upstream against the flow of the river.

Following the successful boat test, Napoléon granted a patent to the brothers. However, despite experiments with other fuel sources, they struggled to find a commercial use for their invention. Nicéphore instead turned his attention to photography, and became the first person to produce a permanent photographic image.

JULY

21

1925

John Thomas Scopes, a substitute science teacher in Tennessee, was found guilty of teaching evolution in school.

In March 1925, Tennessee governor Austin Peay signed the Butler Act into law. This prohibited teachers in state-funded schools from teaching human evolution as it went against the Biblical account of mankind's origins. The American Civil Liberties Union (ACLU) soon announced that it was keen to finance a legal test case to challenge the constitutionality of the Butler Act if a teacher was willing to act as the defendant.

George Rappleyea, the manager of the Cumberland Coal and Iron Company in the small Tennessee town of Dayton, believed that a trial of this type could bring valuable publicity to the town. With the support of other local community leaders, he approached 24-year-old John T. Scopes. Although Scopes couldn't recall specifically teaching evolution he did accept that he may have gone through the state-endorsed textbook chapter and chart relating to it. His students were consequently encouraged to testify against him, which led to his indictment on 25 May and the subsequent trial that began on 10 July.

The 'Monkey Trial' brought enormous crowds to Dayton where their attention was split between carnival entertainments such as performing chimpanzees on the courthouse lawn, and the numerous preachers who converged on the town to address the crowds. The trial's bitter exchanges between the prosecution and defence generated extensive media coverage on both sides of the Atlantic. The case went on for almost two weeks before Scopes was found guilty and ordered to pay a fine of $100, the minimum amount possible. The Tennessee Supreme Court later overruled the verdict on a technicality, but the Butler Act stayed in place until 1967.

JULY

22

1992

Pablo Escobar, boss of the Medellin Cartel, escaped from the luxury *La Catedral* prison and began a 16 month run from the police.

Pablo Escobar became involved in the fledgling cocaine smuggling industry in the early 1970s. He expanded his operations from 1975 onwards and, by the 1980s, was the leading supplier of cocaine to the United States. At the height of his operation he is estimated to have been responsible up to 80% of the entire world's cocaine market.

By 1990, Columbia had become the world's murder capital due to the increasing number of killings by hitmen working for the drugs cartels. Determined to bring the situation under control, the government under President César Gaviria negotiated Escobar's surrender in 1991. With the promise that he would serve a maximum of five years and would not be extradited to the United States he was imprisoned in *La Catedral* prison, which had been built to his own specifications.

Referred to mockingly as 'Hotel Escobar', the prison was staffed by guards chosen by the drugs lord himself. Evidence soon emerged that Escobar was continuing to run his empire while behind bars, with one police report highlighting over 300 unauthorised visits from people that included wanted criminals.

Such reports forced the government to act, leading to the decision to transfer him to a more conventional jail. Escobar, however, refused to go quietly and the operation soon turned violent. He and his henchmen seized hostages and, amidst fighting between cartel members and the Columbian army, Escobar escaped. He remained on the run for 16 months before being found and killed.

JULY 23 1943

Archibald Brown was murdered by his son, who placed an anti-tank grenade under the seat of his bath chair.

47-year-old Archibald Brown had been involved in a motorcycle accident more than twenty years earlier, which caused him to lose the use of both of his legs. He consequently used a bath chair, a luxurious type of wheelchair, and used the large inheritance from his father to pay for three nurses who provided care for him at home in Rayleigh in Essex. Meanwhile he subjected his wife, Doris, and their sons Eric and Colin to years of torment and abuse.

Eric was called up to the 8th Battalion of the Suffolk Regiment in October 1942, where he was trained to use the Number 75 Hawkins grenade that would detonate when a vehicle drove over the pressure plate on top. While at home on leave he grew increasingly angry at the way his father treated his mother. Deciding that the only way to end the situation was for his father to die, Eric placed an adapted stolen Hawkins grenade under the seat of his father's bath chair.

When Nurse Doris Mitchell went to collect the bath chair to take Archibald for a walk around the local area, she was surprised to find the door locked. After a few moments a nervous Eric brought the chair out and Archibald was placed on his seat.

About a mile into the walk, Archibald shifted his weight to retrieve a packet of cigarettes. Nurse Mitchell lit one for him before resuming pushing the chair, but after just a few steps there was an enormous explosion. Archibald and most of the chair were blown to pieces and scattered over a wide area by the anti-tank grenade. Mitchell suffered injuries to her legs but survived. Shortly afterwards Eric was charged with murder. He was found guilty, and was sentenced to a psychiatric hospital where he stayed until 1975.

JULY

24

1911

The Inca city of Machu Picchu was 'rediscovered' by American explorer Hiram Bingham III.

Often referred to as the 'lost city of the Incas', Machu Picchu was constructed in the middle of the 15th century before being abandoned barely a century later in 1572. Believed by modern archaeologists to have been built as a retreat for Incan royalty, the city was never found by the Spanish conquistadors and its existence slowly became known only to those who lived in the local area.

Although there is evidence that the city had been visited by explorers before Bingham, he was the first to conduct an archaeological survey of the area and to secure worldwide publicity for it. He did so as a result of leading the 1911 Yale Peruvian Expedition, having visited the country three years previously on his way home from the First Pan American Scientific Congress.

Bingham's expedition travelled down the Urubamba River, seeking local information about Inca ruins. Eventually he met Melchor Arteaga who led him up the Huayna Picchu mountain. Here the eleven-year-old Pablito, the son of a farmer, led him to the main Machu Picchu ruins.

Bingham first saw the site on 24 July, but the intricate stonework was covered in vegetation from five hundred years of disuse. He therefore only conducted preliminary investigations before continuing the expedition along the river. He returned to the mountain the following year to clear the overgrowth and conduct an archaeological excavation with the support of Yale University and *National Geographic*. Artefacts taken from the site by Bingham have since been returned to Peru, and Machu Picchu continues to be one of the world's leading tourist sites.

JULY
25
1909

French aviator Louis Charles Joseph Blériot made the first flight across the English Channel in a heavier-than-air aircraft.

After graduating from the prestigious École Centrale in Paris, Blériot quickly established himself as a talented engineer. He soon launched his own company to sell the world's first practical car headlamp, the success of this which provided him with the funds to begin developing his own aircraft.

Having started with ornithopters and gliders, by 1905 Blériot had moved on to developing powered aircraft in partnership with Gabriel Voisin. After this business was dissolved the following year, Blériot continued alone. He had already created a number of working aircraft by the time Lord Northcliffe of the *Daily Mail* announced a cash prize for the first powered flight across the Channel.

Blériot was not the only person to express interest in the competition, but he was the first to complete the crossing from Calais after the high winds that had grounded the competitors dropped at dawn on 25 July 1909. Piloting his Blériot XI monoplane without the aid of a compass, he drifted slightly east of his intended course. Blériot landed clumsily near Dover Castle as a result of the windy conditions 36 minutes and 30 seconds after departing France. Having neglected to visit Dover beforehand to identify an appropriate landing site, Blériot touched down where the journalist Charles Fontaine from the French *Le Matin* newspaper stood waving a large Tricolour.

The *Daily Mail* correspondent, meanwhile, was on the other side of the town as he had expected the competitors to land on the beach. He quickly took a car to meet Blériot, whose achievement turned him into an instant celebrity.

JULY

26

1745

The first ever women's cricket match was played on Gosden Common near Guildford in Surrey.

The cricket match was reported in *The Reading Mercury* and featured teams from the villages of Bramley and Hambledon. The newspaper made the point that all the players were dressed in all white, but those from Bramley wore blue ribbons while the Hambledon 'maids' wore red.

Although the identities of the players are unknown, the final result, which saw the team from Hambledon beat Bramley with a score of 127 to 119, was recorded. Furthermore the article highlighted that, 'the girls bowled, batted, ran and catched as well as most men could do in that game'.

The majority of early women's cricket matches were similar local fixtures played in the communities around Sussex, Hampshire and Surrey. Often associated with heavy betting, the sport quickly spread and gained a level of respectability in 1777 when Elizabeth Smith-Stanley, the Countess of Derby, organised a match in which upper-class women made up the two teams.

Despite the growing popularity of women's cricket, the first women's cricket club wasn't formed until 1887. The White Heather Club was established in North Yorkshire, and was followed three years later by the chronologically-confusing Original English Lady Cricketers. However, a national organisation for women's cricket wasn't established until 1926 when the Women's Cricket Association was founded. Under its guidance the England team played its first series of test matches in Australia in 1934-5. The Women's Cricket Association was eventually absorbed by the England and Wales Cricket Board in 1998.

JULY
27
1940

Bugs Bunny made his first appearance in the *Merrie Melodies* cartoon *A Wild Hare*.

A wisecracking rabbit voiced by Mel Blanc had first appeared in 1938's *Porky's Hare Hunt*. However, it wasn't until two years later that director Tex Avery asked the animator Bob Givens to redesign the character as the bold tormentor of the hunter, Elmer Fudd.

In the cartoon *A Wild Hare*, Fudd tries numerous times to shoot Bugs Bunny with his double-barrelled shotgun. In one sequence where Elmer tries to dig out the rabbit from his hole, Bugs emerges from another exit to deliver his catchphrase for the first time. Tex Avery later explained that the phrase 'What's up, Doc?' was a common expression where he grew up in Texas, but audiences around the country found the rabbit's delivery of it hilarious and this guaranteed its inclusion in all subsequent Bugs Bunny cartoons.

A Wild Hare was an immediate hit with the public when it was released in cinemas on 27 July 1940, and later received an Academy Award nomination for Best Cartoon Short Subject. Within two years Bugs Bunny had become the biggest star of the *Merrie Melodies* series of cartoons, and was used during the Second World War in propaganda against the Axis as a well as to advertise War Bonds.

His regular appearances during the war saw Bugs Bunny become a military mascot. He was even made an honorary master sergeant in the United States Marine Corps after appearing in the dress blue uniform of the Marines in 1943's *Super-Rabbit*.

By the time Bugs Bunny was retired from regular releases in 1964 he had appeared in more than 160 short films and won an Academy Award for *Knighty Knight Bugs* in 1958. He only began to appear again in animated specials and films in the late 1970s.

JULY

28

1914

Exactly one month after the assassination of Archduke Franz Ferdinand, Austria-Hungary declared war on Serbia.

The Archduke had been shot and killed while on a visit to Sarajevo in Bosnia. The assassin, Gavrilo Princip, was a Serbian nationalist who opposed Austria-Hungary's annexation of Bosnia that had taken place in 1908.

Austria-Hungary condemned the attack but only began preparations for a formal response after consulting with Germany, its closest ally. Kaiser Wilhelm II met with the Austro-Hungarian Ambassador on 5th July, and gave assurances that Germany would support military action against Serbia in what is known as the 'Blank Cheque'.

Having secured the support of the strongest army in Europe, the Austro-Hungarian Crown Council began preparations to force a military conflict with Serbia. The intention was to secure a swift Austrian victory before Serbia's powerful ally, Russia, was able to intervene.

The Crown Council decided that an ultimatum containing unacceptable demands would be the best course of action, and presented the terms to Serbia on 23 July. Austria-Hungary's Emperor Franz Josef ordered mobilisation after Serbia agreed to all but one of the demands at the end of the 48-hour deadline.

This response alarmed the other countries of Europe, including Britain who called for mediation. This was rejected by Vienna on the advice of Germany and, at 11am on 28 July, Emperor Franz Josef signed the declaration of war against Serbia. It was sent by telegram to the Serbian government in Belgrade ten minutes later, making it the first declaration in what was to become the First World War.

JULY

29

1588

The Battle of Gravelines, the decisive battle of the Spanish Armada, took place off the coast of Flanders.

In May 1588, King Philip II of Spain sent a fleet of 130 ships to support the invasion of England by 30,000 troops based in the Spanish Netherlands. Commanded by the Duke of Medina Sidonia, their objective, which had the support of Pope Sixtus V, was to overthrow Queen Elizabeth I and reinstate Catholicism.

Elizabeth was expecting an invasion attempt, so had sent Sir Francis Drake to the Bay of Cádiz the previous year to disrupt the Spanish preparations. By the time the Spanish Armada was finally ready set sail in 1588 the English fleet, based in Plymouth, outnumbered the Spanish but had lower overall firepower.

Harried by the English, the Armada sailed along the English south coast and reached Calais on 27 July. The fleet then anchored in a defensive crescent formation. At midnight the next day the English sent ships, packed with wood and pitch and then set alight, directly into the middle of the Spanish fleet. This resulted in them scattering and breaking the crescent formation to escape the flames.

With the Spanish fleet in disarray, the English closed for battle on 29 July. They repeatedly provoked the Spanish, and then used the wind to sail out of range of their guns before closing in again to unleash a broadside. In this manner the Spanish were gradually worn down, losing five ships while sinking none of the English.

Having run dangerously low of ammunition, Medina Sidonia took advantage of a change in the wind and fled north. Chased by the English fleet, the Armada was forced to sail around the north coast of Scotland and return to Spain via Ireland. Less than half the ships that had set out made it back.

The city of Baghdad was founded by the Abbasid Caliph Al-Mansur.

The Abbasids overthrew the Umayyad Caliphate in 750, and quickly consolidated their power by removing potential opponents. By 762 the new Caliph, Al-Mansur, had secured his position, and set about building a new administrative capital on the banks of the Tigris at a site previously occupied by an ancient village. Situated at a junction with the Sarat Canal that connected to the Euphrates, the new city benefited not only from plentiful access to water but also control over important trade routes.

Construction began on 30 July 762 after two royal astrologers determined that the city would fare best if built under the sign of Leo. Many thousands of workers, ranging from architects and engineers to unskilled labourers, were brought from around the Empire to complete the task. Four straights roads led directly to the centre of the city through concentric circular walls, the outer of which stood 80 feet high. The circular layout of Baghdad was said to be the only one of its type in the world at the time.

Construction was completed in 766 and the city was named Madinat al-Salaam (City of Peace), although the ancient name Baghdad was also used. The city soon established itself as a centre of learning and trade. A sophisticated system of commerce also quickly developed, fuelled by the city's connections to the east. This led to Baghdad becoming a multicultural hub as merchants settled to benefit from these links. The growing population in turn fuelled the development of schools, which included the unrivalled House of Wisdom. This acted as a catalyst for the Golden Age of Islam that is widely accepted to have lasted until the Siege of Baghdad in 1258.

JULY

31

1703

The English writer Daniel Defoe was put in the pillory for seditious libel after publishing a politically satirical pamphlet.

Defoe had authored a number of political pamphlets by the time he published *The Shortest Way with the Dissenters*, which satirised the increasing hostility towards religious Dissenters after Queen Anne succeeded to the throne. Also known as nonconformists, the term applied to a range of Protestant denominations that had broken away from the Anglican High church over the course of the previous century, and who were often the target for criticism and persecution.

Shortly after Anne came to the throne, Parliament began to debate a Bill that would make it more difficult for Dissenters to hold public office. In its wake, High church clergymen and the Tory press published numerous sermons and pamphlets warning against Dissenters assuming positions of political power.

Defoe himself was a Presbyterian, who responded with a pamphlet of his own. Written as a satire from the point of view of the High church and Tory arguments, Defoe later explained that he sought to mock them by taking their arguments to the extreme. However, the pamphlet was initially taken seriously by both sides and ultimately led to the Tory ministry of the time coming under scrutiny for their handling of the issue of Dissenters.

Despite publishing the pamphlet anonymously, Defoe was identified and later found guilty of seditious libel. He was sentenced to endure public humiliation in a pillory, and then to be imprisoned until he paid a punitive fine that he was unlikely ever to afford. While in the pillory the public allegedly threw flowers at him instead of the customary unpleasant objects. He was later released from prison after his fine was paid in return for him agreeing to work for the Tories.

AUGUST

AUGUST

1

1714

George, Elector of Hanover, became King George I of Great Britain.

George's mother, Sophia, was a granddaughter of King James I of England, and his father Ernest Augustus was the Elector of Hanover. George succeeded his father as Elector on his death in 1698 and, three years later, in 1701, became third in line to the English throne after Parliament passed the Act of Settlement.

This Act was designed to ensure a Protestant succession to the throne in case Princess Anne, who would later become Queen Anne, had no surviving heirs. Bypassing Anne's exiled Catholic half-brother James Edward Stuart, as well as a further 50 other Catholic claimants, the Act made George's mother Sophia the heiress after Anne.

Sophia died in spring 1714, putting George second in line to the English throne. Queen Anne died just a few months later on 1 August and the Whig politicians in Westminster, fearful that the Tories still held broad support for James, moved quickly to proclaim George king.

The new monarch arrived in England on 18 September, accompanied by two mistresses and a reported eighteen cooks. His coronation was held at Westminster Abbey on 20 October 1714 but, the following year, his position was threatened by a Jacobite rebellion that sought to replace him with the Catholic James Edward Stuart. Despite securing the support of a few Tories in Westminster, the uprising was suppressed by the end of the year. In response, George turned to the Whigs, who went on to dominate British politics for the next few decades. Under the leadership of Robert Walpole, widely recognised as the first *de facto* Prime Minister, they began the shift towards the modern system of cabinet government.

Hannibal's army inflicted a devastating defeat on the numerically superior Roman army at the Battle of Cannae.

The start of the Second Punic War had seen the Carthaginian general Hannibal lead his forces, which famously included a number of war elephants, across the Alps to Italy. After suffering early defeats in pitched battles at the hands of Hannibal's men, the Romans under Quintus Fabius attempted to wear the Carthaginians down by adopting a strategy of attrition.

By 216 BCE the failure to drive the invaders out of Italy was frustrating those Romans who desired a decisive victory. After the election of Gaius Terentius Varro and Lucius Aemilius Paullus as co-consuls, the Senate provided an unprecedented eight legions to create the largest army in the history of the Roman Republic.

Aware of his numerical disadvantage, Hannibal marched south and seized the important supply depot at Cannae. The Romans gave pursuit and, at the start of August, the two armies met at the River Aufidus. Hannibal arranged his troops to exploit his surroundings, forcing the enormous Roman army into a narrow space that limited the length of their line. Varro adopted the traditional block formation with his infantry in the centre and the cavalry on each side.

Meanwhile, Hannibal positioned his weakest troops at the centre with his more experienced Africans further back and to the side. His cavalry stayed on the wings, but they engaged first and scattered their Roman counterparts. When the infantry engaged, Hannibal's weak centre gave way and the Romans surged forward into the gap where they were surrounded in one of the first examples of a military pincer movement. The ensuing slaughter lasted for most of the day, resulting in over 50,000 Roman deaths and just 6,000 Carthaginians.

AUGUST
3
1936

American athlete Jesse Owens won the first of four gold medals at the Berlin Olympics.

The International Olympic Committee had taken the decision to grant the 1936 Olympics to Berlin in 1931, two years before Hitler was appointed Chancellor. On assuming power, he embraced the idea of the Games as an opportunity to promote the Nazi regime and its ideology. However, he was forced to allow black and Jewish athletes to attend after other nations threatened to boycott the competition.

On the other side of the Atlantic, American athlete Jesse Owens had already established himself as a track and field sensation. On 25 May 1935 at the Big Ten athletics meeting he had set three world records in the space of an hour. Despite pressure to boycott the Olympic Games over Germany's discriminatory policies that had even seen the Nazis bar world-class athletes of Jewish and Roma descent from the German team, he chose to compete.

The Berlin Olympics saw the first torch relay ahead of the lighting of the Olympic flame at the specially-built 100,000 seater stadium on 1 August. Two days later Owens won his first Olympic gold medal in the 100m dash. He went on to win a further three golds in the 200m dash, the long jump, and the 4 x 100m relay after he and Ralph Metcalfe were added to the team in place of Jewish-American sprinters Marty Glickman and Sam Stoller.

An urban legend states that Owens' victories were snubbed by Hitler. In reality, the Nazi leader opted not to attend any medal presentations after only congratulating the German medallists on the first day. The IOC insisted he needed to either greet every medallist or none. Owens himself later stated that he was snubbed more by the USA's President and the country's policies of segregation than Hitler.

RAF Flight Officer T. D. Dean became the first Allied jet pilot to achieve a combat victory when he flipped over a Nazi German V-1 'doodlebug' flying bomb with his Gloster Meteor jet fighter.

The V-1 was specifically designed for terror bombing civilians, and had first been used on 13 June 1944. The RAF began to investigate ways to intercept and destroy the Nazis' new weapon, and soon found that they could be tipped over by positioning an aircraft's wing to within 6 inches of the V-1's wing. This manoeuvre used the changing airflow of the interceptor's wing to force the V-1 upwards, confusing the flying bomb's gyroscope and resulting in it diving into the ground before reaching its target. The first aerodynamic flip manoeuvre was performed by Major R. E. Turner on 18 June, using a North American P-51 Mustang.

The following month, No. 616 Squadron of the RAF received the first ever Gloster Meteor jet planes. This new aircraft, equipped with Sir Frank Whittle's revolutionary turbojet engines, could reach speeds in excess of 400 miles per hour which placed it well within reach of the average speed of a V-1. The hope was that the new Meteors would be able to shoot the flying bombs down using their 20mm cannons, but the guns had a habit of jamming.

On 4 August Flight Officer T. D. Dean experienced a problem with his Meteor's cannons as he approached a V-1. He consequently resorted to the tipping manoeuvre and successfully sent the bomb off course. It is believed to have crashed on farmland near Headcorn in Kent, where shrapnel said to be from the explosion can be detected deep inside the trunk of a nearby oak tree. The destruction of the V-1 marked the first ever 'kill' for an RAF jet plane.

Scottish independence leader William Wallace was captured by English forces at Robroyston near Glasgow.

William Wallace was a member of the Scottish nobility who rose to prominence during the First War of Scottish Independence. The war was prompted by King Edward I of England extending his influence over Scotland in the aftermath of a succession crisis that brought John Balliol to power. In 1296 Edward attacked the border town of Berwick-upon-Tweed and went on to defeat John's army at the Battle of Dunbar, seemingly securing English domination of Scotland.

However, Scottish resistance soon emerged under the leadership of Andrew de Moray and William Wallace. Wallace's first action is known to have been the assassination of William de Heselrig, the English High Sheriff of Lanark, in May 1297. He later joined with Moray ahead of the Battle of Stirling Bridge where their combined forces defeated the significantly larger English army of Edward I on 11 September 1297. Moray died a short time later from wounds suffered during the battle, while Wallace continued to lead raids and skirmishes as the Guardian of the Kingdom of Scotland.

Sometime after the Scottish defeat at the Battle of Falkirk in 1298, Wallace resigned as Guardian of Scotland and little is known of his movements over the next few years. However, on 5 August 1305 he was captured by the English at Robroyston near Glasgow. Having been betrayed by the Scottish knight John de Menteith, Wallace was taken to London where he was found guilty of treason. Condemned to death by being hung, drawn and quartered he reportedly replied to the charge that, 'I could not be a traitor to Edward, for I was never his subject'.

AUGUST

6

1890

William Kemmler became the first person to be executed using an electric chair.

Buffalo dentist Alfred Southwark began experimenting with electrocution as a new and humane form of execution in the aftermath of a number of botched hangings. After hearing reports of a drunk worker who died from touching a high voltage electrical generator, Southwark began work on the first 'electric chair'. The design was later refined by the New York Medico-Legal Society, and New York lawmakers formally replaced hanging with electrocution on 1 January 1888.

Meanwhile, William Kemmler had moved to Buffalo, New York, from Pennsylvania after the death of his parents. He became a vegetable peddler and began a relationship with Matilda 'Tillie' Ziegler, but was also a violent alcoholic. On 29 March 1888, the day after a drinking binge, Kemmler attacked and killed his common-law wife with a hatchet during a particularly aggressive argument. He was arrested later that day and was subsequently found guilty of murder. He was sentenced to death using the new electric chair.

At 5am on 6 August 1890, Kemmler was woken from his cell in Auburn Prison. After dressing and eating breakfast he entered the execution chamber, where the new chair had been successfully tested on a horse the previous day. Having been strapped to the chair and attached to electrodes, 1,000 volts were passed through his body for 17 seconds. Although initially believed to be dead, witnesses noticed that he was still breathing. The generator was subsequently charged with 2,000 volts, resulting in Kemmler's skin beginning to bleed. A foul smell started to fill the room as his hair and flesh singed before he died. The entire procedure took around eight minutes.

AUGUST

7

1909

Alice Huyler Ramsey became the first woman to drive an automobile across a continent when she completed a 59-day road trip from New York to San Francisco.

Ramsey was 22 years old when her husband bought her a Maxwell runabout car in 1908. She quickly found a love of driving, covering more than 6,000 miles around New Jersey during her first summer. In September she was one of only two women to enter the 200-mile Montauk Point endurance race, and her competent handling of the car led to her being approached to undertake a coast-to-coast drive by the Maxwell-Briscoe company's publicist Carl Kelsey.

Ramsey took up the offer of an all-expenses-paid road trip, which Kelsey intended to demonstrate the reliability of Maxwell cars and entice women to consider purchasing a vehicle. The company provided Ramsey with a brand new four-cylinder, 30-horsepower 1909 Maxwell DA touring car, and ensured that Maxwell dealerships along the route were ready to assist with any repairs as necessary.

Departing New York City on 9 June 1919, Ramsey was joined on the journey by three other women. However, she was the only one who could drive and so was responsible for piloting the car along more than 3,500 miles of roads, the vast majority of which were unpaved. With few maps of the country at the time, the travellers were forced to rely on landmarks to navigate, and on occasion had to retrace their route after finding the conditions impassable.

The Ramsey team arrived in San Francisco on 7 August to large crowds assembled outside the St James Hotel. Their journey had lasted 59 days, 3 weeks more than anticipated, and had seen them carry out numerous auto maintenance tasks that included repairing a brake pedal, cleaning the spark plugs, and changing 11 tyres.

Traffic was stopped on the B507 road in London so The Beatles could pose for their iconic *Abbey Road* album cover.

The Beatles began work on the *Abbey Road* album in February 1969, starting just 3 weeks after the last session for what would become *Let It Be*. Consequently, *Abbey Road* was the last Beatles album to be recorded although *Let It Be* ended up being released later.

George Martin had agreed to produce the album, and many of the backing tracks were recorded with the band playing live as an ensemble. The schedule was loose, and overdubs weren't completed until 20 August – 12 days after Scottish photographer Iain Macmillan took his photograph of the band on the zebra crossing outside EMI Studios on Abbey Road.

The image was based on a sketch by Paul McCartney, and the final album cover featured one of the six photographs taken by MacMillan. He had been granted permission to close the road for just 10 minutes. A single policeman held back traffic as the photographer climbed a stepladder in the middle of the road.

The band crossed the road a number of times and, although the shoot began at 11:35am, the day was already getting hot. Consequently in four of the photos McCartney famously didn't wear any shoes. One of these images, in which McCartney is out of step with the other three band members, was eventually chosen for the cover. This fuelled the 'Paul is Dead' conspiracy theory that John Lennon later acknowledged was valuable free publicity for the album.

Abbey Road was released on 26 September, and the zebra crossing soon became a popular location for visiting Beatles fans. Because of its status as one of the most famous locations in pop music, the crossing itself was given Grade II listed status in 2010.

AUGUST

9

1173

Construction began on the campanile of the Cathedral of Pisa, now better known as the Leaning Tower of Pisa.

By the twelfth century, the city of Pisa had become an important sea port and one of the four main historical maritime republics of Italy. Its sizeable fleet secured a commercial and political influence that extended across the Mediterranean, allowing Pisa to gain considerable wealth.

As a sign of this prosperity the city began construction of a religious complex, the Square of Miracles, which would be dominated by a mighty cathedral and its free-standing bell tower or campanile. The cathedral was consecrated in 1118, but work didn't begin on the campanile for another five decades. The foundations were eventually laid on 9 August 1173.

The most notable feature of the tower is its tilt, which first became apparent with completion of the second floor in 1178. The ground beneath the tower is weak and unstable and, with the building having just 3 metres of foundations, its weight had begun to compress the soft subsoil.

In an attempt to correct the lean, the upper floors of the tower were built with one side slightly taller than the other. However this only led to the tower sinking even further, increasing the angle of the tilt that eventually reached more than 5 degrees in the 1990s.

In response to the imminent threat of the tower toppling over, a team of engineers eventually chose to remove more than 70 tons of soil beneath the raised side of the structure. This allowed the famous tower to straighten slightly, returning to an angle where it became safe for the public to climb the 294 steps inside. It continues to be one of the most popular tourist attractions in Italy.

AUGUST

10

1793

The Louvre museum in Paris opened to the public.

The Louvre was originally built as a fortress on the banks of the River Seine at the end of the 12th century, and became the main residence of the French royal family under Francis I three centuries later. After Louis XIV, the 'Sun King', moved the court to the Palace of Versailles in 1682, the Louvre was primarily used to house the royal collection which, by that time, already featured Leonardo da Vinci's *Mona Lisa*. At the same time, use of the numerous rooms in the palace was granted to artists working for the king.

By the time the French Revolution began in 1789, Louis XVI had approved the idea of the Louvre housing a royal museum. As the monarchy fell into terminal decline this plan never came to fruition but, following the arrest of the royal family after the Storming of the Tuileries on 10 August 1792, the royal collection became national property. The National Assembly subsequently decreed that the Louvre should house a public museum, and appointed a committee to 'preserve the national memory' who set about preparing the collection for display.

On 10 August 1793, exactly one year after the fall of the monarchy, the Louvre museum opened to the public. For three days every week the public were granted free access to view more than 700 pieces of art that had been confiscated from the royal collection, the nobility, and the Church. This collection soon began to expand as the revolutionary armies swept across Europe and, with a budget of 100,000 livres a year, obtained new works of art before the museum was temporarily closed in 1796 due to problems with the building.

The Louvre reopened under Napoléon and is now the largest art museum in the world, receiving over 10 million visitors a year.

AUGUST
11
3114 BCE

The Mesoamerican Long Count Calendar, most famously used by the Maya civilisation, began.

The ancient civilisations of Central America used their astronomical skills to develop a complex series of incredibly accurate calendars. These pre-Columbian societies used both ritual and civil calendars in parallel to perform ceremonies and rituals during a person's lifetime. However, for events beyond this they used the Long Count Calendar that could be used to accurately pinpoint dates in both the distant past and future.

The Maya used the Long Count Calendar to identify dates from their mythical creation date, which scholars later identified as 11 August 3114 BCE by extending the Gregorian calendar backwards. This date has been widely accepted through the use of separate historical, archaeological, and astronomical evidence, and is known as the GMT constant after the scholars Goodman, Martinez and Thompson whose research was combined to create this correlation.

The Long Count Calendar itself consists of a series of units that function together and clock up like the numbers of a car's odometer. Beginning with one day, known as a kin, the five units culminate in a baktun which represents 144,000 days. The calendar itself began with the completion of 13 baktuns, when Mayan theology claims the world of humans began.

The previous Long Count Calendar consequently finished with the completion of the 13th baktun. This 5,126-year-long cycle finished in December 2012 but, despite some sections of the media promoting fears of a Mayan-predicated apocalypse, the 21 December saw the world continue to turn and another Mayan calendar cycle begin.

AUGUST

12

1969

The Battle of the Bogside began in Derry, Northern Ireland, marking one of the first major conflicts of The Troubles.

The city of Derry had a large Catholic and nationalist population, but the local government was dominated by unionists. Frustrated by the situation, in 1968 the Derry Housing Action Committee joined with the Northern Ireland Civil Rights Association to press for improved conditions for the Catholics in the city.

Many unionists saw NICRA as a front for radical republican groups. The ensuing tensions spilled over into violence in late 1968 and early 1969 as NICRA staged marches and protests in Derry that were attacked by unionists, while the police refused to intervene. Marches by NICRA and other protest groups were subsequently banned, but the tensions remained and reached a climax on 12 August, when around 15,000 members of the Protestant Apprentice Boys of Derry were given permission for their 'customary' march to take place in the city against police advice.

The march celebrated an historic Protestant victory and was described as a 'calculated insult to the Derry Catholics' as it ran very close to the Catholic area of the city known as the Bogside. Some of the marchers threw pennies at the Catholic residents, who responded with marbles fired from slingshots. The violence soon intensified with both sides hurling stones and, later, petrol bombs at each other. Members of the Royal Ulster Constabulary arrived to find barricades erected by the Catholics, prompting direct battles between the two.

The rioting continued for three days. The police flooded the area with tear gas, and the army was eventually brought in to restore order on 14 August. By the time the violence subsided over 1,000 people had been injured.

AUGUST

13

1876

The first complete performance of Wagner's *Ring* cycle took place in the Bavarian town of Bayreuth.

Richard Wagner was born in the city of Leipzig in 1813 and developed a love of theatre after his mother began a relationship with Ludwig Geyer following the death of his father. Although he initially found his creative outlet as a playwright like his stepfather, the young Wagner soon became heavily influenced by the work of Beethoven and began composing music.

Wagner first came up with the idea of what would become his famous *Ring* cycle in 1848. He intended his creation to be a 'total work of art' that would combine music, dance and dramatic storytelling. Basing his work on early Norse and German heroic poetry, Wagner wrote both the libretti and the music. Combined with a 12-year hiatus from the project, this meant he didn't complete the fourth and final part of the cycle until November 1874.

By the time Wagner had finished composing the entire cycle, 'special previews' of earlier parts had already been staged. This was despite Wagner's insistence that the four parts should be unveiled together as a four-night sequence. Nevertheless, the composer had already set about preparing for the premiere by building a new opera house specifically for the purpose. The town council of Bayreuth gave him a plot of land, and the building opened on 13 August 1876 after Ludwig II of Bavaria provided a financial loan.

The opening night of the new opera house hosted a performance of *Das Rheingold*, the first part of the *Ring* cycle. Despite a number of technical problems, Wagner finally got to show his 15-hour masterpiece as a complete series over the course of the next week. It continues to be performed today.

AUGUST

14

1941

The Atlantic Charter was issued by US President Franklin D. Roosevelt and British Prime Minister Winston Churchill.

More than three months before the Japanese attack on Pearl Harbor, the leaders of the United States and Great Britain met aboard ships in Placentia Bay, off the coast of Newfoundland. Codenamed Riviera, the Atlantic Conference was the first time the two men had met as leaders of their respective countries. It led to them agreeing eight 'common principles' that their nations would uphold in the post-war world.

First among these was an agreement that neither country would seek to expand its territory in the aftermath of the war, and that they would help to re-establish borders in accordance with the will of the people living in those areas. The Charter also helped to determine the direction of future world politics, as it was widely accepted by the Allied nations. Consequently the Atlantic Charter helped to lay the foundations for the modern United Nations Organisation.

The document was initially published as the 'Joint Declaration by the President and the Prime Minister' and only became known as the Atlantic Charter thanks to the press. At the time it acted as a symbol of America's moral support for Britain against the Axis powers, but it failed to persuade the American public to support joining the war. Furthermore, the promise of self-determination to Nazi-occupied territories raised tensions between Britain and her colonies since many subjects demanded similar rights for themselves.

Of the Axis powers, it was arguably Japan that felt the most threatened. Believing that the Charter set the scene for a new Anglo-American alliance, the Japanese military adopted aggressive policies that culminated in the attack on Pearl Harbor in December that year.

AUGUST

15

1914

The Panama Canal was officially opened to traffic with the transit of SS *Ancon*.

The Panama Canal, which joins the Atlantic and Pacific oceans, crosses the narrow Isthmus of Panama. The waterway cuts thousands of miles off journeys which would otherwise need to sail around Cape Horn. Stretching 51 miles from deep water at either end, more than 20 miles of the waterway is along the large artificial Gatún Lake to which ships are raised through a series of enormous canal locks.

The idea of building a canal to join the two oceans stretches back to the 16th century. However, it wasn't until 1881 that a French team under engineer Ferdinand de Lesseps began to build a sea-level canal. Although Lesseps had previously constructed the Suez Canal, his attempt to cut across the Isthmus of Panama made slow progress. The project was abandoned, and canal building only resumed after the United States took on the project having supported the independence movement in Panama to break free of Colombia.

American construction began in 1904, and enormous funds were spent on all aspects of the project. These ranged from improved medical facilities to heavy machinery such as steam shovels that were used to excavate the deep channel. It was such an important project that Theodore Roosevelt became the first sitting president to travel outside the United States when he went to inspect progress in 1906.

On 10 October 1913, President Woodrow Wilson detonated the explosives that blew up the last remaining dyke and joined the waters of the two oceans together. Although ships involved in the construction passed along the waterway first, the Panama Canal was officially opened on 15 August 1914 with the passage of the cargo ship SS *Ancon*.

AUGUST

16

1858

Queen Victoria sent the first telegram using the newly-installed transatlantic telegraph cable to US President James Buchanan.

The electrical telegraph had first been conceived in the early 19th century, but it wasn't until the late 1830s that commercial systems began to gain traction. The importance of fast messaging systems grew alongside the rapid expansion of the railways and, by the 1840s, engineers had begun experimenting to find ways to transmit messages across the sea using submarine cables.

One of the first challenges was finding a material that could sufficiently insulate the cable and stop the current dissipating in the surrounding water. Using a thick cable coated with gutta-percha, the non-conductive sap of the palaquium gutta tree, an undersea link was successfully laid between Britain and France in 1850.

At the time it took ten days for a message to travel between North America and Europe by ship, so efforts soon intensified to connect the continents by telegraph. In 1856 St John's and Nova Scotia were joined by a cable and, later that year, the Atlantic Telegraph Company was created to lay the first transatlantic link.

The cable weighed 550 kg/km and could withstand enormous forces, but the first few attempts to lay the cable on the seabed resulted in it breaking. The connection was eventually completed in August 1858 and, after several tests that included a message from the Directors of the Atlantic Telegraph Company in Britain to their counterparts in America, the first transatlantic telegram was sent by Queen Victoria to President Buchanan. Contemporary reports state that the 98-character message of congratulations took 16 hours to send and decipher, but this still made it the fastest system of transatlantic communication.

Parliament passed the Marriage Act that legalised civil marriages and introduced their formal registration.

Prior to the previous Marriage Act of 1753, the government had little control over marriage. It was possible for anyone to marry, providing the ceremony was conducted by an ordained clergyman of the Church of England. However, the early 18th century saw a growing number of 'irregular' and clandestine marriages involving people who were either underage or did not have their parents' permission. Consequently, the government introduced legislation that only recognised marriages performed by a minister in a parish church or chapel of the Church of England.

Although Jews and Quakers were exempt from the 1753 legislation, other religions and Christian congregations had to be married in an Anglican ceremony. This restriction was increasingly opposed by Catholics and people of other denominations and religions who sought the same legal right to marry according to their traditions as Anglicans. The 1836 Marriage Act subsequently allowed other buildings, including those belonging to other religious groups, to be used for weddings if they were licensed by the Registrar General.

As well as providing the same legal status to non-Anglican marriages, the 1836 Marriage Act was also the catalyst for a huge amount of demographic data. From 1 January 1837, when the law came into force, records of all marriages conducted in England and Wales were to be kept by the newly-created General Register Office. This had already been established by the earlier Births and Deaths Registration Act. Nevertheless, centralised birth registrations began slightly later than marriages, and were only made compulsory in 1875.

AUGUST
18
1920

The 19ᵗʰ Amendment to the US Constitution was ratified, guaranteeing all American women the right to vote.

The women's suffrage movement had been gathering pace in America since the 1830s, although most commentators say it formally began at the 1848 Seneca Falls Convention organised by Elizabeth Cady Stanton and Lucretia Mottin in New York.

The convention's resolution to seek female suffrage sparked decades of lobbying and activism. This eventually led to Republican Senator Aaron A. Sargent of California introducing a constitutional amendment to guarantee women the vote in 1878. However, despite having found a supporter within government, the women's suffrage bill didn't make it beyond the committee stage until 1887 when it was voted down.

While the battle for a federal law for female suffrage continued to rage, the newly-formed National American Woman Suffrage Association began to focus on state-level change. By 1914 eight states had passed woman's suffrage legislation. Nevertheless, a new constitutional amendment was rejected at federal level. This prompted a more militant campaign from some suffrage supporters.

Four years later, and having recognised the enormous impact of female support for the war effort, in 1918 President Woodrow Wilson expressed his support for women's suffrage. Although the federal amendment continued to face opposition, it was eventually passed by the Senate on 4 June 1919. It took nearly another year, however, for the amendment to be ratified. Tennessee's House of Representatives, the last to vote, eventually approved the amendment on 18 August 1920 by 50 votes to 49. This secured the two-thirds of states required for ratification.

AUGUST

19

1989

The Cold War border between Austria and Hungary was opened for a short period of time for the Pan-European Picnic.

In the years following Churchill's famous Fulton speech of 1946, in which he spoke of a metaphorical Iron Curtain dividing Europe, a physical border had been erected between the East and West. As the Cold War progressed, however, the demand for change in the countries of the Eastern Bloc grew. By 1989, and influenced by the policy of perestroika that had been introduced by Soviet premier Mikhail Gorbachev, the people of Eastern Europe had increased their calls for democratic elections and an end to Soviet influence.

Meanwhile, the Hungarian government had found that the maintenance of the fortified border had become economically unsustainable. By the late 1980s Hungary had also relaxed travel restrictions, and it became increasingly common for citizens from places such as East Germany to spend their summer holidays with their western friends and relatives by the Hungarian Lake Balaton.

To celebrate this increasing spirit of collaboration, the government of Austria agreed to hold a symbolic event with members of the growing Hungarian anti-communist opposition. On 19 August 1989, the border gate on a road a few miles outside the Hungarian city of Sopron was opened for three hours. Taking the Hungarian government by surprise, approximately 600 East Germans took advantage of the opportunity to cross to the West.

Although the gate was later closed as agreed, the Hungarian government later permanently opened the border. This prompted the steady defection of tens of thousands of East Germans who used the crossing to return to West Germany. Within just a few months the Berlin Wall itself was opened by the East German government.

Leon Trotsky was fatally wounded with an ice axe wielded by Spanish communist Ramón Mercader.

Leon Trotsky had been one of the architects of the Russian Revolution. As chairman of the Supreme Military Council he went on to lead the Red Army, and successfully defeated the combined anti-communist forces of the White Army in the Russian Civil War. Many assumed that he would succeed Lenin as the Soviet leader, but he lost out to Stalin in a bitter power struggle.

Trotsky disagreed deeply with Stalin's ideology and approach to government. Although the new leader adopted a policy of 'Socialism in One Country' through which he sought to strengthen the USSR against potential external threats, Trotsky favoured a more classically Marxist approach of a world revolution to achieve global socialism.

As Trotsky's criticisms of Stalin grew, he was made the target of an intensive propaganda campaign. By 1927 he had been expelled from the Communist Party and, following his exile from the USSR, he settled in Mexico in 1936. Despite being thousands of miles away, Trotsky was found guilty of treason and sentenced to death.

After the failure of previous assassination attempts, Trotsky was finally killed when Spanish communist and NKVD agent Ramón Mercader attacked him with an ice axe. Mercader had used his relationship with Trotsky's friend Sylvia Ageloff to build the trust of Trotsky and his bodyguards, and so managed to enter the heavily-defended compound without the weapon being discovered.

Trotsky died the next day, having persuaded his guards not to kill his attacker. Mercader was later found guilty of murder and served nearly 20 years in prison. Following his release, he was awarded the title of Hero of the Soviet Union.

AUGUST
21
1959

Hawaii became the 50th state to join the United States of America.

The Hawaiian Islands had been ruled as a kingdom since the late 18th century but, as American businesses began to dominate the economy over the next hundred years, the authority of the monarch was gradually eroded. Queen Liliuokalani was deposed in 1893, in what was recognised a century later as an illegal overthrow, and was replaced by a provisional government before lawyer Sanford B. Dole was appointed as the first President of the Republic of Hawaii.

In 1898 Hawaii was annexed as a US territory, but soon afterwards the first attempt to formally recognise it as a state stalled in Congress. It wasn't until the 1950s that a concerted campaign for statehood began, by which time the Japanese attack on Pearl Harbor had highlighted the importance of the territory as an American possession. The population of Hawaii had also shifted to be dominated by the descendants of immigrant labourers who aspired to full representation in Congress. Nevertheless there were still a number of Native Hawaiians who protested against statehood.

Concerned that Hawaii might be dominated by the Republican Party, it was agreed that its admission to the Union would be matched with Alaska since the latter was assumed to be a Democratic Party stronghold. Consequently, after Alaska was admitted in January 1959, the government passed the Hawaii Admission Act in March. Signed into law by President Dwight D. Eisenhower, the Act was confirmed by a referendum on 27 June that offered the choice between accepting the Act, or remaining a US territory. Of 155,000 registered voters over 140,000 went to the ballot. 93% of these voted in favour of statehood, which became effective on 21 August 1959.

AUGUST 22 1791

Slaves in the French colony of Saint-Domingue on the Caribbean island of Hispaniola began the Haitian Revolution.

Christopher Columbus landed on the Caribbean island of Hispaniola during his first transatlantic voyage in 1492, and the island and its population were soon exploited for their gold. However, by the 17th century Spanish interest in the island had waned and French settlers soon rose to dominance with the creation of large sugar plantations.

By the outbreak of the French Revolution in 1789, the plantations on Saint-Domingue were producing 60% of the world's coffee and 40% of all the sugar imported by Britain and France. This economy was built on the slave labour of approximately 500,000 black Africans who lived in incredibly harsh conditions. They were regularly subjected to extreme cruelty and brutality at the hands of their masters.

Tensions between the different groups in the colony had often led to violence, and there had been several slave uprisings prior to the Haitian Revolution that began on 22 August 1791. Influenced in part by the new ideology expressed in the Declaration of the Rights of Man, the slaves of Saint-Domingue rose against the plantation owners on an unprecedented scale and had seized control of a third of the entire island by 1792.

Desperate to end the revolt and regain control over the island's wealth, the French National Assembly abolished slavery. Although Napoléon later attempted to reintroduce it to the colonies, he failed to do so in Saint-Domingue. The people there declared independence on 1 January 1804 under the name Haiti, making it the first country to be established by former slaves.

AUGUST
23
1944

King Michael I of Romania led a *coup d'état* that removed the Nazi-aligned government of Ion Antonescu.

Michael was proclaimed King of Romania after his father, Carol II, was forced to abdicate by the newly-appointed Prime Minister General Ion Antonescu on 6 September 1940. In practical terms, however, the 18-year-old king was nothing more than a figurehead in Antonescu's military dictatorship that went on to join the Axis powers on 23 November 1940.

On 22 June 1941, the Romanian army supported the German attack on the Soviet Union. By the summer of 1944 more than 1 million Romanian troops had fought on the Eastern Front, although the war as whole was going badly for the Axis powers. King Michael had already begun talks with conspirators seeking to topple Antonescu and bring an end to the war when, on 20 August, Soviet troops launched their offensive on eastern Romania.

Three days later, on 23 August, the king summoned Antonescu to his palace where he was dismissed from the post of Prime Minister and arrested. That evening, Michael went on the radio to issue a cease-fire and declare Romania's loyalty to the Allies. Although German forces responded with force, they were soon overwhelmed by the combined armies of Romania and the advancing USSR.

By 31 August the Red Army had reached Bucharest and, less than two weeks later, an armistice was signed on terms virtually dictated by the USSR. Nevertheless, King Michael was presented with the Order of Victory by Stalin and made Chief Commander of the American Legion of Merit by President Harry S. Truman. Antonescu was later found guilty of war crimes, crimes against the peace, and treason. He was executed on 1 June 1946.

AUGUST
24
1967

Political activist Abbie Hoffman and a group of protesters threw dollar bills onto the trading floor of the New York Stock Exchange.

Prior to gaining notoriety as a leader of the Yippie movement, Abbie Hoffman had protested in favour of Civil Rights and been involved in demonstrations against the Vietnam War. Influenced by the Diggers, a San Francisco-based group of community activists, he soon realised the importance of attracting media attention to a cause by creating a spectacle. Such 'guerrilla theatre' activism had first been written about in 1965, but it wasn't until Hoffman's protest at the New York Stock Exchange two years later that such performances began to receive national attention.

As American involvement in the Vietnam War escalated, so too did both the human and financial cost. In keeping with the spirit of guerrilla theatre, Hoffman later said 'If you don't like the news, why not go out and make your own?'

Having assembled a group of fellow protesters, he gave them each a handful of dollar bills before going inside the stock exchange building. Despite being challenged by a security guard, the crowd of activists were able to make their way to the gallery overlooking the trading floor where they began throwing the money over the railing.

The stunt was met with a mixture of laughter and anger from the traders below, while the press assembled outside were quick to give it widespread coverage. The activists gave often contradictory answers to their questions, fuelling the mythology of the demonstration to the point where nobody is entirely sure who was involved or how much money was thrown. Nevertheless, the stunt at the New York Stock Exchange cemented Abbie Hoffman as a master of political protest.

AUGUST
25
1875

Captain Matthew Webb became the first person to successfully swim across the English Channel.

Webb learnt to swim in the River Severn outside the English industrial village of Coalbrookdale, near modern Telford. When he was twelve years old he began training on board the school ship HMS *Conway*, leading to a career as a sailor on board merchant and passenger vessels. It was while sailing from New York to Liverpool that he first showed his strength as a swimmer by diving into the Atlantic to save a man who had gone overboard. Although the man was never found, Webb was celebrated for his courage.

Webb later became captain of the *Emerald*, and it was during this time that he read of J. B. Johnson's failed attempt to swim across the Channel. Quitting his job, Webb began preparations to make his own crossing in the summer.

On 12 August, Webb covered himself in porpoise oil to act as insulation against the cold water and entered the Channel at Dover's Admiralty Pier. He was forced to abandon this first attempt after a storm at sea made the swim particularly difficult but tried again twelve days later, shortly before 1pm on 24 August.

Accompanied by three boats, Webb finally stepped ashore near Calais after swimming for approximately 21 hours and 45 minutes. His crossing had seen strong currents regularly move him off course, while a painful jellyfish sting was dealt with by drinking a glass of brandy. Altogether he had swum 64 kilometres.

Matthew Webb's cross-Channel swim secured his position as a Victorian celebrity, and he soon found fortune by undertaking other extreme water-based challenges. He died in 1883 during a failed attempt to swim across the Whirlpool Rapids below Niagara Falls.

The National Constituent Assembly of France adopted the Declaration of the Rights of Man and of the Citizen.

The National Constituent Assembly was established in France on 9 July 1789, in the aftermath of the Tennis Court Oath. Its power grew following the storming of the Bastille on 14 July, after which the Assembly set about drafting a new constitution.

Emerging from the ideals of the Enlightenment and the original principals of the French Revolution, the Declaration of the Rights of Man and of the Citizen contains 17 articles that make it one of the most important documents in the history of human rights. Based on the principle of 'natural rights' that had been advanced by philosophers such as Locke, Montesquieu, and Rousseau, the Declaration was drafted jointly by the Abbé Sieyès and the Marquis de Lafayette. Its authors also consulted with Thomas Jefferson, one the American Founding Fathers.

Described in its preamble as a 'solemn declaration [of] the natural, inalienable, and sacred rights of man', the Declaration nevertheless found opposition from those members of society who were excluded. Of particular significance was the issue of 'active' and 'passive' citizens, since the rights of the Declaration only applied to them. Active citizens were French men who were at least 25 years old and were wealthy enough to pay taxes equal to three days of work.

The Declaration did not, therefore, recognise the rights of women. The first article, which stated 'men are born and remain free and equal in rights', also became an important focus for the anti-slavery movement. Nevertheless, the Declaration provided a political and social ideal that continues to influence and inspire democracies throughout the world.

AUGUST

27

1883

One of the most destructive volcanic events in modern history occurred when Krakatoa's eruption reached its climax.

Krakatoa consists of a mostly-sunken caldera that lies within the Sunda Strait, between the Indonesian islands of Java and Sumatra. Situated on the subduction zone of the Eurasian Plate and the Indo-Australian Plate, the island and its surrounding archipelago were formed by previous volcanic eruptions.

In May 1883, clouds of ash and steam were seen venting from the volcano by the captain of the German warship *Elizabeth*. The intensity of the volcano's activity varied over the next three months until, on Sunday 26 August, the eruption became significantly more violent and debris was thrown an estimated 15 miles into the air. The earlier celebratory mood of people on the nearby islands soon turned to fear as hot ash and rock began to fall.

The eruption reached its climax the next day. Over the course of five and a half hours, beginning at 5:30am, four enormous explosions occurred. The third of these was the most powerful, with the sound being heard up to 3,000 miles away in the Indian Ocean. The explosive power of the eruption is believed to have been the equivalent of 200 megatons of TNT, while the pressure wave is estimated to have travelled around the globe three and a half times. The force of the eruption and the amount of material displaced also caused a number of tsunamis, the effects of which could be felt as far away as South Africa. Over 36,000 people are known to have died.

Over two-thirds of the island of Krakatoa itself disappeared. In the aftermath, the effect of unusually high quantities of ash and sulphur dioxide that had been expelled into the atmosphere disrupted global weather patterns for more than five years.

AUGUST

28

1955

Black teenager Emmett Till was murdered for allegedly flirting with a white woman in Mississippi.

When Chicago-born Emmett Till was fourteen years old, his mother agreed that he could visit his great uncle in the small Mississippi settlement of Money. Before travelling south, she warned her son that life for black people in the South was dramatically different to that of their black neighbourhood in Chicago.

On 24 August, Till and some other black teenage boys gathered outside Bryant's Grocery and Meat Market which was staffed by 21-year-old Carolyn Bryant. All sources confirm that Till entered the store to buy some bubble gum, but what happened next is disputed. Depending on the source it is alleged that that he then either wolf-whistled, flirted with, or touched Carolyn.

Carolyn's husband Roy Bryant was away on a business trip but, on his return, heard the allegations about Till. Incensed that he had crossed the 'color line', Bryant and his half-brother J.W. Milam drove to the home of Till's great uncle Mose Wright in the early hours of 28 August. They abducted the teenager and beat him severely before shooting him in the head. They then tied his body to a heavy fan and threw it into the Tallahatchie River.

Till's body was found three days later, and was only identifiable from an initialled ring on his finger. Bryant and Milam went on trial for murder but, despite Mose Wright bravely identifying them in court, the all-white jury acquitted them. Protected against double jeopardy, they admitted to the crime in a magazine interview in 1956.

Till's mother insisted on an open-casket funeral so that people could see for themselves what had happened to her son. His brutal murder soon became a rallying point for the Civil Rights Movement.

AUGUST
29
1842

The First Opium War formally ended when Britain and China signed the Treaty of Nanking, the first of the 'unequal treaties'.

Britain and China had been at war since September 1839, the conflict having been triggered by Chinese attempts to halt the lucrative opium trade that was causing significant social and economic problems in the country.

By the summer of 1842 almost all Chinese ports were blockaded or under British occupation and, after the fall of Shanghai in June, the British sailed up the Yangtze River. Having reached the outskirts of Nanking on 9 August, Chinese officials agreed to negotiate. After a week of discussions the Daoguang Emperor granted permission for his diplomats to sign the treaty, which they did on board the British ship HMS *Cornwallis* on 29 August.

Consisting of thirteen articles, the Treaty of Nanking saw China pay an indemnity of 20 million silver dollars, grant Hong Kong to Britain, and abolish the Canton System by opening up a further four 'treaty ports' to unrestricted trade. Since the treaty was seen to have been imposed on China as a result of war, it became known as one of the first of the 'unequal treaties' that were signed between China and various foreign nations in the 19th and 20th centuries.

Ironically, however, the Treaty of Nanking did not resolve the original dispute over the opium trade and failed to bring about the improved trade and diplomatic relations that Britain had hoped to benefit from. Instead, the aftermath of the First Opium War saw rampant Western imperialism target China and its valuable trading ports. Consequently, having failed to persuade the Qing government to renegotiate the Treaty of Nanking, the Second Opium War between Britain and China began in 1856.

AUGUST

30

1963

The Moscow–Washington hotline entered operation, providing a direct link between the Kremlin and the Pentagon.

The idea for a direct system of communications between the world's two largest superpowers had been discussed since at least the late 1950s, but became more urgent in the aftermath of the Cuban Missile Crisis. Many officials found that the slow pace at which the existing diplomatic communication system operated had undermined their attempts to reach a peaceful conclusion in the standoff, with messages taking upwards of six hours to be delivered.

On 20 June 1963, the Soviet premier Nichita Khrushchev and American President John F. Kennedy met in Geneva where they signed a Memorandum of Understanding to establish a direct communication link between their governments. The primary route would take messages from Washington to Moscow via a 16,000km long cable via London, Copenhagen, Stockholm and Helsinki.

Contrary to the urban legend, the hotline did not see a red telephone placed on the respective leaders' desks. Instead the first system used a telex link to type messages that would be decoded and translated by military interpreters at the other end prior to being forwarded to the country's commander-in-chief. The first message, sent from Washington on 30 August 1963, ensured the system was working properly: 'The quick brown fox jumped over the lazy dog's back 1234567890'.

To ensure the system was functioning as intended, test messages continued to be sent every hour. The first official message was sent from Washington on 22 November 1963 to report the assassination of President Kennedy. The system now uses satellites to provide a secure email connection between the two countries.

AUGUST

31

1907

Britain and Russia signed the Anglo-Russian Entente, which led to the formation of the Triple Entente.

For much of the second-half of the nineteenth century, Britain and Russia had been involved in a series of disputes over colonial acquisitions in Persia, Tibet and Afghanistan. By the start of the twentieth century, however, the increasing threat of the relatively-young German Empire saw the two great powers seek to settle what had become known as 'The Great Game'.

Russia had already ended years of tension with France through the Franco-Russian Alliance of 1894. Meanwhile, the Entente Cordiale of 1904 saw Britain and France settle a number of longstanding colonial disputes. Consequently, the signing of the Anglo-Russian Entente on 31 August 1907 completed a series of agreements that loosely tied the three nations together.

The Anglo-Russian Entente itself consisted of three separate agreements which were bundled together for ratification. The first divided Iran into three zones, two of which were part of the British and Russian spheres of influence respectively, while the third – which separated the other two – was neutral. In the second agreement the two nations agreed not to interfere in Tibet's domestic affairs. The third agreed that Afghanistan was 'outside Russia's sphere of influence' – effectively a recognition of British influence there.

The Anglo-French and Anglo-Russian Ententes did not formally make the signatories allies. Nevertheless the Triple Entente, as the network of agreements between the three powers became known, acted as a counterweight to the existing Triple Alliance between Germany, Austria-Hungary and Italy. These two huge power blocs played a prominent role in the outbreak of the First World War.

SEPTEMBER

SEPTEMBER

1

1604

The *Adi Granth*, the original holy scripture of Sikhism now known as *Guru Granth Sahib*, was first installed at the Harmandir Sahib Golden Temple.

Beginning with Guru Nanak, the founder of Sikhism, the gurus had distributed collections of hymns to distant Sikh communities. The *Adi Granth* was a compilation of these texts assembled by Guru Arjan, the fifth Sikh Guru, who had inherited the role from his father, Guru Ram Das, in 1581.

While collating the work of his predecessor, Guru Arjan realised that some of the legitimate writings had been infiltrated by forged works from other people who sought the guruship. Keen to stop the illegitimate texts from spreading, Guru Arjan set about compiling the writings of Guru Ram Das and the first three gurus into a single volume.

The *Adi Granth* manuscript was completed in 1604 and was installed at the Golden Temple, which Guru Arjan had also designed, on 1 September that year. Copies were sent to Sikh communities across northern India. The book remained unchanged until the tenth guru, Guru Gobind Singh, added the writings of his predecessor to it. Guru Gobind Singh later ended the human line of gurus by announcing the text itself as his successor on 20 October 1708. Consequently this second rendition of the *Adi Granth* became known as *Guru Granth Sahib*.

Guru Gobind Singh instructed Sikhs to respect the Guru Granth as an embodiment of the ten Gurus who had come before it. Consequently *Guru Granth Sahib* is considered within Sikhism to be the final Guru, since it contains answers to all questions regarding religion and morality.

SEPTEMBER

2

31 BCE

Octavian defeated the combined forces of Marc Antony and Cleopatra at the Battle of Actium.

The Second Triumvirate of Marc Antony, Octavian and Marcus Lepidus emerged out of the civil war that had erupted following the assassination of Julius Caesar in 44 BCE. However, the power-sharing agreement broke down as Antony grew closer to Queen Cleopatra VII Egypt. He eventually separated from his wife Octavia – Octavian's sister – in favour of the Egyptian queen. Together they and Caesarion, Cleopatra's son by Julius Caesar, were soon portrayed as a threat to the stability of the Roman Republic.

Swayed by the publication of Antony's will, which had come into Octavian's hands after the defection of Plancus, the Senate declared war against Cleopatra in 31 BCE. It was clear that Antony too would be drawn into battle and, on 2 September, the opposing forces met for the decisive naval battle outside the Gulf of Actium in Greece.

Antony's fleet of larger ships was undermanned due to a malaria outbreak, leading to them being easily out-manoeuvred by Octavian's smaller 'Liburnian' vessels. Octavian further benefited from the defection of Antony's general, Quintus Dellius, who brought with him Antony's plans.

Both sides attempted to outflank the other for much of the afternoon without any decisive breakthrough. Eventually Cleopatra's Egyptian galleys, which had stayed behind Antony's fleet, fled the battle. Antony followed soon afterwards, and the remainder of his fleet were forced to surrender.

Antony's land forces deserted him as Octavian advanced on Egypt. Both Antony and Cleopatra subsequently committed suicide, leaving Octavian to consolidate his control over Rome.

SEPTEMBER
3
1783

The Treaty of Paris, which ended the American Revolutionary War, was signed by representatives of King George III of Great Britain and representatives of the United States of America.

The American Revolutionary War, also known as the American War of Independence, began on 19 April 1775 between Great Britain and her Thirteen Colonies that had declared independence as the United States of America.

The conflict lasted for over eight years from its first shot to the signing of the Treaty. The Americans, having formed an alliance with France in 1778, had accepted the surrender of British troops under Charles Cornwallis on 17 October 1781. This resulted from the decisive victory at Yorktown by a combined force of American troops, led by General George Washington, and French Army troops under the Comte de Rochambeau.

A vote of 'no confidence' in the British government under Lord North soon led to the creation of a new government that began peace negotiations in April 1782. By the end of the summer the Americans had begun to negotiate directly with the British Prime Minister, Lord Shelburne. This move forced France to agree a separate peace with Britain, and had the effect of weakening the relationship between the two allies.

The Treaty of Paris was drafted on 30 November 1782, and was signed the following year. It formally recognised that the United States would be free, sovereign, and independent. The land granted under the agreement to the United States by Britain has subsequently been described as 'exceedingly generous'. However, in an excellent piece of diplomatic prediction by Lord Shelburne, this went on to provide Britain with a fast-growing and lucrative trading partner.

Thomas Edison began operating the first permanent commercial electrical power plant in New York.

Edison created his incandescent light bulb in October 1879, and was quick to realise that he also had to develop a system to generate and distribute the required electricity to consumers. Having successfully fitted a number of small private systems in the United States and Britain, Edison bought two adjoining commercial buildings on Pearl Street in the area known as the First District in New York to house his commercial power plant. Installing the six dynamos and their coal-powered reciprocating steam engines was a significant technical challenge, but one of the most expensive aspects of the venture was the laying of almost 100,000 feet of wiring in specially-dug underground conduits.

By the time the system was ready to begin operation on 4 September 1882, Edison had signed up around 80 customers with a total of 400 light bulbs. *The New York Times*, one of the first users, described the 'soft, mellow' light in a short article the next day. However, the inauguration of the world's first commercial power plant did not receive the media fanfare many might have expected, and the report was filed under 'Miscellaneous City News'.

Edison's customer base increased to almost 500 users within twelve months of the Pearl Street Station opening, but it ran at a loss for the first two years. The system did, however, generate demand for electrical energy elsewhere and kick-started the electrical age. The shortcomings of Edison's direct current soon became apparent, however, as it was prohibitively expensive to provide such power over long distances. Within just a few years, competitors using high voltage alternating current had begun to dominate the market.

SEPTEMBER
5
1793

The Reign of Terror began in France when Bertrand Barère, a member of the Committee of Public Safety, made a speech that ended with the exclamation, 'Let's make terror the order of the day!'

Although there is debate amongst historians regarding the exact date that the Reign of Terror began, Barère made his speech at a time when the Paris Commune was agitating for a more proactive way to deal with enemies of the revolution. Less than two weeks later the National Convention passed the Law of Suspects. This led to the arrest of both proven and suspected opponents of the government. This was one of the key causes of the more than 16,000 executions that took place during the Terror.

The following February, Robespierre himself justified the government's policy as 'nothing more than speedy, severe and inflexible justice'. While some historians disagree with Robespierre's argument that the Terror was necessary to combat counter-revolutionary elements in French society, there can be little doubt that France's fortunes improved during this time.

However, the Terror soon began to face opposition. Within just a few months two factions – one calling for an escalation, the other for moderation – had emerged. Although the leaders of both groups were executed, Robespierre's dominance of the Committee of Public Safety was soon seen as a threat to the National Convention itself.

In the session on 27 July 1794, members of the Convention turned against Robespierre and his allies. Shouts of 'Down with the tyrant! Arrest him!' were heard in the chamber. Robespierre and 21 followers were arrested, and later executed, in what became known as the Thermidorian Reaction.

The ship *Victoria* returned to Spain as the only survivor of Ferdinand Magellan's fleet that circumnavigated the globe.

Despite Magellan being Portuguese, his voyage was funded by the Spanish king Charles I. Better known as the Holy Roman Emperor Charles V, Charles was determined to find a westward route to the Indies in order to avoid violating the Treaty of Tordesillas that reserved the eastward route around Africa for Portugal.

Known as the Armada de Molucca, the expedition departed Seville on 10 August 1519. After crossing the Atlantic Ocean, the five ships succeeded in finding what became known as the Strait of Magellan that took them through the South American land mass and into the South Pacific.

The expedition finally reached the Spice Islands on 6 November 1521, by which time the fleet had been reduced to just two ships. Magellan himself had also been killed in the Battle of Mactan. Six weeks later, and fully-laden with spices, the ship *Victoria* departed the Moluccas under the command of Juan Sebastián Elcano. The other surviving vessel, *Trinidad*, followed in April 1522 but was later captured by the Portuguese.

Victoria returned to Spain across the Indian Ocean before rounding the Cape of Good Hope and heading home. She arrived in Sanlúcar de Barrameda on 6 September 1522, and returned to Seville two days later as the first ship to circumnavigate the globe. The final leg of the voyage had seen the remaining crew forced to survive by eating nothing but rice, and altogether only 18 men returned from the initial expedition of around 265. Meanwhile the 26 tons of spices on board the ship survived the homeward voyage. Their sale more than covered the entire cost of the expedition.

SEPTEMBER

7

1940

The Nazi German *Luftwaffe* launched the first of 57 consecutive days and nights of bombing raids on London in what became known as the Blitz.

The *Luftwaffe* had been attacking British targets in the Battle of Britain since June 1940. This was an attempt to achieve air superiority over the RAF to enable a land invasion by the Nazis, or force the British government to sue for peace.

Having failed to defeat the RAF in the Battle of Britain, Hitler and Göring instead ordered a policy designed to crush civilian morale. The first raid of the Blitz took place on 7 September. Over 337 tons of bombs were dropped on London, and 448 civilians were killed. The earlier decision by Hugh Dowding, Air Officer Commanding Fighter Command, to focus on day fighter defences meant that Britain was woefully unprepared for German bomber attacks at night when they became the official policy on 7 October.

The *Luftwaffe* used technology known as beam navigation to locate their target, in which the crews had to detect converging radio signals from two or more ground stations. Britain countered this by transmitting false navigation signals that were designed to send the incoming crews off course. They also created a number of dummy targets such as diversionary airfields and industrial targets that used lighting effects to simulate factories and transport.

By the end of the Blitz on 11 May 1941, approximately 41,000 tons of bombs had been dropped by the *Luftwaffe* and more than 40,000 civilians had been killed. Yet, despite the psychological pressures of the situation in which class divisions and anti-Semitism often surfaced, British society continued to function. Morale remained high, and British industrial production actually rose.

SEPTEMBER

8

1941

The Siege of Leningrad, one of the longest and most destructive sieges in history, began.

Nazi Germany's *Lebensraum* foreign policy sought to secure living space for future generations of Germans in the 'thousand-year Reich'. Hitler intended the fertile lands of the western USSR to provide food for his new empire, while the native Slavic population would be destroyed and replaced with ethnic Germans.

Leningrad, which is now known as Saint Petersburg, was a politically significant Soviet city due to its role in the Bolshevik Revolution. Furthermore, it was a centre of industrial production, and had military significance as a base for the Baltic Fleet of the Soviet navy. Consequently, when the Nazi invasion of the Soviet Union - known as Operation Barbarossa – began on 22 June 1941, the capture of Leningrad was a key strategic goal.

By September, Army Group North under the command of German Field Marshal Wilhelm Ritter von Leeb had reached the southern outskirts of the city whilst the Finnish army had approached from the north. Meanwhile, more than a million civilians from Leningrad prepared extensive fortifications to assist the approximately 200,000 Red Army defenders.

Although the city's defences held, by the start of September Leningrad was almost entirely surrounded and its communication lines had been severed. The Germans attempted a final push but, unable to overcome the defensive fortifications, Hitler ordered the city to be starved into submission.

Over one million civilians died as a result of the ensuing siege that lasted for more than 870 days. The Red Army was eventually able to repel the German forces and lift the siege in January 1944.

Elvis Presley appeared on *The Ed Sullivan Show*, the USA's most popular television show, for the first time.

Ed Sullivan was a former New York entertainment columnist who had once vowed never to have Elvis Presley appear on his variety show. He had previously turned down an opportunity to hire the singer for $5,000 but realised his mistake when his show ratings were crippled by Elvis' appearance on a rival show hosted by Steve Allen.

Sullivan consequently agreed to pay the unprecedented sum of $50,000 for three appearances, the first of which took place on the new season premiere. Sullivan, however, was not able to host the show as he was recovering from a head-on collision that had almost killed him. British actor Charles Laughton was recruited as the stand-in host, and introduced the rock n roll star with the words '…and now, away to Hollywood to meet Elvis Presley!'

Elvis needed to perform at CBS Television City in Los Angeles, rather than the New York studio where *The Ed Sullivan Show* was based, because he was in the middle of filming his debut movie. Having opened with his recent hit 'Don't Be Cruel', Elvis went on to perform the title song from the forthcoming film, 'Love Me Tender'.

He appeared again later, performing Little Richard's hit 'Ready Teddy' and a shortened version of 'Hound Dog'. This segment included some full-body shots of Elvis, but when he began dancing the cameras tended to focus only from his waist upwards.

Sullivan's decision to hire Elvis to appear on the show paid off. 60 million people tuned in to watch the show, representing 82.6% of the evening's television audience. Knowing they would be unable to compete, Steve Allen's network chose only to show a movie.

SEPTEMBER
10
1991

American rock band Nirvana released the critically acclaimed single 'Smells Like Teen Spirit'.

Kurt Cobain and Krist Novoselic formed Nirvana in 1987. After a succession of drummers they recruited Dave Grohl in 1990, with whom they signed to DGC Records and soon began recording the album *Nevermind*. Cobain was initially reluctant to include 'Smells Like Teen Spirit' as he was reportedly concerned that it sounded too similar to songs by the Pixies, a band whose music he had long admired and attempted to emulate. However, he was eventually persuaded by the other band members and producer Butch Vig.

The song title was inspired by graffiti scrawled on Cobain's wall by Kathleen Hanna, singer with feminist punk band Bikini Kill. The message, 'Kurt Smells Like Teen Spirit' was a reference to how the Nirvana frontman had been marked by his girlfriend's deodorant, the popular Teen Spirit brand produced by Mennen.

When Cobain first shared the main guitar riff and chorus melody with the rest of the band, Novoselic is said to have described it as 'ridiculous'. Despite such blunt criticism, the band played the riff repeatedly and, after an hour and a half of experimentation, they had agreed to slow down the tempo while Grohl added his iconic drum intro. A rough demo recording was sent to their producer, who immediately heard the song's potential.

The single was released to radio on 27 August, and to the public on 10 September. Intended to consolidate and build Nirvana's core following, neither DGC Records nor the band members themselves expected the single to take off in the way it did. The music video took MTV by storm, and within weeks it had catapulted alternative rock and the grunge genre as a whole into the mainstream.

SEPTEMBER

11

1789

Alexander Hamilton was made the first United States Secretary of the Treasury by President George Washington.

Alexander Hamilton was born on the Caribbean island of Nevis to a Scottish-born father and a half-British, half-French Huguenot mother who had left her husband and son on the Danish-ruled island of St. Croix in the Virgin Islands. Alexander's parents were consequently unmarried when he was born, and he became an orphan around the age of twelve following his mother's death. His father had left the family a number of years earlier, and Hamilton moved to live first with his older cousin and later a wealthy merchant.

Hamilton secured work as a clerk at a local shipping company, where he developed an interest in writing. A letter to his father recounting a violent storm was later published in a newspaper, and this attracted the attention of wealthy locals who provided funds for him to continue his education in New York City.

Hamilton believed strongly in independence for the Thirteen Colonies and, following the outbreak of the American Revolutionary War, he joined a local militia from which he rose to become the senior aide to General Washington. The end of the war saw Hamilton elected as New York's representative to the Congress of the Confederation, where he argued for a strong central government and the creation of a new constitution.

Hamilton went on to become a highly influential member of President Washington's cabinet, and was appointed as the first Secretary of the Treasury on 11 September 1789. He continued in this role for almost five years, during which he had a key role in defining the structure of the government of the United States and created the country's first national bank.

SEPTEMBER

12

1977

South African anti-apartheid activist Steve Biko died in Pretoria prison from injuries inflicted while in police custody.

Bantu Stephen Biko established the South African Students' Organisation, and developed the ideology of Black Consciousness to challenge the system of racial segregation and white-minority rule known as apartheid. Having voted in favour of the Black People's Convention in 1972, by 1973 Biko's activities had caught the attention of the authorities. The government were concerned that the Black Consciousness Movement, and Biko himself, were a threat to the political situation in South Africa. In response, a banning order was placed on him and a number of other anti-apartheid activists.

Despite the banning order severely limiting Biko's activities by restricting him from leaving King William's Town, he continued to be involved in the anti-apartheid movement and was arrested and held without charge four times between 1975 and 1977. However, on 17 August 1977 he broke the terms of his banning order by driving to Cape Town in the hope of meeting the leader of the Unity Movement, Neville Alexander. On his return the next day, Biko was stopped at a police roadblock and taken into custody.

While held in Port Elizabeth, Biko was interrogated while shackled, handcuffed and naked. The exact details of the interrogation have never been established, but it has since been acknowledged that Biko was violently assaulted to such an extent that he suffered brain injuries that led to a haemorrhage. Having been sent to Pretoria for medical treatment, on 12 September he died in his cell of what the autopsy referred to as an 'extensive brain injury'. Biko's death attracted global attention and intensified international criticism of apartheid.

Michelangelo began work on his celebrated statue of the biblical hero, David.

Michelangelo's *David* is considered to be one of the greatest examples of Renaissance sculpture. Carved from a piece of marble from a quarry near the Tuscan town of Carrara, the statue is a nude male standing 517cm tall without his pedestal.

Michelangelo was not the first artist to begin carving a statue of David from the marble block. The Florentine sculptor Agostino di Duccio had first been contracted by the Overseers of the Office of Works of Florence Cathedral in 1464 to create the statue as one of twelve figures to appear on the buttresses of the recently-completed cathedral. Despite having shaped the feet and legs, he stopped work on the statue in 1466. Work only resumed a decade later when Antonio Rossellino took over.

Rossellino did not do much more to the marble before his contract was terminated shortly after it had been awarded. The block then remained on its back in the cathedral yard for 25 years before Michelangelo was eventually recruited to complete the statue, two years after he finished work on the *Pietà*.

The 26-year-old was given two years to produce *David* and, according to the written contract, was to be paid 'six broad florins of gold in gold for every month'. Dr Barrie Cook of the British Museum has since used the Bank of England's price inflation index to calculate that Michelangelo was therefore paid just £40,000 at today's prices for the finished piece.

On its completion the sculpture was placed next to the entrance to the Palazzo Vecchio, although it has been displayed in the Accademia Gallery since 1873 to protect the fragile marble.

Shortly after midnight in Moscow, the Soviets became the first to successfully send a human-made object to the Moon.

The Luna 2 probe was developed under the supervision of Sergei Korolev. Korolev was the Chief Designer of the Soviet space program, and he had previously created the R-7 rocket that launched both the Sputnik 1 satellite and Laika the dog in to space.

The Soviets had attempted to reach the Moon earlier in 1959 with Luna 1, but this probe missed its target due to a malfunction on the ground that caused an error in its rocket's burn time. With the problem fixed, the spherical design of Luna 2 was almost identical to its predecessor. Numerous antennas and instruments protruded from the probe to measure and transmit data about radiation, magnetic fields and meteorites.

The original launch on 9 September was aborted due to the core booster failing to reach full thrust at ignition, but a replacement was successfully installed for the second attempt three days later. Travelling in a direct path to the Moon, rather than entering orbit first, Luna 2 reached its destination less than 36 hours after launch.

Having monitored the signals coming from Luna 2 on its journey, Soviet scientists correctly predicted that the satellite would crash into the Moon shortly after midnight on 14 September. It was clear that the mission had been a success when the signals suddenly stopped.

Luna 2 was seized upon as pro-communist propaganda, but also opened the way for American developments in the Space Race that intensified over the next decade. Less than ten years later this culminated in astronaut Neil Armstrong becoming the first person to walk on the Moon's surface.

The British MP William Huskisson died as a result of a fatal accident on the opening day of the Liverpool and Manchester Railway.

The Liverpool and Manchester Railway was created in order to link Manchester, a major industrial city in the north west of England, with the nearby port of Liverpool. Intended to lower the cost of transporting imported cotton to the Manchester textile mills, the 35-mile railway was an incredibly expensive project as it was the first railway to use locomotives to haul goods and passengers.

William Huskisson was the MP for Liverpool, and fought hard to secure parliamentary representation for the new industrial towns. As former President of the Board of Trade he also had an acute awareness of the likely positive effects of the creation of the railway.

The Liverpool and Manchester railway used four equally spaced rails along the length of the route. George Stephenson, the designer and builder intended that under normal circumstances this would allow two-way traffic using a pair of rails in each direction, but also meant that the centre two rails could be used in case of a wide load or a problem with one of the outer rails.

The railway was opened on 15 September 1830 with great fanfare. Arthur Wellesley, Duke of Wellington, the Prime Minister, was riding in a special carriage when his train stopped to take on water. Having invited Huskisson over, the passengers noticed the prototype engine *Rocket* approaching on the adjacent track. Huskisson attempted to climb into Wellington's carriage, but the door swung open and the approaching locomotive crashed into it. Huskisson fell on to the track and *Rocket* ran over his right leg and thigh. He died of his injuries later that evening.

SEPTEMBER

16

1955

The *Revolución Libertadora* began in Argentina, resulting in the end of Juan Perón's second term as President.

Juan Perón had been elected President of Argentina in 1946 with overwhelming support from the country's working class thanks in large part to his wife, Evita. Perón went on to win a second term but, before long, the economy began to falter. This coincided with Evita's death from cancer in July 1952, and Perón soon found his support amongst the working classes declining.

By 1955 Perón's government had become increasingly repressive. The Catholic Church began to turn against the President in the face of controversial legislation that would legalise prostitution and divorce, and in return was threatened with the separation of church and state.

Meanwhile Perón lost the support of large swathes of the military. Just days after 100,000 people joined a Corpus Christi procession that turned into an anti-Perón demonstration, thirty navy and air force planes killed more than 300 people when they bombed the Plaza de Mayo and Casa Rosada in Buenos Aires.

Although this revolt was put down, tensions continued to mount. On 16 September, the military in Cordoba seized control of the city, and large swathes of the country's armed forces came out against the President. Within two days Buenos Aires was facing a blockade, and the country was on the brink of civil war.

With no other options open to him, Perón resigned the Presidency on 19 September and fled to exile in Paraguay. Four days later General Eduardo Lonardi, one of the coup's leaders, became the provisional president after being greeted in Buenos Aires by the largest crowd in the city's history.

SEPTEMBER 17 1859

Joshua Abraham Norton declared himself Norton I, Emperor of the United States.

Norton moved to San Francisco from South Africa sometime around the end of 1849 and, within three years, had amassed a significant fortune as a result of shrewd real estate investments and various commodities deals.

A famine in China, leading to a ban of rice exports at the end of 1852, led to Norton's purchase of an entire shipment of Peruvian rice. The cost of rice rose as a result of the lack of Chinese imports, and he hoped to benefit from this. However, numerous other rice shipments from Peru arrived shortly after he signed the contract and the market value of his own purchase plummeted. These losses, combined with the cost of a court case that eventually ruled against his attempt to void the contract, forced him into bankruptcy.

Frustrated by what he perceived as the failings of the American political and legal system, Norton declared himself Emperor on 17 September 1859. The *San Francisco Bulletin* printed his decree in full, sparking media interest that led to him becoming a celebrity in the city. Norton often dined for free and received theatre tickets in return for the publicity that his imperial seal of approval would provide.

Norton maintained the role of self-declared Emperor until his death on 8 January 1880. Within this time he added the additional title of 'protector of Mexico', and issued a range of decrees ranging from the abolition of the United States Congress to the imposition of a fine for anybody who referred to San Francisco as 'Frisco'. Although these decrees were ignored, a bridge and a tunnel between San Francisco and Oakland, both of which he called for in 1872, were eventually opened in 1933 and 1974 respectively.

SEPTEMBER

18

1932

The body of actress Peg Entwistle was found in a ravine below the Hollywoodland sign in Los Angeles.

Millicent Lillian Entwistle was born in Wales to English parents, but had settled in New York with her actor father by 1916. After he died in 1922, the fourteen-year-old Peg and her two half-brothers were cared for by their uncle who had also moved to New York.

Within a few years Entwistle had followed her father into the theatre, and she appeared in ten Broadway plays between 1926 and 1932. She also toured the United States, but in 1932 settled in Los Angeles where she lived with her uncle on Beachwood Drive. Entwistle's performance in a sold-out production of *The Mad Hopes* secured glowing reviews and, having lost out on the lead role in *Bill of Divorcement* to Katharine Hepburn, she was given a supporting role in the RKO film *Thirteen Women*. However, her contract with the studio was not renewed. The actress's uncle later told the police that by September she was 'suffering an intense mental anguish'.

By 1932 a large advertising sign on Mount Lee for the new Hollywoodland housing development had become an iconic feature of the Los Angeles skyline. It was here that the distraught Entwistle headed on 16 September, having told her uncle that she was walking to a nearby drugstore and then paying a visit to some friends.

Two days later LAPD received an anonymous call from a hiker informing them that she had found a woman's purse, shoes and jacket near the sign. Inside the purse was a suicide note. Officers soon located the body of a young blonde woman in the ravine below, which was later identified by Entwistle's uncle. The police came to the conclusion that the 24-year-old had climbed a workman's ladder behind the letter 'H' and thrown herself to her death.

SEPTEMBER
19
1879

The Illuminations at the British seaside resort of Blackpool were turned on for the first time.

The Illuminations, which continue to be an annual light festival, have grown considerably since their inception. Now stretching for 6 miles along the Promenade, and featuring over one million bulbs, the very first event consisted of just eight carbon arc lamps that were used to light the seafront.

The lamps were positioned 320 yards apart, and were powered by 16 Robey steam engines that drove 8 Siemens dynamo-electric machines. Described at the time as 'artificial sunshine', the first Illuminations were turned on almost a year before Thomas Edison patented the electric light bulb. At the time the streets of Britain were lit by gas lamps, assuming they were lit at all. Since the eight Blackpool amp lamps were each equivalent to the light of 48,000 candles, their installation was an incredible novelty and it is estimated that over 70,000 people travelled from all over Britain to see them.

The Illuminations didn't become an actual display until May 1912, when Blackpool was visited by a member of the British royal family for the first time. Princess Louise opened the Princess Parade section of the Promenade, and her visit was marked by 'festoons of garland lamps' that used more than 10,000 bulbs. The spectacle was so impressive that the local Chamber of Trade urged the council to stage the display again in September to mark the end of the season.

The Illuminations were such a commercial success that they were turned on again the following year, but the Promenade stayed dark throughout both the First and Second World Wars. The Illuminations were restarted in 1949 and have been an annual event ever since.

SEPTEMBER
20
1835

The Ragamuffin War began when Brazilian rebels in the southern province of Rio Grande do Sul captured Porto Alegre.

The early 1830s had seen gaucho ranchers in southern Brazil growing increasingly frustrated with the country's central government. Their primary grievance concerned a tax on the province's main product, a type of dried and salted beef known as *charque*, that had led to the market being flooded with cheaper imported versions from Uruguay and Argentina.

As criticism of the government grew, the gauchos joined together under the leadership of Bento Gonçalves da Silva. Disparagingly referred to as *farrapos* or 'ragamuffins', due to their fringed leather clothing, the rebels seized control of the provincial capital of Porto Alegre on 20 September 1835. The local governor fled, while the rebels began demanding secession and independence.

As the uprising turned into a civil war, the rebels received assistance from the Uruguayan government of José Fructuoso Rivera who sought to form a political union with the separatist state. Attracted by the radical republicanism of the southern rebels, the Italian revolutionary Giuseppe Garibaldi also joined the fight and gained military experience that would later prove invaluable in the cause of Italian Unification.

The Ragamuffin War raged for ten years and caused the deaths of tens of thousands of people, making it both the longest war against the Imperial Brazilian government and also the second most costly in terms of casualties. The conflict was finally brought to an end with the signing of the Ponche Verde Treaty in 1845 that, along with granting a full amnesty for the rebels, introduced a 25% import tax on imported *charque*.

SEPTEMBER

21

1915

Cecil Chubb became the last private owner of Stonehenge after buying the Neolithic monument at auction.

Chubb grew up four miles away from the famous stones in the English village of Shrewton, where his father was the village saddler and harness maker. He won a place at a grammar school and later attended Christ's College, Cambridge, before becoming a barrister.

Chubb had amassed a considerable fortune by the time he attended an auction at the Palace Theatre in Salisbury on 21 September 1915. The company Knight Frank and Rutley auctioned Stonehenge on behalf of its former owners, the aristocratic Antrobus family, who had owned the stones and surrounding land for generations. Lieutenant Edmund Antrobus, the heir to the Baronetcy, was serving with the Grenadier Guards in Belgium when he was killed in action on 24 October 1914. His father, Sir Edmund Antrobus, the fourth Baronet, died just a few months later on 11 February 1915. With no surviving male heirs the line passed to the elder Edmund's brother Cosmo, who put Stonehenge up for auction.

According to Stonehenge's curator, Chubb had gone to the auction to buy a pair of curtains and claimed that he only bought the monument 'on a whim'. There is competing speculation that he may have bought the stones as a romantic gesture for his wife, or that he did so in order to stop a foreign bidder from taking ownership.

Whatever the reason for Chubb's purchase, on 26 October 1918 he gifted the monument to the nation. As part of the terms of the donation, he stipulated that local people should get in for free and that outsiders should pay no more than one shilling per visit. English Heritage, which now runs the site, claims that the current entry price is still within this limit due to wage inflation.

SEPTEMBER

22

1888

The first edition of the *National Geographic Magazine* was published by the National Geographic Society.

The National Geographic Society was established in Washington D.C. in January 1888. Founded by just thirty-three men, the Society's first President was the lawyer and financier Gardiner Greene Hubbard, whose lay interest in science and geography perfectly embodied the Society's creation 'for the increase and diffusion of geographical knowledge'.

Nine months after the Society's foundation, the first edition of its journal was sent to 165 charter members. Consisting mostly of short technical articles, the magazine struggled to increase its readership for the first few years of its existence. However, following the election of Alexander Graham Bell as President and the appointment of the new editor Gilbert H. Grosvenor, the early 1900s saw the magazine begin to focus more on pictorial content. Although criticised by some members of the Board of Managers for being 'unscientific', the increasing use of often pioneering photographs soon helped to secure a much wider audience.

The magazine was initially only available to members of the National Geographic Society, but can now be purchased on newsstands and through direct subscription around the world. The creation of nearly 40 different local-language editions has resulted in a global circulation of more than 6.5 million copies per month, reaching an estimated 60 million readers. Revenue from sales of the magazine help to fund scientific expeditions and scientific research as well as sponsor travelling exhibitions, making the National Geographic Society one of the largest non-profit scientific and educational organisations in the world.

SEPTEMBER

23

1338

The first recorded naval battle featuring artillery took place in the first naval engagement of the Hundred Years' War.

The Battle of Arnemuiden saw five slow but stable single-masted English cogs face 48 galleys of The Grand Army of the Sea. This huge French fleet had already sacked English coastal towns such as Portsmouth and Southampton in an attempt to cripple the English economy and stop Edward III's attempts to gain the French crown.

Edward relied on income from the valuable wool trade to ensure he could pay for his army and maintain the support of his allies on the continent. The five ships that sailed from England to the Flanders port of Arnemuiden were unloading this cargo when they were overwhelmed by the French fleet.

Realising that their best chance of avoiding capture was to put to sea again, the ships quickly left their moorings. Under the command of John Kingston on board the *Christopher*, the English then attempted to fight off the French. Four of the five ships were forced to adopt the established tactic of attempting to ram the sides of the opposing ships, but the *Christopher* was able to employ a new type of offensive: artillery.

The ship was equipped with three canons and one handgun and, against overwhelming numbers, the crew members were able to use these to hold off the enemy for much of the day. Nevertheless, Kingston was eventually forced to surrender. The French admirals Hugues Quiéret and Nicolas Béhuchet captured the five ships with their valuable cargo and executed the crews.

The French navy went on to dominate the Channel for almost two years before its decisive defeat at the Battle of Sluys on 24 June 1340, during which the English were able to recapture the *Christopher*.

SEPTEMBER

24

1789

The Judiciary Act was passed by the United States Congress and signed into law by President George Washington.

Article III of the United States Constitution created the Supreme Court, and stated that it would be vested with 'the judicial Power of the United States'. As it was to be the head of a federal court system, the Constitution further specified that the Supreme Court's composition was to be determined by Congress.

The Judiciary Act of 1789 was consequently adopted by the First United States Congress in late September, having been reported out of committee in June. The Act called for the court to consist of six judges, later to be known as justices, made up of one Chief Justice and five Associate Justices. Shortly after signing the Act, President Washington nominated the first six judges. Although all six were confirmed by the Senate two days later, Robert H. Harrison declined the appointment citing ill health and family commitments and so an alternative member had to be found.

In addition to establishing the composition of the Supreme Court, the Judiciary Act also created the Office of the Attorney General, whose role was to 'prosecute and conduct all suits in the Supreme Court' as the representative of the United States. Originally intended to be a part-time job for one person, the scope of the role quickly expanded. However, it didn't become a full-time position with the support of a newly-created Department of Justice until 1870.

The Supreme Court met for its first session in February 1790 in New York City's Royal Exchange Building. There were no cases to consider and so the court was adjourned until September. In contrast the Supreme Court now hears around 100 cases per term, drawn from the many thousands of requests that are made.

SEPTEMBER

25

1956

The world's first submarine transatlantic telephone cable system was inaugurated.

Known as Transatlantic No. 1, or TAT-1, the £120 million system actually consisted of two identical cables to allow transmission in each direction. Prompted by the successful installation of a submarine cable between Florida and Cuba in 1952, a consortium of the UK's General Post Office, the American Telephone and Telegraph Company, and the Canadian Overseas Telecommunications Corporation had agreed to investigate the feasibility of a transatlantic cable.

It was already possible to make a transatlantic telephone call when the 1,950 nautical mile long cable began to be laid in 1955. However, this involved numerous radio links to be booked in advance and was consequently an expensive method of communication that required significant advance planning.

Stretching from Oban in Scotland to Clarenville in Newfoundland, the new TAT-1 was able to carry 35 simultaneous telephone calls while a 36th channel provided an additional 22 telegraph lines. Calls from the UK were charged at £1 per minute, which was a significant saving compared to the radio alternative.

Having gone into operation almost as soon as the two ends were connected, TAT-1 went on to carry over 600 transatlantic calls in the first 24 hours of public service. In 1963, following the de-escalation of the Cuban Missile Crisis, TAT-1 also carried the Moscow-Washington hotline that linked the Kremlin to the White House.

TAT-1 was eventually retired in 1978, having been superseded by other transatlantic cables that were capable of transmitting a greater number of concurrent signals.

SEPTEMBER 26 1960

The first United States presidential debate took place between John F. Kennedy and Richard Nixon.

Political debates had taken place in the United States as far back as 1858's series of seven meetings between Senate candidates Abraham Lincoln and Stephen A. Douglas. Despite this, it wasn't until 1956 that university student Fred A. Kahn first suggested a national presidential debate. Nevertheless, it still took four years before Kennedy and Nixon met at the CBS studios in Chicago.

At the start of the election campaign Nixon had been the favourite to win. He had served for eight years as Eisenhower's vice president, whereas Kennedy had only served for one term as a Massachusetts senator. However, prior to the televised debate Nixon had spent two weeks in hospital after suffering an injury to his knee. Combined with an exhausting campaign schedule, he arrived for the debate looking much more drawn and tired than his opponent. Adding to the difference in the men's appearances on screen, Nixon turned down the offer of stage makeup whereas Kennedy opted for it. Nixon's appearance was reportedly so poor that, after the debate, his mother called him to ask if he was ill.

The debate was moderated by journalist Howard K. Smith and lasted for an hour. Polls showed that Kennedy's performance in front of an estimated 70 million television viewers had moved him slightly ahead in the race, while Nixon had fared better on the radio.

Over the next few weeks the candidates faced off in a further three debates, for which Nixon was both in better health and opted to wear makeup. The gap between the two men narrowed but, when the ballots from the 8 November election were counted, Kennedy emerged victorious with a popular vote majority of just 0.17%.

The shortest papacy in history ended after just twelve days when Pope Urban VII died, shortly after he introduced Europe's first smoking ban.

Giovanni Battista Castagna was elected as Pope on 15 September 1590. Despite his reign lasting for less than two weeks, he was responsible for introducing a range of financial reforms that benefited the poor. Ranging from bread subsidies to public works projects, these were partly funded through restrictions on luxury items and partly from his own pocket.

As well as these charitable acts, Urban VII was also responsible for Europe's first smoking ban. Tobacco had arrived in Europe less than a century earlier, and the new Pope threatened to excommunicate anyone who was caught 'chewing it, smoking it with a pipe or sniffing it in powdered form through the nose' in the porchway of, or inside, a church.

An earlier smoking ban had been introduced by the leaders of the Roman Catholic Church in Mexico in 1575, specifically prohibiting smoking inside churches. It was Urban VII's ban, however, that gained most attention due to the growing popularity of tobacco in Europe in the 16th century. The ban was later extended by Urban VIII in 1624 when he completely prohibited the use of snuff due to the sneezing it prompted resembling 'sexual ecstasy'.

Urban VII's ban on tobacco in churches and their porches stayed on the books until the early 18th century, far outlasting the Pope himself. Following his death from malaria, which it is believed he contracted within two days of his election as Pope, Urban VII was buried in the Vatican. His remains were later moved to the church of Santa Maria sopra Minerva, near the Pantheon in Rome.

William, Duke of Normandy, landed in England to begin the Norman Conquest.

Edward the Confessor died childless in January 1066, prompting a succession crisis that had a dramatic effect on the course of English history. William was a distant cousin of Edward and claimed that he had been promised him the throne of England in 1051. He further maintained that Harold Godwinson, the king's brother-in-law and the most powerful man in England after the king, had sworn in 1064 to support William's claim.

Shortly before he died, Edward is said to have instead entrusted his kingdom to Harold. At a meeting of the Witenagemot – the 'meeting of wise men' – on 6 January, Harold was elected king and his coronation as Harold II took place later the same day. Almost immediately after hearing this news, William began making plans to invade.

Meanwhile the Norwegian king Harald Hardrada also made preparations to seize the English throne. While Harold II waited on the south coast for the expected invasion by William, a fleet of approximately 300 Norwegian ships landed in the north east where they joined forces with Harold's brother Tostig and defeated an English army at Fulford.

Receiving news that the city of York had also been taken, Harold marched his army to Stamford Bridge where the English repelled the invaders on 25 September. Three days later, William's fleet of around 7,000 troops and cavalry landed unopposed at Pevensey on the south coast. Although exhausted from the Battle of Stamford Bridge, Harold II had no choice but to march his troops 250 miles to meet the Normans. On 14 October they fought the Battle of Hastings.

SEPTEMBER

29

1829

The Metropolitan Police, which is often considered to be the first modern police force, began operating in London.

Informally known as 'the Met', the Metropolitan Police Act 1829 established the first structured system of law enforcement. Policing had previously been the responsibility of unpaid parish constables, although paid 'thief-takers' were sometimes employed by the victims of crime to catch criminals.

The appointment of Sir Robert Peel as Home Secretary in 1822 brought about the reinvigoration of a committee tasked to investigate the current system of policing. Peel immediately acted upon the committee's findings, distilling the key aspects of his approach into a series of 'Peelian principles' that involved the payment of police officers who were organised along civilian lines.

Peel's ideas for the system of policing were approved by Parliament in the Metropolitan Police Act, and Royal Assent was granted on 19 June 1829. The 895 constables of the new force, nicknamed 'Peelers' or 'Bobbies' after their founder, were responsible for law enforcement and public order within a seven-mile radius of Charing Cross. They were overseen by a progressing hierarchy of Sergeants, Inspectors, Superintendents and two Commissioners who reported directly to Peel himself.

Deliberately given blue uniforms to distinguish them from the red used by the military, the first police officers were equipped with only a wooden truncheon and a ratcheted rattle to raise the alarm. Despite these attempts to avoid the image of a totalitarian police force, some members of the public argued that the Met was a threat to civil liberties. Within a decade, however, the force had begun to prove itself, and its powers were increased.

The Battle of the Baggage saw the defeat of an army from the powerful Umayyad Caliphate by Turgesh forces.

The Umayyads had seized the region of Transoxiana, now in northern Afghanistan, in the early 700s. They were unpopular rulers, and by 720 the native Iranian and Turkic populations had begun to revolt with the support of the nearby Turgesh kingdom.

Over the next two decades the Umayyads faced a number of attacks and revolts in Transoxiana. In 724 they were forced to retreat across the river Jaxartes in the Farghana Valley, in a defeat known as the Day of Thirst. Four years later another uprising forced the Caliphate out of even more of Transoxiana.

Further revolts in the early 730s led to the appointment of the Umayyad governor Asad ibn Abdallah al-Qasri, who set about stamping out opposition. Having successfully halted the revolts, in 737 Asad turned his attention to capturing the principality of Khuttal where the inhabitants had sided with the rebels. Initial victories soon turned sour, however, when the Turgesh ruler sent his forces against the Umayyads.

Asad had time to send his baggage train of valuables looted from Khuttal ahead of his army, but when his men saw the Turgesh troops they fled for the River Oxus. The Turgesh soon caught up with the retreating Umayyads and, having crossed the river, attacked their camp. After withdrawing overnight, the next morning the Turgesh turned their attention to the baggage train, which they easily captured after overwhelming the train's defenders. Although the Turgesh were later crushed by the Umayyad regime, the Caliphate had lost direct control over the region and laid the foundation for their overthrow at the hands of the Abbasid Revolution a decade later.

OCTOBER

OCTOBER
1
1949

Mao Zedong, the Chairman of the Communist Party of China, declared the establishment of the People's Republic of China.

The Chinese Communists in the People's Liberation Army had been fighting the second stage of a long and costly civil war against the Nationalist forces of Chiang Kai-shek, known as the Kuomintang, since shortly after the end of the Second World War. The first stage had been suspended in 1937 in order to focus a combined Chinese army against the Japanese, but relations between the two Chinese contingents had remained poor.

Even before the Japanese surrender, the Kuomintang and the PLA had begun to receive support from the USA and the USSR respectively. In the aftermath of the Second World War this division continued until the two Chinese armies resumed full-scale war on 26 June 1946. A quarter of China's land area and a third of the population were already under Communist control, and the PLA soon expanded to over 1.2 million troops supported by a militia of almost double that.

With the resumption of the Civil War, the Communist Party itself promised land reform to the peasantry. In return for supporting the PLA, peasants were told that they would be given possession of their own land instead of needing to rent it from unscrupulous landlords. This secured more support for the Communists and, combined with the effective 'passive defence' strategy, led to the gradual expansion of Communist control and a Kuomintang retreat.

By October 1949 almost all of mainland China was under Communist control and Mao Zedong declared the foundation of the People's Republic of China. Chiang Kai-shek and the retreating Kuomintang fled to the island of Taiwan in December.

OCTOBER

2

1919

United States President Woodrow Wilson suffered a stroke that left him paralysed on his left-hand side.

Following the conclusion of the Treaty of Versailles in June 1919, Wilson returned to the United States. There he found stiff opposition to the treaty from Republican and Irish Catholic Democratic senators. Determined to convince the public of the importance of ratifying the treaty and joining the League of Nations, the President embarked on a national speaking tour in September.

Wilson was exhausted before the presidential train even departed Washington yet stuck to the punishing schedule for 22 days before his private secretary, Joseph Tumulty, announced the tour's cancellation on 26 September. Although he publicly blamed 'a nervous reaction in his digestive organs', the President had in fact been suffering from splitting headaches and uncontrollable twitching in his facial muscles.

Wilson returned to the White House to rest on 28 September but, just four days later, fell unconscious in his private quarters. Although the exact details are unclear, within a few minutes his wife Edith had called for his doctor, Cary T. Grayson. Having attended the patient, Grayson is reported to have remarked, 'My God, the president is paralysed.'

A stroke had left Wilson paralysed on his left-hand side, and with a visual impairment. With the President confined to his bed, Mrs Wilson began what she referred to as her 'stewardship'. For a number of months she oversaw all communication to and from her husband, giving her unprecedented control over the direction of both domestic and foreign policy. Edith Wilson has consequently been referred to by her biographer as the first female president.

OCTOBER

3

1918

Tsar Boris III of Bulgaria came to the throne following his father's abdication.

Boris III became Tsar of Bulgaria four days after his father, Ferdinand I, signed the Armistice of Thessalonica with the Allied Powers at the end of the First World War. In order to save the monarchy he handed power to Boris, who had gained great respect from both Bulgarian and German troops during the First World War.

The new Tsar found himself leading a country that faced enormous economic and political problems as a result of the war and the subsequent Treaty of Neuilly that was signed in November 1919. Bulgaria was forced to hand territory to both Greece and the newly-formed Yugoslavia, resulting in approximately 300,000 Bulgarians finding themselves in new countries. The army was also reduced and the country was forced to pay reparations.

The first decade of Boris' reign saw tensions between the monarchy and the powerful forces of both the Agrarian Union and the Communist Party. By the end of 1935 he had begun to secure his hold on power and establish the 'King's Government' in which he personally dominated the political system.

The outbreak of the Second World War was followed a year later by Bulgaria allying itself with the Axis powers in an attempt to win back territories lost at the end of the First World War. However, Boris refused to lend unconditional military support to Germany and infuriated Hitler with his refusal to declare war on the USSR. In early 1943 Boris angered Hitler again by refusing to deport Bulgarian Jews. He insisted that they should stay in Bulgaria where they were needed for labouring tasks, saving approximately 50,000 lives. Boris died of apparent heart failure later that year, on 28 August.

OCTOBER

4

1936

The Battle of Cable Street saw demonstrators block a march by Oswald Mosley's British Union of Fascists.

Oswald Mosley had formed the British Union of Fascists, known as the BUF, in 1932. In the 1920s he had served as a Conservative Member of Parliament before crossing the floor to the Labour Party. By the start of the 1930s, however, he had formed his own party that was strongly influenced by the ideas of Fascism.

The presence of Nazi sympathisers within the party meant that the BUF became increasingly anti-Semitic, while anti-fascist opposition began to mount. When Mosley proposed that his uniformed Blackshirts march through the East End of London, anti-fascists quickly petitioned the Home Secretary to ban the march.

Unwilling to ban the march, the government instead provided 7,000 police officers to clear the route for the BUF. Yet when the march began on 4 October, the 3,000 Blackshirts and their police escort were massively outnumbered by anti-fascist protesters drawn from a variety of political and religious groups.

As the police attempted to clear a route through the improvised barricades, violence erupted. The worst fighting took place on Cable Street where protesters attacked the heavy-handed police with improvised weapons. Cable Street is situated in the Whitechapel area of East London, and had a large Jewish population at the time. Unable to clear the route, Mosley and the BUF were eventually persuaded by Sir Philip Game, the Commissioner of Police, to abandon the march and leave the area.

Although the Battle of Cable Street was a success for the anti-fascists in the short-term, membership of the BUF grew and the violent 'Mile End Pogrom' took place a week later.

OCTOBER

5

1936

The Jarrow March departed the north east of England with a petition calling on Parliament in London to respond to the unemployment crisis that was crippling the community.

The Tyneside town of Jarrow had been the site for Palmer's Shipyard that was responsible for a large proportion of the town's employment. Having operated since 1851, the yard was sold in 1933 due to a collapse in the British shipbuilding industry and the impact of the Great Depression.

The shipyard closed shortly afterwards and, although American entrepreneur T. Vosper Salt proposed turning the site into a steelworks, he was forced to withdraw after members of the British Iron and Steel Federation lobbied to make the project unfeasible.

The collapse of the steelwork plan was a devastating blow to the people of Jarrow, where unemployment had hit 70% in the months following the closure of the shipyard. In response David Riley, the chairman of Jarrow Borough Council, proposed a march to London in order to raise the profile of the economic disaster.

The marchers had the full support of their local Labour MP, Ellen Wilkinson, and secured funding for the march from the local community including all the political parties. Over 1,200 men volunteered to take part in the march, of which 200 were chosen to take the petition to London. They marched for 25 days and received a generally positive reception wherever they passed through.

Arriving in London on 31 October the marchers entrusted the petition of 11,000 names to Wilkinson, who presented it in the House of Commons on 4 November. It achieved no immediate response from the government, and the marchers returned home feeling that they had failed.

Germantown was founded in the Pennsylvania Colony by immigrant Quaker and Mennonite families.

Large numbers of German nationals began moving to the British colonies in America in the 1670s and, by the early 1680s, they had established a notable presence in the states of Pennsylvania, New York, and Virginia.

George Fox, the founder of the Quaker movement, had visited a community of Mennonites in Germany's Rhine valley the previous decade. His companion, William Penn, convinced thirteen of the families to join his 'Holy Experiment' in the newly-established Province of Pennsylvania. Penn, who had been granted the land by King Charles II of England, sought to establish a community based on religious freedom.

Thirteen families of German Quakers from the area around Krefeld arrived in Pennsylvania in the summer of 1683. Francis Daniel Pastorius, the agent of the Frankfurt Land Company, negotiated the purchase of 15,000 acres of land from Penn himself and soon set about developing a settlement. On 6 October the thirteen families from Krefeld founded Germantown, the first notable German settlement in North America.

Having survived the harsh winter, the first Germantown settlers were joined by more immigrant families the following spring. Less than six years later Germantown was incorporated as a borough, by which time it had already established itself as the birthplace of the anti-slavery movement.

Germantown was absorbed into the city of Philadelphia through the Act of Consolidation of 1854, but many buildings have survived and continue to be important landmarks in the area.

OCTOBER

7

1879

The Dual Alliance was formed by Germany and Austria-Hungary.

A series of three wars in less than a decade had seen the creation of a unified Germany directed by the *Realpolitik* of Chancellor Otto von Bismarck. Keen to consolidate the newly-united country, he turned to diplomacy in an attempt to ensure the status quo in Europe.

Despite forming the *Dreikaiserbund* with Austria-Hungary and Russia in 1873, a power struggle over territory in the Balkans from 1875-78 led to Bismarck playing the role of 'the honest broker' at the Congress of Berlin to resolve tensions between his allies. The congress was a diplomatic defeat for Russia and left the *Dreikaiserbund* in tatters, leading Bismarck to negotiate the new Dual Alliance with Austria-Hungary.

Although specific details of the Dual Alliance were kept secret until 1888, it was a defensive alliance in which both countries agreed to assist each other if they were attacked by Russia. Bismarck and Austria-Hungary's Secretary of State, Count Julius Andrássy, also agreed to remain neutral in the case of an attack from another country in what is known as benevolent neutrality.

The announcement of the alliance surprised some observers, who noted the threat that the burgeoning German nationalism posed to the Habsburg Empire. The Austro-Prussian War had only been fought between the two countries thirteen years earlier, but the relatively generous peace terms that had been agreed in its wake left the door open to future cooperation. This, combined with Germany and Austria's shared linguistic and cultural connections, ensured the Dual Alliance lasted until the end of the First World War.

OCTOBER

8

1480

The Great Stand on the Ugra River marked the start of the decline of the Great Horde.

The first half of the 15th century saw the once-powerful Golden Horde disintegrate in to separate khanates. The steppe remnant, known as the Great Horde, was ruled by Akhmat Khan who grew increasingly frustrated by Grand Prince Ivan III of Muscovy who refused to pay the customary tribute.

Ivan's rule as Grand Prince of Moscow had begun in 1462, and the early years of his reign saw him bring several territories under the direct control of Moscow. His refusal to pay tribute to Akhmat from 1476 was significant as it showed that he no longer recognised the Horde's authority over the area.

While Akhmat formed an alliance with Casimir IV, Grand Duke of Lithuania, Ivan made his own alliance with Crimea. Determined to re-establish control, Akhmat prepared to invade Moscow in 1480. Knowing that the best chance of defending the city was by stopping the Horde from crossing the rivers that separated their realms, by 6 October the Muscovite army had established positions along the Ugra River 150 miles southwest of Moscow.

While Akhmat waited in vain for his Lithuanian allies to arrive, the two sides shot little more than light explosives and insults at each other. When the Horde finally attempted to cross the river on 8 October it was repeatedly repulsed. With winter fast approaching, Ivan eventually began to move his troops north and east. Meanwhile, Akhmat and the army of the Great Horde withdrew south. The two withdrawals were independent, but they signalled the end of the Great Stand on the Ugra River, as well as a marked decline of Tatar-Mongol influence over Russia.

The Prague Astronomical Clock, the oldest surviving example in the world, was first recorded in a medieval document.

Known as the Orloj, the astronomical clock was designed and built by the Imperial clockmaker Mikuláš of Kadaň and Charles University professor Jan Šindel. Consisting of three main components, the astronomical dial and the mechanical clock itself were first noted in a document on 9 October 1410. The third component – a calendar dial – was added around 1490 when the façade was decorated with additional gothic sculptures.

One of the most famous features of the clock is the hourly 'Walk of the Apostles' in which carved figures of the Apostles appear in procession at two windows above the main clock face. These were added to the Orloj during a major repair on the clock in 1787-1791, while some of the other moving allegorical statues such as Death had been added beforehand. Further statues were added in later years, including the golden crowing rooster that didn't appear until 1866.

The clock is a masterpiece of medieval engineering. It also provides useful evidence of the European view of the universe at the time, since the Earth is positioned at the centre. Against this background are the four key moving parts of the astronomical dial: the zodiacal ring, the Old Czech time scale, and two clock hands representing the Sun and the Moon and their position on the elliptic. The half-black, half-silver Moon even contains a mechanism to show the lunar phases.

The Orloj suffered serious damage in the Second World War when German forces attempted to suppress the Prague Uprising of May 1945. Restoration successfully returned the clock to working order in 1948, since when it has been renovated another two times.

OCTOBER

10

1957

US President Dwight D. Eisenhower apologised to Ghanaian finance minister Komla Agbeli Gbedemah after he was refused service in a Delaware restaurant.

Ghana was the first Sub-Saharan black African nation to gain independence from colonial rule on 6 March 1957. Komla Agbeli Gbedemah had held the position of Minister of Finance in Dr Kwame Nkrumah's government since 1954, and he soon began seeking outside funding for the ambitious Akosombo Dam that was intended to supercharge the country's economy.

In October 1957 Gbedemah visited the United States in an attempt to secure money for the project. Aluminium companies were interested in using power from the hydroelectric dam to process bauxite, but they needed reassurances about the cost of electricity. This was dependent on how much foreign investment could be secured to fund the dam's construction.

Having stopped at a Howard Johnson restaurant in the Delaware city of Dover, Gbedemah and his secretary ordered a glass of orange juice. After serving their drinks in takeaway containers, the waitress told them that 'colored people are not allowed to eat in here'.

Despite being shown proof that Gbedemah was the finance minister of Ghana, the manager refused to compromise. Gbedemah reportedly left the restaurant saying that 'the [white] people here are of a lower social status than I am but they can drink here and we can't. You can keep the orange juice and the change, but this is not the last you have heard of this.'

When news of the incident reached the President, Eisenhower apologised to Gbedemah and invited him to breakfast at the White House where he warmed to the idea of the Akosombo Dam project.

OCTOBER

11

1975

The late-night American television show *Saturday Night Live* was broadcast for the first time.

Saturday Night Live was originally known as *NBC's Saturday Night* to avoid any confusion with the ABC show *Saturday Night Live with Howard Cosell*. Having been developed to fill the gap left by Johnny Carson's request to stop showing reruns of *The Tonight Show* at the weekend, the new show was intended to be a variety show featuring a mix of comedy sketches, political satire, and guest musical performances.

Dick Ebersol had been brought in by NBC president Herbert Schlosser to create the show, and he in turn approached Canadian television producer Lorne Michaels to oversee the show. Together they refined the show's concept and recruited young comedians to join the cast who would later become household names. Cast members such as Dan Aykroyd, John Belushi and Chevy Chase had been recruited from The Second City improvisational theatre troupe and *The National Lampoon Radio Hour*. The original theme music was composed by Howard Shore, who has since become a renowned film composer and Academy Award winner.

The very first episode was hosted by stand-up comedian George Carlin and featured music from Janis Ian and Billy Preston. Comedy sketches featuring the cast, known as the 'Not Ready for Prime Time Players' were not a prominent feature, although the episode did begin with a cold open sketch which has become a tradition.

The show was renamed to *Saturday Night Live* in March 1977, having gradually developed the format and built a dedicated following. It has continued to be broadcast from Studio 8H at 30 Rockefeller Center ever since.

OCTOBER

12

1915

British nurse Edith Cavell was executed by a German firing squad during the First World War.

Edith Louisa Cavell had worked as a nurse in England before taking up the position of matron at the Berkendael Institute in Brussels. This was Belgium's first nurse training school, and Cavell soon began to bring about dramatic improvements in the standard of nursing in the country.

Although she was visiting her family in Norfolk when the First World War broke out, Edith Cavell soon returned to Belgium where she began working in a Red Cross hospital in occupied Brussels. She and her nurses treated any injured soldier, irrespective of which side they were fighting on, but Cavell soon joined an underground network that helped British, French and Belgian soldiers escape to the neutral Netherlands.

Having grown suspicious of her activities, the occupying German authorities arrested Cavell in early August 1915. After being kept in Saint-Gilles prison, she and 34 other people connected to the network were tried at court martial on 5 October. She had already made a full confession, but was found guilty of treason under the terms of German military law and sentenced to death.

International law usually protected medical personnel, but the fact that Cavell was helping members of the military meant that this was forfeited. Nevertheless, her sentence was met with outrage both at home and in neutral countries. Despite attempts to secure amnesty, Edith Cavell was executed by firing squad on 12 October alongside her fellow defendant Philippe Baucq. The previous night she had told a visiting chaplain, 'Patriotism is not enough. I must have no hatred or bitterness towards anyone.'

OCTOBER

13

54

The Roman Emperor Claudius died, supposedly after being poisoned.

Claudius was the grandson of Marc Antony and the great-great-grandnephew of Gaius Julius Caesar on his mother's side. His father was the legal stepson of his mother's second husband, Emperor Augustus. However, his physical disabilities that some argue were related to cerebral palsy, saw him disowned by his mother and raised by his grandmother who employed the historian Livy as his tutor.

Claudius subsequently spent a number of years as an historian, despite making various attempts to enter public office. Under Caligula he was finally appointed co-consul and, after Caligula's assassination in 41 CE, was proclaimed as the new Emperor. It was Claudius who was responsible for expanding the Roman Empire to Britannia in the north, with the Emperor himself crossing the Channel in 43 CE to witness the attack on modern-day Colchester.

Claudius' fourth wife, Agrippina the Younger, was one of the few remaining descendants of Emperor Augustus. This made her twelve-year-old son from her previous marriage one of the last male heirs of the imperial family. Claudius adopted him and proclaimed him joint heir with his own nine-year-old son Britannicus.

The ancient sources generally claim that Claudius was killed on the orders of Agrippina. These same sources state that the Emperor was poisoned, although who administered the poison - and on whose orders - continues to be fiercely debated by scholars.

Claudius was succeeded by his adopted son – Agrippina's child from a previous marriage – who became known as Emperor Nero. Four months after Nero became Emperor, Britannicus also died of suspected poisoning.

A U-2 spy plane captured images of the construction of a missile site on Cuba, triggering the Cuban Missile Crisis.

Under the leadership of Fidel Castro, Cuba had forged links with the communist government of the USSR. Angered by the presence of an increasingly socialist country so close to the United States, the Kennedy administration launched the failed Bay of Pigs Invasion, but this only further strengthened Cuba's relationship with the Soviets.

By 1962, the Cold War had become a bitter fight for technical and nuclear supremacy. Fuelled by tensions over a perceived 'missile gap' between the USA and the USSR, the USA had placed medium-range ballistic missiles in Turkey that were capable of hitting the Soviets before they had chance to react. When combined with other factors, Soviet premier Nichita Khrushchev decided the best course of action was to place his own missiles on Cuba.

Soviet specialists began to arrive in Cuba to begin construction from July 1962. Although the USA quickly began to suspect that the Soviets were building missile bases, they didn't take any action beyond ordering U-2 spy plane missions. However, in the aftermath of two international incidents involving U-2s, US reconnaissance flights over Cuba were reduced to avoid prompting a confrontation.

This coincided with the arrival of the Soviet missiles themselves. Consequently, it wasn't until 14 October, five days after the U-2 missions resumed, that the extent of the missile development was revealed. The photographs from Major Richard Heyser's U-2 were reviewed by the CIA on the 15 October and, the following morning, President Kennedy was informed of the presence of nuclear missile bases on Cuba. The next thirteen days became known as the Cuban Missile Crisis.

OCTOBER

15

1764

Edward Gibbon first considered writing *The History of the Decline and Fall of the Roman Empire* while a group of friars sang vespers in the Temple of Jupiter.

Gibbon's six volume history traces the collapse of the Roman Empire from the rule of the Five Good Emperors until the end of Byzantium. Gibbon, like Machiavelli who had coined the term over two centuries earlier, believed that Rome had reached its peak during the period from the Emperor Nerva to Marcus Aurelius and that a decline in civic virtue had led to the Empire being gradually overrun by barbarians.

Having previously served with the South Hampshire militia during the Seven Years' War, the 25-year-old Gibbon was in the midst of the Grand Tour when he arrived in Rome in October 1764. Known as the 'Capitoline vision', Gibbon later recounted the inspiration for his *magnum opus* in his autobiography:

'It was at Rome, on the fifteenth of October 1764, as I sat musing amidst the ruins of the Capitol, while the barefooted friars were singing Vespers in the Temple of Jupiter, that the idea of writing the decline and fall of the City first started to my mind.'

The first volume of *The History of the Decline and Fall of the Roman Empire* was published on 17 February 1776. It was immediately greeted with praise and made Gibbon a celebrity. The sixth and final volume finally reached the press over a decade later, in May 1788, six years before his death. Gibbon's extensive use of primary sources, and the relative objectivity of his writing, has had a lasting impact on the methodology of historians. Consequently, he has been called the first 'modern historian of ancient Rome' though others have gone further by describing him as truly the first modern historian.

OCTOBER

16

1846

The first well-publicised public demonstration of inhaled ether anaesthesia was given at the Massachusetts General Hospital.

Herbal remedies have been used for pain relief and, in extreme cases, to bring about unconsciousness since antiquity. However, it wasn't until the 19th century that scientific developments directly impacted modern general anaesthetic techniques.

In the 18th century Joseph Priestley's discovery of nitrous oxide led to research by scientist Humphry Davy that identified its analgesic effects and potential for use in surgery. Known colloquially as 'laughing gas', nitrous oxide was later adopted by American dentist Horace Wells to perform painless extractions. However, a public demonstration of the technique at the Massachusetts General Hospital went wrong when the patient cried out in pain.

Around the same time as nitrous oxide was being employed as an analgesic, experiments were taking place with diethyl ether. William T. G. Morton had worked as a dentist in Wells' surgery and news of his painless work on music teacher Eben Frost convinced Boston surgeon Henry Jacob Bigelow to invite him to demonstrate ether as a surgical anaesthetic.

The demonstration took place in the amphitheatre of the Massachusetts General Hospital, the same place as Wells' failed demonstration just a few months earlier. After Morton administered the ether to patient Edward Abbott, surgeon John Collins Warren removed a tumour from his neck. On regaining consciousness Abbott stated it felt only as if his neck had been scratched.

News of the successful demonstration spread fast, and doctors across the world soon began to adopt similar anaesthetic techniques. The amphitheatre was subsequently named the Ether Dome.

OCTOBER

17

1933

Albert Einstein moved to the United States following Hitler's appointment as Chancellor of Germany earlier that year.

Einstein, who was Jewish, was undertaking a visiting professorship at the California Institute of Technology in Pasadena when Adolf Hitler was appointed Chancellor on 30 January 1933. With the Nazis expanding their power in Germany, Einstein chose not to go home when he returned to Europe in March. When his ship docked at the Belgian port of Antwerp on 28 March he renounced his German citizenship by handing in his passport at the German Consulate.

The Nazis seized Einstein's cottage and converted it to a Hitler Youth camp. Meanwhile the government barred Jews from teaching at universities, and the German Student Union burned his books. With a bounty on his head, Einstein stayed in Belgium for a few months before moving to Britain where he was guarded by his friend, naval officer Commander Oliver Locker-Lampson.

While a refugee in Britain, Einstein lobbied foreign governments and universities to find employment for former German Jewish scientists. Many positions were found around Europe with over 1,000 German Jewish scientists being placed in Turkish universities alone, but Einstein himself was refused British citizenship and instead accepted an offer from the Princeton Institute for Advanced Study in New Jersey. He departed England on 17 October 1933.

Although Einstein initially intended to only stay in the United States for a short time, in 1935 he chose to seek American citizenship which he gained in 1940. By this time he had warned President Roosevelt about the danger of Hitler developing nuclear weapons, and encouraged the United States to begin its own research.

OCTOBER

18

1565

European and Japanese naval forces fought for the first time at the Battle of Fukuda Bay.

Portuguese traders on board a Chinese ship belonging to a Chinese pirate were the first to reach Japan when they were shipwrecked on the island of Tanegashima in 1543. The discovery of Japan provided the Portuguese with a new market for their goods, as well as potential converts for Jesuit missionaries.

Having established trade to the already-warring states with the introduction of the arquebus, an early portable gun, the Portuguese soon set about finding suitable harbours for their large carracks. Known by the Japanese as 'black ships' due to the pitch painted on their hulls, they initially found harbour at the port of Hirado on the island of Kyushu, ruled by the feudal lord Matsura Takanobu.

Although Takanobu was keen to welcome the Portuguese traders, he was less enthusiastic about the Jesuit missionaries who travelled with them. Prompted by the destruction of Buddhist imagery, he expelled the missionaries in 1558. With tensions heightened, the Portuguese soon began to look for alternative ports.

By 1562 they had found a suitable harbour in territory controlled by Takanobu's rival, Ōmura Sumitada. In revenge, Takanobu conspired with visiting Sakai merchants to launch a flotilla against a carrack under the command of João Pereira that had moored at the Ōmura bay of Fukuda.

The Japanese attack on 18 October saw some troops successfully board the carrack, but they were turned back when an accompanying Portuguese galleon opened fire on the fragile Japanese ships. The Hirado forces lost over 70 men, and more than 200 were injured. In comparison, only eight Portuguese lives were lost.

The Roman Republic defeated Carthage at the Battle of Zama, effectively ending the Second Punic War.

The Second Punic War is famed for the Carthaginian commander Hannibal leading his troops and elephants over the Alps to face the Roman armies. After seventeen years, the war was finally brought to an end with the decisive victory of the Roman general and consul Scipio Africanus over Hannibal at the Battle of Zama.

Scipio proposed an invasion of the Carthaginian Empire itself, and gradually built a force of volunteers to mount the offensive. These Roman forces secured victories at the battles of both Utica and the Great Plains in 203 BCE, resulting in an armistice between the two sides and Hannibal being called back to Carthage. However, the Carthaginians soon broke the armistice, and the stage was set for the decisive Battle of Zama in modern day Tunisia.

Hannibal arrived first and arranged his army, consisting of 36,000 infantry, 4,000 cavalry, and 80 war elephants, in three lines. Scipio's smaller force of 29,000 infantry and 6,100 cavalry was arranged in three broken lines, with gaps between groups of soldiers hidden from the Carthaginians by loose collections of other troops.

Hannibal opened the battle by sending his war elephants at the opposing Roman forces. The Romans blew loud horns to confuse the elephants, and then channelled them through the prepared gaps in the lines and away from the battle. Meanwhile the Roman cavalry drove the Carthaginian cavalry from the field and, later, returned to attack Hannibal's troops from the rear. Hannibal and many of his men managed to escape, but up to 20,000 others were killed. The ensuing peace treaty crippled Carthage and paved the way for the Roman victory in the third and final Punic War fifty years later.

OCTOBER

20

1740

Maria Theresa inherited the Austrian throne, prompting the War of the Austrian Succession.

Maria Theresa was the eldest daughter of the Holy Roman Emperor Charles VI, who had issued the Pragmatic Sanction to ensure that a female heir could inherit his possessions. This superseded an existing agreement that would have made his niece – and her husband – the heir presumptive, and it took Charles ten years to convince the European powers to agree to his edict.

Even before Charles' death, some states had begun to privately rescind their support for the Pragmatic Sanction. Despite this Charles continued to focus on seeking European acceptance of a female heir rather than preparing his daughter for the role. He similarly made no attempt to ensure the imperial treasury or army were in a strong enough state to withstand challenges to her position. Consequently, when he died on 20 October 1740, Maria Theresa inherited an almost bankrupt government that she had little idea how to run.

Despite her father's attempts to avoid a succession crisis, France, Prussia, Bavaria, and Saxony almost immediately contested Maria Theresa's claim. Charles Albert, the Elector of Bavaria, was married to Maria Theresa's disinherited cousin Maria Amalia and had secured the support of France for his 'just claims'. However, it wasn't until December that any action was taken against Maria Theresa when Frederick II of Prussia invaded the prosperous Habsburg-controlled province of Silesia.

The war continued for almost eight years, and finally ended with the signing of the Treaty of Aix-la-Chapelle in 1748. This confirmed Maria Theresa as Archduchess of Austria and Queen of Hungary, but left Silesia under the control of Prussia.

OCTOBER
21
1966

116 children and 28 adults were killed when a colliery spoil tip above the Welsh village of Aberfan collapsed.

At 9.15am, approximately 150,000 cubic meters of mining debris from waste tip No. 7 surged down the mountainside, of which 40,000 cubic metres swept in to the village. Within seconds a large area of the village was inundated with a thick slurry up to 12 metres deep.

A farm, and twenty houses on Moy Road, disappeared under the surging waste. However, the most devastation was wrought on Pantglas Junior School. The landslide smashed into the school and filled the classrooms, which were on the side of the school facing the mountain, with rubble. The children and teachers, who had only arrived a few minutes earlier, were buried alive. Over half the children enrolled at the school died.

Hundreds of people including parents, miners and rescue workers struggled to rescue those trapped beneath the waste. Their efforts were hampered by the flow of water and mud that continued to spill from the tip, as well as the lack of space in which to work due to the large number of people who subsequently travelled to the village in an attempt to help.

The National Coal Board and its chairman, Alfred Lord Robens, were heavily criticised in the aftermath of the disaster. Lord Robens didn't go to the scene of the disaster until the evening of the next day, and claimed that the landslide was caused by 'natural unknown springs', despite evidence that the NCB was fully aware that the ground beneath the tips was unstable.

The remaining tips were only removed after government intervention, while the public donated over a million pounds to a disaster relief fund that was later embroiled in controversy.

OCTOBER
22
1797

Frenchman André-Jacques Garnerin performed the first high-altitude parachute descent.

Garnerin had a background in physics and, after studying under the balloon pioneer Jacques Charles, became a keen proponent of the use of balloons by the military during the French Revolutionary Wars. Although he was captured and imprisoned by the British, on his release Garnerin resumed his interest in balloons. He soon began practical experiments with rigid frame parachutes which had been successfully demonstrated by fellow Frenchman Louis-Sébastien Lenormand in 1783.

Lenormand had demonstrated his device by jumping from the tower of the observatory in Montpellier, and only ever intended his parachute to help people escape from burning buildings. While being held as a prisoner of war Garnerin adapted Lenormand's idea to devise a parachute that could help a military balloonist evade capture.

On 22 October 1797 Garnerin attached his parachute beneath a balloon that he launched from Parc Monceau in Paris. The device was closed like an umbrella as it ascended, and Garnerin rode in a basket underneath. When the balloon reached an altitude of approximately 3,000 feet or 1,000 metres, he detached the parachute from the balloon.

As the balloon, free of its load, accelerated upwards the parachute and its passenger began to fall. Nevertheless, within just a few seconds the canopy expanded. Although the parachute did succeed in slowing the decent, the lack of a vent in the material caused violent oscillations that almost threw the inventor from the basket. He landed safely to a hero's welcome, however, and was later appointed the Official Aeronaut of France.

OCTOBER

23

1911

Italian pilot Captain Carlo Piazza made the first use of an aircraft in wartime during the Italo-Turkish War.

The Italian government of Prime Minister Giovanni Giolitti launched its invasion of Libya in order to formalise its influence in the provinces of Tripolitana and Cyrenaica amidst the declining power of the Ottoman Empire. Having sent an ultimatum to the Ottoman government that was not accepted in full, war was declared on 29 September 1911.

Meanwhile, Carlo Piazza had formally qualified as a pilot in April of the same year, and soon took control of the Royal Italian Army air detachment having proved himself as a talented racing pilot. When the Italo-Turkish War broke out later that year, the Italian military transported its entire fleet of nine aircraft to Tripoli following the prediction of aviation theorist Giulio Douhet that aircraft would cause significant problems for the enemy.

Having arrived in Libya by steamship, the Italian aircraft were brought on shore after the 20,000 ground troops began disembarking their ships on 10 October. The Italians soon found that the Ottoman defence was stronger than they had expected and, during a standoff near Benghazi, Piazza made history's first reconnaissance flight when he observed the Turkish lines from a Blériot XI aircraft. This type of machine, powered by a 25-horsepower, three-cylinder engine, had famously made the first flight across the English Channel in a heavier-than-air aircraft in 1909.

Barely a week after the first wartime flight, the first ever aerial bombing occurred when Italian Lieutenant Giulio Gavotti dropped four grenades from his Taube monoplane. Later in the conflict, the Turkish military was the first to shoot down an aircraft with rifle fire.

World-renowned escapologist Harry Houdini performed his final show.

Houdini started his magic career in 1891, but his popularity only rose after he began focusing on escapology on the advice of vaudeville theatre owner Martin Beck. Within just a few years he was regularly appearing in both the United States and Europe, and had begun to devise increasingly challenging escape scenarios that are still performed today.

Having spent most of his career in vaudeville, in 1926 Houdini teamed up with notable theatre manager L. Lawrence Weber to stage his first full evening show. Billed as '3 Shows In One', Houdini performed magic and escapes before then demonstrating and exposing the methods used by fraudulent spirit mediums.

Houdini broke his ankle during a show in mid-October. He nevertheless continued the tour, and was visited in his dressing room by three students whilst in Montreal on 22 October. The details of the meeting are unclear, but the most common account says that at one point Houdini was repeatedly punched in the stomach by one of the students to test his ability to withstand such blows. This was despite him not being prepared due to lying down to rest his ankle.

Although left in great pain, Houdini performed his remaining shows in Montreal and travelled to Detroit on 24 October. A doctor who examined him at the Garrick Theatre found him running a fever of 104°F (40°C) and diagnosed acute appendicitis. Houdini nevertheless took to the stage that night, but was unable to complete the show. He was later taken to Detroit's Grace Hospital for surgery but his appendix had already burst, leaving him with peritonitis. Houdini died a few days later, on 31 October.

OCTOBER
25
1940

Benjamin Oliver Davis Sr. became the first African-American general in the United States Army.

Davis was born in Washington D.C. and, although his army records and gravestone claim that he was born in 1877, his biographer has found a census document that suggests he was actually born three years later and falsified his birth year in order to join the army.

Davis first entered military service following the outbreak of the Spanish-American War in 1898. He later served as Professor of Military Science and Tactics at both Wilberforce University in Ohio and Tuskegee University in Alabama, as well as serving tours of duty around the world. Having been assigned to the 369th Regiment, New York National Guard in 1938, he soon took command of the unit and was promoted to brigadier general by President Franklin D. Roosevelt on 25 October 1940.

During the Second World War, Davis was an influential member of the Advisory Committee on Negro Troop Policies. Having been tasked with improving race relations and securing the morale of black soldiers in the European theatre, he lobbied to end segregation and introduce full racial integration. Davis was awarded the Distinguished Service Medal (DSM) on 22 February 1945 for his 'wise advice and counsel' that 'brought about a fair and equitable solution to many important problems which have since become the basis of far-reaching War Department policy'.

Benjamin O. Davis Sr. died on 26 November 1970 and was buried in Arlington National Cemetery. His son, Benjamin O. Davis Jr., had already followed in his father's footsteps by becoming the first African-American general in the United States Air Force.

OCTOBER
26
1881

The gunfight at the O.K. Corral took place between the Earp brothers and a gang of outlaws in Tombstone, Arizona.

Wyatt, Morgan, and Virgil Earp arrived in the booming silver-mining town of Tombstone in December 1879. Virgil had been appointed Deputy US Marshal for eastern Pima County, and within two years he had been made Tombstone's town marshal which made him the equivalent of a modern-day police chief. His brothers also held positions related to law enforcement in the town. This put them into conflict with the Cochise County Cowboys, a loosely organised group of outlaws who had been accused of crimes ranging from cattle rustling to murder.

Throughout 1881 the Earp brothers received a number of death threats from the Cowboys with whom there were long-running tensions for a combination of interpersonal, family and wider political reasons. The situation came to a head on the afternoon of 26 October when five of the Cowboys – Billy Claiborne, Ike and Billy Clanton, and Tom and Frank McLaury – were spotted by the Earps and their friend Doc Holliday in a vacant lot behind the O.K. Corral.

Although Cochise County Sheriff John Behan initially tried to diffuse the situation, a gunfight soon erupted. Accounts of the fight are contradictory and it is unclear which side opened fire first, but in total more than 30 shots were discharged. Of the Cowboys, both Tom and Frank McLaury, along with Billy Clanton, were killed while Ike Clanton and Billy Claiborne were able to run away.

Wyatt Earp emerged unscathed from the gunfight but Virgil, Morgan, and Doc Holliday were all injured. They were charged with murder by Sheriff Behan, who had witnessed the whole fight, but less a month later a justice of the peace found them not guilty.

US President Ronald Reagan publicly called for construction of the new United States embassy in Moscow to stop, due to the presence of Soviet listening devices in the structure.

Negotiations over the building of new embassies for the two superpowers were completed in 1969. Bugs had been discovered in the old US building in Moscow just three years earlier but, amidst the improving relations of détente, the Nixon administration permitted the Soviets to have an unprecedented amount of input into the design and construction of the new American building.

By the time construction began in 1979, the USSR had already manufactured concrete pieces for the building in their own factories. Since these were made away from US supervision, they were fitted with bugs that could not be easily spotted by a visual inspection when they arrived at the construction site. American technical experts still raised concerns, but the presence of Soviet devices could not be proved until a team of trained rock-climbers began to X-ray the concrete pillars and beams in situ from 1982 onwards.

News of the situation reached Congress in 1985 and, by the summer of 1987, it had become public knowledge that the Soviets had bugged the new building with technology that the United States was struggling to disable. The Senate Intelligence Committee voted in favour of demolishing the entire building the next year and, on 27 October, Reagan formally called for a halt on construction. A decision over the future of the new embassy was left until after the Presidential election two weeks later.

Robert E. Lamb, Assistant Secretary of State for Diplomatic Security, later stated, 'we knew the Russians were going to bug it, but we were confident we could deal with it. Obviously, we were wrong.'

OCTOBER

28

1971

The Prospero satellite was launched, becoming the first and only British satellite to be launched using a British rocket.

During the 1960s, while the USA and the USSR were engaged in the Space Race, British engineers began working on the Black Arrow carrier rocket. Intended as a way to carry payloads into low Earth orbit, it was based on technology developed for the Black Knight rocket that formed part of Britain's ballistic missile program.

Meanwhile, the Royal Aircraft Establishment in Farnborough built a satellite to conduct a series of experiments that would help to guide the development of later communication satellites. Originally given the name X-3, the squat 1.2m diameter satellite soon became known as Puck after the character from Shakespeare's *A Midsummer Night's Dream*.

Puck was to be launched by a Black Arrow, but the rocket project was cancelled in July 1971 after just one successful launch and two failures. By the time the cancellation was announced, however, the rocket intended to carry the satellite had already been shipped to the launch site at Woomera in Australia, so permission was given to continue as planned. The satellite was consequently renamed Prospero in reference to Shakespeare's sorcerer giving up his powers.

The satellite was launched shortly after 4am GMT on 28 October, and was successfully deployed into low Earth orbit. However, the second stage booster rocket continued firing, resulting in a collision with the satellite that broke off one of its radio antennas. Despite this damage, and the failure of the on-board tape recorder two years later, Prospero was only officially deactivated in 1996. Nevertheless, amateur radio operators reported hearing its radio transmissions as late as 2004.

OCTOBER
29
1618

Sir Walter Raleigh was beheaded, fifteen years after he was found guilty of treason for his involvement in the Main Plot against King James I.

Raleigh had been a favourite of Queen Elizabeth I, who granted him permission to lead three expeditions to the Americas. Although he had inspired the queen's fury after secretly marrying one of her ladies-in-waiting, Raleigh had returned to her favour by the time she died in March 1603.

In November, Raleigh was found guilty of treason for his involvement in the Main Plot that sought to depose Elizabeth's successor James I and replace him with his cousin Arabella Stuart. Nevertheless, the king suspended the death sentence and instead imprisoned Raleigh in the Tower of London, where he lived for thirteen years before being pardoned.

Raleigh was freed and granted permission by James to undertake an expedition in search of the fabled city of El Dorado, which began in 1617. In January 1618 a group of his men ignored an order to avoid confrontation with Spanish settlers when Lawrence Keymis, one of Raleigh's closest companions, led an attack on the Spanish outpost of Santo Tomé de Guayana on the Orinoco River. This was in direct contravention of peace treaties signed between England and Spain. Raleigh's son, Walter, was also killed in the attack.

Although Raleigh himself had specifically ordered his men not to attack, he knew that their actions had broken a key condition of his pardon. On his return to England the Spanish ambassador demanded the earlier death sentence be reinstated, and King James had little option but to order Raleigh's execution. He was beheaded in the Old Palace Yard at the Palace of Westminster on 29 October 1618.

The Tsar Bomba, the most powerful explosive weapon ever created, was detonated by the USSR.

The Soviet Union tested its first nuclear bomb in 1949, four years after the USA became the world's first nuclear superpower. Determined to catch up with their rival in the West, successive Soviet governments invested heavily in the nuclear program. By 1961 they had successfully detonated more than 80 devices.

Nichita Khrushchev, who had been the Soviet leader since 1953, was particularly keen to position the USSR as the dominant nuclear power. With his encouragement, a team of physicists designed what was to become the most powerful man-made weapon ever created. Known by various codenames, it was soon referred to in the West as the Tsar Bomba.

A specially adapted Tu-95V bomber carried the bomb to the remote Novaya Zemlya archipelago in the Barents Sea, north of the Arctic Circle. Measuring 8 metres (26 ft) long by 2.1 metres (6 ft 11 in) in diameter, the weapon weighed 27 metric tons and contained three stages that had a combined yield of more than 50 megatons. This was more than 1,500 times the power of the Hiroshima and Nagasaki bombs combined, but it would have been capable of twice this if some of the uranium had not been replaced with lead.

The bomb was dropped from an altitude of 34,000ft. A parachute then slowed its descent to give the aircraft time to get away before detonation at 13,000ft. Even so, the crew had only a 50% chance of survival. The explosion caused a fireball that was visible 630 miles away, while the shock wave orbited the world three times and broke windows as far away as Norway and Finland. No weapon of this power has been detonated since.

The cabinet of Italian Prime Minister Benito Mussolini took the oath of office and formally assumed control of the government.

Mussolini, who was determined to restore the glory of the Roman Empire following the 'mutilated victory' of the First World War, had formed the precursor to the Fascist Party in 1919. His skill as an orator, the intimidating power of his Blackshirts, and the relative weaknesses of the existing liberal government all contributed to the speed at which the Fascists gained influence.

On 24 October 1922, Mussolini went on stage at the Fascist Congress in Naples to declare his willingness to use the power of the Fascist movement to overthrow the government of liberal Prime Minister Luigi Facta. Four days later, approximately 30,000 Blackshirts from around the country gathered in the capital in an event known as the March on Rome. As they filled the streets and occupied public buildings, they called for Facta's resignation.

The Prime Minister chose to oppose the attempted revolution, but King Victor Emmanuel III refused his request to declare martial law. Stunned by the king's rejection of military action, Facta offered his resignation. It was immediately accepted. Victor Emmanuel later invited Mussolini to form a government. The cabinet was sworn in on 31 October in front of the King himself.

The establishment of Mussolini's government was greeted by a victory march by tens of thousands of Blackshirts. In time the March on Rome would achieve mythical status among Fascists as a revolutionary seizure of power, but the reality is that Mussolini was granted power by the king. Within a few years, however, he would transform the country into a dictatorship.

NOVEMBER

The public saw the ceiling of the Sistine Chapel for the first time when Pope Julius II celebrated All Saints Day mass.

Construction of the Sistine Chapel was completed in 1481 during the reign of Pope Sixtus IV. He commissioned a number of the Renaissance's leading artists to decorate the walls, while the ceiling was covered with gilt stars on a blue sky.

In 1508 Michelangelo was commissioned by Pope Julius II to repaint the ceiling with the twelve Apostles. Michelangelo saw himself more as a sculptor than a painter, but he later accepted the job after negotiating with the Pope to portray his own choice of Biblical scenes that went on to feature over 300 characters.

Michelangelo laboured for four years to complete the work, supported by scaffolding that was held by brackets above the windows. His working position was so uncomfortable that he wrote a sonnet about it, and later complained that the task had aged him so much his friends barely recognised him.

After numerous arguments with the Pope over how long the work was taking due to his desire to realise his creative vision, Michelangelo finished the ceiling after he was threatened with being thrown from the scaffolding if he didn't hurry up.

Julius celebrated All Saints Day mass in the Sistine Chapel on 1 November 1512 at which a small number of distinguished laity were present. They were to first to see the finished ceiling and marvelled at the breath-taking frescoes that famed art historian Helen Gardner regarded as one of the most important pieces of art ever created. Following restoration of the chapel's frescoes that was completed in 1994, the Sistine Chapel is now visited by up to 20,000 people a day determined to gaze upon Michelangelo's achievement.

NOVEMBER

2

1868

The government of New Zealand became the first to officially adopt a national standard time, which became known as New Zealand Mean Time (NZMT).

Prior to the adoption of universally accepted time zones, the vast majority of settlements around the world observed local mean solar time. Because of variations in geographical longitude, this meant that different towns and cities had slightly differing time standards. Although Greenwich Mean Time had been established in 1675 to help mariners navigate at sea, no law existed to mandate its use for local time.

The arrival of the railways in the mid-19th Century increased the need for a standardised time across the network, since local time would differ in all the towns the train visited. In Great Britain, Greenwich Mean Time was first adopted by the Great Western Railway and it is estimated that by 1855 up to 98% of all public clocks in the country displayed Greenwich Mean Time.

The use of a standard time in Britain was, however, not mandated by law. It was the New Zealand government that first introduced such legislation in order to allow the easier synchronisation of railways, steam ships, and the electric telegraph. Having consulted with Scottish-born scientist and explorer James Hector, the government adopted his recommendation of a time zone based on New Zealand's mean longitude 172° 30' east of Greenwich. Originally established at 11½ hours ahead of Greenwich Mean Time, New Zealand Mean Time was adopted on 2 November 1868.

Britain eventually implemented a standardised national time in 1880, while the US Congress passed the Standard Time Act on 19 March 1918.

NOVEMBER
3
1534

The Parliament of England passed the First Act of Supremacy which made Henry VIII the head of the Church of England.

Henry had been married to Catherine of Aragon, his older brother Arthur's widow, since 1509. Although she was pregnant seven times only one of Catherine's children, the future Mary I, survived. Frustrated by the lack of a male heir, by 1527 Henry had switched his affections to Anne Boleyn, who was young enough to bear children. Determined to make Anne his wife and produce a male heir, the king soon began to seek an annulment of his marriage to Catherine.

Despite enormous pressure, Pope Clement VII steadfastly refused to grant the annulment and clear the way for Henry's marriage to Anne. The king's use of Bible verses and historic documents in support of his case made little impact on the Pope and, despite failing to secure the annulment, Henry married Anne in early 1533. He did so on the basis that, if Catherine had consummated her marriage to Arthur, her marriage to Henry must have been invalid.

Within five months Thomas Cranmer, the newly-appointed Archbishop of Canterbury, declared the marriage to Catherine illegal and the marriage to Anne lawful. Shortly after the birth of the couple's daughter, Elizabeth, Henry began preparations to formally break from Rome. When the Pope declared in March 1534 his marriage to Anne illegal, Henry responded that the Pope had no authority in England.

Consequently on 3 November 1534 Parliament passed the Act of Supremacy that recognised Henry as the 'Supreme Head of the Church of England'. Largely political in its origin, the Act nevertheless marked the beginning of the English Reformation.

NOVEMBER
4
1839

The last large-scale armed rebellion against authority in Britain occurred during the Newport Rising in south Wales.

Focusing on reform of the electoral system to improve the conditions of the working class, the release of the People's Charter in 1838 had prompted the creation of the national working-class Chartist protest movement. William Lovett from the newly-established London Working Men's Association had written the majority of the document, but a petition in favour of it was rejected by the House of Commons on 12 July 1839.

Parliament's apparent refusal to listen to the concerns of the working class led to increased anger. Just three weeks later the Chartist leader Henry Vincent was jailed by the Welsh Monmouth Assizes for making inflammatory speeches. In Wales the Chartists soon began to organise and equip themselves for a mass protest.

Between three and five thousand Chartists marched into Newport on 4 November, by which time the authorities had prepared for a violent confrontation. The marchers made for the Westgate Hotel where they heard a number of Chartist prisoners were being held, but their chant to 'surrender our prisoners' was met only with gunfire from the soldiers stationed there. An estimated 22 Chartists were killed in the battle, and dozens more were injured.

Approximately 200 Chartists were arrested for their involvement in the march. The three principal leaders, John Frost, Zephaniah Williams, and William Jones, were found guilty of high treason and sentenced to be hung, drawn and quartered. Although their sentences were later reduced to transportation for life following a national outcry, they were the last people to be sentenced to this punishment in England and Wales.

NOVEMBER

5

1940

Franklin D. Roosevelt was elected for an unprecedented third term as President of the United States.

Franklin D. Roosevelt was inaugurated as the 32nd President of the United States on 4 March 1933, and quickly introduced initiatives designed to counter the effects of the Great Depression. Known as the New Deal, the combination of 'relief, recovery and reform' introduced Social Security and unemployment benefits that proved popular with the American people. This led to Roosevelt being elected to a second term in 1936 with 98.49% of the electoral vote.

Four years later there was speculation about whether Roosevelt would run again. George Washington had established the two-term tradition when he declined to run for a third in 1796. However, this limitation wasn't formally imposed until the 22nd Amendment in 1947. Consequently Roosevelt chose to run again, having decided that only he was capable of leading the United States at a time when Europe was battling the Nazi threat.

Roosevelt easily won the Democratic nomination, and joined with Henry Wallace as his running mate. He secured a boost to his popularity in September with the announcement of the Destroyers for Bases Agreement that gave a number of aging American battleships to a desperate Britain, in return for access to military bases that would improve American continental defences.

Nevertheless the Republican candidate, Wendell Willkie, warned that electing Roosevelt risked involving the United States in another European war. The president promised that this would never happen, however, and went on to win an unprecedented third term with almost 85% of the electoral vote. America joined the war just over a year later, prompted by the Japanese attack on Pearl Harbor.

NOVEMBER

6

1860

Abraham Lincoln was elected as the 16th President of the United States of America.

Abraham Lincoln was elected barely five months before the outbreak of the American Civil War, and was assassinated less than a month before its end. During this time he paved the way for the abolition of slavery through the Emancipation Proclamation and also delivered the Gettysburg Address, one of the most famous speeches in American history.

Having originally come from Kentucky, Lincoln's family settled in Illinois shortly after his twenty-first birthday. He soon moved to the town of New Salem where he became involved in local politics and began to teach himself law. He was admitted to the Illinois bar in 1836, by which time he had already been elected to the Illinois House of Representatives.

Lincoln served just one term in the United States House of Representatives in 1847-49, and it wasn't until 1856 that he re-embraced politics and joined the newly-formed anti-slavery Republican Party. The high profile Lincoln–Douglas debates in 1858 earned Lincoln national recognition and, two years later, he secured the Republican nomination for President on the third ballot.

The 1860 election saw four candidates vying for the Presidency, of whom only Lincoln did not make any campaign speeches. He instead harnessed the enthusiasm of the young adults in the Wide Awakes organisation to generate support for the new Republican Party. With his anti-slavery ideology Lincoln didn't receive a single vote from 10 of the 15 Southern slave states, but emerged victorious in the election thanks to overwhelming support in the North and West that translated into a decisive majority in the Electoral College.

NOVEMBER

7

1492

The oldest meteorite with a known date of impact crashed into a wheat field outside the Alsatian town of Ensisheim.

A boy from the modern-day French town which, at the time, was in a region known as Further Austria, reportedly witnessed the meteorite crash into the ground. Weighing 127 kilograms (280 pounds), its fall through the atmosphere created a fireball that could be seen from over 100 miles away, and the impact left a 1-metre deep hole.

Locals soon arrived at the site to collect souvenirs, but before long they were stopped by the local magistrate who kept the stone safe until the arrival of King Maximilian I, who became Holy Roman emperor the following year. Declaring the meteorite to be a positive omen from God for success in his wars against France and Turkey, he chipped off some pieces as gifts before entrusting the remainder to the people of Ensisheim.

Meanwhile, contemporary satirist Sebastian Brant composed a poem about the meteorite that was circulated in printed broadsheets in both German and Latin. He suggested that its arrival was a manifestation of God's anger at humankind's wayward and sinful behaviour. In response the meteorite was fixed to the wall of the church with strong iron crampons to ensure it couldn't escape and cause mischief.

The meteorite currently resides in Ensisheim's sixteenth-century Musée de la Régence, although the intervening years have seen souvenir hunters remove more than half of its original mass. These fragments of the oldest meteorite with a precise date of impact can now be found in both museum and private collections around the world.

NOVEMBER
8
1520

Danish soldiers under the command of King Christian II arrested numerous Swedish nobles, marking the start of the Stockholm Bloodbath.

Christian II had invaded Sweden in an attempt to preserve the Kalmar Union that joined the Scandinavian countries of Denmark, Sweden and Norway under a single monarch. Sweden's anti-unionist party under the regent Sten Sture the Younger opposed the pro-Danish group who were nominally led by Archbishop Gustav Trolle.

Christian had twice failed to subdue Sweden before his successful invasion at the head of a mercenary army in early 1520. Trolle, who had been under siege since his removal from the office of Archbishop by Sten Sture, was soon reappointed. After being hit by a cannonball that ricocheted into his leg at the Battle of Bogesund, Sture himself died of his wounds and the Swedish anti-unionist cause was severely weakened. Sture's widowed wife held out against the invasion for a number of months, but she eventually surrendered and Christian was crowned King of Sweden on 4 November.

Three days later Christian invited leading Swedes to a banquet at the palace. At dusk on 8 November his soldiers entered the building and arrested many of the guests. They had all been identified by Archbishop Trolle on a proscription list. Having been condemned to death as manifest heretics, around eighty people were drowned, hanged or beheaded by the Danes. Some sources also claim that Sten Sture's body, along with that of one of his children, was subsequently exhumed and burned.

The new king became known in Sweden as Christian the Tyrant, and before long he faced a new revolt under Gustav Vasa who led Sweden to victory in the Swedish War of Liberation.

NOVEMBER

9

1918

Kaiser Wilhelm II abdicated as German Emperor and King of Prussia after the German Revolution took hold.

The latter years of the First World War had seen Wilhelm's role reduced to that of a 'shadow Kaiser' who handled ceremonial duties while generals Hindenburg and Ludendorff dominated what historian Gordon A. Craig referred to as 'a military dictatorship'.

By September 1918 the German military commanders began to acknowledge that the war was lost. Prince Maximilian of Baden was appointed as the new Chancellor of Germany on 3 October and, the next day, sent out a message requesting an armistice in the hope that it would be accepted by US President Woodrow Wilson. As the end of the month approached it became increasingly clear that the Allies would only negotiate if Wilhelm II abdicated.

Meanwhile the situation within Germany was rapidly declining. Years of enduring the hardships of war had reduced morale and, when the Imperial Naval Command in Kiel issued an order on 24 October to prepare for a final battle against the British Royal Navy, the sailors mutinied. The revolt quickly spread throughout Germany leaving Maximilian little choice but to confront Wilhelm, who had fled to the military headquarters in the Belgian town of Spa, and request his abdication.

Before he was able to depart for Belgium, however, the growing German Revolution prevented Maximilian from leaving Berlin. On 9 November he unilaterally announced the abdication of the Kaiser. Having been informed by his military commanders that they would not fight to keep him on the throne, Wilhelm had little option but to consent. He left Belgium the next day and went into exile in the Netherlands, where he died in 1941.

NOVEMBER

10

1871

Henry Morton Stanley, a Welsh-American journalist and explorer, allegedly greeted missing Scottish missionary David Livingstone with the phrase, 'Dr Livingstone, I presume?'

David Livingstone was born in 1813 and, having completed training as a doctor, made his first journey to Africa in 1841. He converted his first and only African eight years later, after which he became convinced that further missionary work could only succeed if Africa's rivers were mapped to become 'highways' to the interior.

Livingstone sent his family back to Britain in 1852 prior to beginning an expedition to explore the Zambezi. Over the course of the next four years he crossed the African continent and mapped almost the entire Zambezi. He also became the first European to see the Mosi-oa-Tunya waterfall, which he renamed Victoria Falls.

Livingstone returned to Britain in 1856, but sailed back to Africa in 1858 with the intention of opening the Zambezi to 'legitimate' British trade to combat slavery. After this expedition failed in its aim to find a navigable route to the interior Livingstone again returned to Britain. He began his final journey to Africa in January 1866.

Hoping to find the source of the Nile, the expedition began to fail as Livingstone's assistants deserted him. With the outside world having heard nothing of him for over three years, Henry Morton Stanley was sent to find the Scot by the *New York Herald* newspaper in 1869. He was eventually found on 10 November 1871 in the town of Ujiji. Stanley is alleged to have greeted him with the words 'Dr Livingstone, I presume?' although this phrase is likely a fabrication. The relevant pages in Stanley's diary were torn out, and Livingstone himself never mentioned those words in his own papers.

NOVEMBER

11

1865

American surgeon Dr Mary Walker became the first, and so far only, woman to receive the Medal of Honor.

Mary Walker was awarded her Doctor of Medicine degree in 1855 from Syracuse Medical College in New York, having been the only woman in her class. After working in private practice, the outbreak of the Civil War led her to travel to Washington D.C. where she hoped to join the Union Army as a surgeon.

The army rejected her application due to her being a woman, so she was forced to volunteer as a nurse at the Patent Office Hospital. She moved to the field as an unpaid civilian surgeon in 1862 and was finally employed as a civilian assistant surgeon in the Army of the Cumberland by General George H. Thomas the following year.

While employed by the Union, Walker often crossed enemy lines to treat civilians. On 10 April 1864, she was arrested by Confederate troops as she was returning from one such trip. Accused of being a spy, she was imprisoned in the notoriously brutal Castle Thunder prison. Walker was eventually freed as part of a prisoner exchange on 12 August.

Dr Walker left government service within a year of her release. Nevertheless, she was awarded the newly-introduced Medal of Honor by President Andrew Johnson after it was determined that she could not receive a retroactive commission for her service.

The Medal of Honor is the highest award given to members of the United States military, and is only presented for exceptional acts of valour. At the time, however, there were no regulations regarding how and when it should be awarded. Consequently in 1917 Walker's was among 911 awards that were 'deleted' during an eligibility review. Her medal was restored in 1977, almost sixty years after her death.

NOVEMBER

12

1927

Leon Trotsky was expelled from the Communist Party of the USSR.

Trotsky had been a key figure in the Bolshevik Revolution of 1917. He soon became one of the members of the first Politburo that was created to manage the transition to a communist state, alongside the Bolshevik founder Vladimir Lenin, and the USSR's future leader Joseph Stalin.

As Lenin's health began to fail in the early 1920s, it initially appeared as though Trotsky would be his successor. Following Stalin's alliance with Zinoviev and Kamenev in the *troika*, however, Trotsky soon found himself marginalised. He also became the subject of rumours about his health and capability to serve in government.

Stalin subsequently emerged as the leader of the USSR following Lenin's death in 1924. Trotsky's Left Opposition faction was a vocal critic of many of Stalin's policies but, with Trotsky himself being increasingly side-lined from government decisions, he was removed from his position as War Commissar in 1925 and from the Politburo itself the following year.

Having organised a demonstration by the Left Opposition to celebrate the tenth anniversary of the Bolshevik Revolution, Trotsky was accused of fomenting and organising a counter-revolution. He, along with his recent ally Zinoviev, was expelled from the Communist Party on 12 November 1927 while 98 of his supporters met the same fate a month later.

Trotsky was soon exiled to Alma Ata in Kazakhstan, but within a year had left the USSR completely. He never returned, eventually being granted asylum in Mexico where he was eventually tracked down and assassinated with an ice pick by an NKVD agent.

NOVEMBER

13

1956

The United States Supreme Court upheld the District Court's ruling in *Browder v. Gayle* that segregation on public buses and transportation in Alabama was illegal.

Jim Crow laws firmly established racial segregation on buses in the Southern states, and this continued despite the growth of the national Civil Rights movement. In Alabama's capital, Montgomery, the arrest of seamstress and local NAACP secretary Rosa Parks for refusing to give up her seat sparked a city-wide boycott of the buses.

Shortly after the Montgomery Bus Boycott began, local civil rights leaders began to prepare a legal challenge to the segregation laws. Rather than focus on the case of Rosa Parks, Civil Rights lawyer Fred Gray instead filed a federal civil action lawsuit on behalf of five other black women who had been discriminated against on the Montgomery buses.

Aurelia Browder had been arrested and fined for sitting in the white section of a bus over seven months before Rosa Parks' act of defiance. The case of which she was the lead plaintiff was filed against the mayor of Montgomery, W. A. Gayle, on 1 February 1956 under Reconstruction-era civil rights legislation. Four months later, on 5 June, the three judges of the District Court ruled 2-1 that segregation of the buses was unconstitutional under the Fourteenth Amendment.

Both the state and the city appealed the decision but, on 13 November 1956, the Supreme Court upheld the District ruling and ordered the desegregation of buses in Alabama and Montgomery. The boycott finally ended on 20 December when the buses were desegregated. This marked an important victory in the battle for Civil Rights and stimulated the national movement.

NOVEMBER

14

1960

Ruby Bridges became the first African-American child to integrate an all-white elementary school in the American South.

Bridges was born in 1954, the same year that the Supreme Court unanimously ruled in the landmark case of *Brown v. Board of Education of Topeka, Kansas* that racially segregated schools were unconstitutional. Although the court ordered schools to desegregate 'with all deliberate speed' there was significant opposition, and some local school districts placed further legal obstacles in the way of desegregation.

Despite her father's initial reluctance to expose his daughter to the potential trouble that integration was expected to cause, six-year-old Ruby Bridges was put forward for an academic entrance test to determine whether she should be allowed to attend the all-white William Frantz Elementary School. The school was situated just five blocks from her home in New Orleans, yet Bridges had previously needed to attend a segregated kindergarten several miles away.

Having passed the entrance exam, and with the school district unable to delay integration any longer, Ruby Bridges and her mother were driven the short distance to the school accompanied by four federal marshals. Crowds of protesters lined the streets and, with the threat of violence hanging over the young girl and her family, she spent the entire first day in the principal's office.

Only one teacher at William Frantz Elementary agreed to teach Ruby and, although some white families that had boycotted the school slowly returned to classes, for an entire year Ruby was taught on her own. Outside school the Bridges family also experienced hardships including Ruby's father being made redundant, but other members of the community rallied round to support them.

NOVEMBER 15 1969

Over 500,000 protesters marched on Washington D.C. as part of the national Moratorium to End the War in Vietnam.

In the summer of 1969, anti-war activists Sam Brown and David Hawk formed the Vietnam Moratorium Committee and began organising a national protest against the Vietnam War. Having joined with the New Mobilization Committee to End the War in Vietnam, Brown was able to target potential supporters using lists that he had gained from his previous position as youth coordinator for Democratic Senator Eugene J. McCarthy's presidential campaign the previous year.

The first Moratorium event took place on 15 October and an estimated two million people across the United States took part in rallies, marches, and prayer vigils. Meanwhile Americans overseas, including future President Bill Clinton who was studying at Oxford University at the time, organised parallel protest events.

The success of the first Moratorium was followed by an enormous march in Washington the next month. The rally was preceded by the March against Death that began on the evening of Thursday 13 November in which protesters carried placards bearing the names of dead American soldiers and Vietnam villages that had been destroyed.

On Saturday 15 November an estimated half a million people gathered at the Washington Monument for speeches and performances in which the singer Pete Seeger led the crowd in a ten-minute rendition of John Lennon's 'Give Peace a Chance' while calling on President Nixon to end the war. Nixon later acknowledged the amount of opposition to the war but refused to be swayed by the protests. The war continued for another six years.

German pop duo Milli Vanilli were stripped of the Grammy Award for Best New Artist after it emerged that they did not sing any of the vocals on their debut album.

Milli Vanilli had been founded by German record producer and songwriter Frank Farian in 1988. He had previously created the disco-pop group Boney M., for whom he provided all the male recorded vocals. This was despite another man, Bobby Farrell, being the male 'face' of the band during live performances.

In the late 1980s Farian began to record a number of songs for a new album, using session musicians and vocalists. Having decided that the vocalists did not have a marketable image, Farian recruited two good-looking male dancers to lip-sync to the tracks. Rob Pilatus and Fab Morvan later claimed that they were 'trapped' by the contract they had signed with Farian.

The group's debut album, *All or Nothing*, was released in Europe in November 1988 and was followed by an American release, *Girl You Know It's True*, four months later. Unlike the European release the American packaging explicitly stated that Morven and Pilatus were the vocalists. During a live performance for MTV that summer, however, the public witnessed a key sign of lip-syncing when the backing track began to skip and repeat part of a vocal line over and over again.

In December one of the vocalists on the recordings, Charles Shaw, revealed his involvement to a reporter. Despite a rumoured $150,000 payment by Farian to retract the claim, rumours about lip-syncing continued. On 12 November 1990 Farian finally admitted that Morvan and Pilatus did not sing Milli Vanilli's songs. Just four days later the group's Grammy Award was withdrawn.

NOVEMBER
17
1903

The Russian Social Democratic Labour Party split into the Bolshevik and Menshevik factions.

The RSDLP was a Russian Marxist group that was established in 1898 to oppose the revolutionary populism that fuelled the Socialist Revolutionary Party. Drawing on the theories of Karl Marx and Friedrich Engels, the RSDLP sought to achieve revolution through the actions of the industrial working class even though this accounted for barely 3% of the population at the turn of the century.

The party was illegal in Russia, and the nine delegates of the first Party Congress in 1898 were arrested by the Imperial Russian Police. Consequently the 57 delegates of the Second Party Congress that began in July 1903 initially met in Brussels, but soon moved to London due to concerns over attention from the Belgian authorities.

Vladimir Ilyich Ulyanov, better known as Vladimir Lenin, had laid out his vision for the party's revolution in the book *What Is To Be Done?* He called for a dedicated revolutionary leadership to keep the workers focused on achieving the transition to a socialist state. In contrast Julius Martov was willing to adopt what Lenin referred to as a 'soft' approach with a looser and more democratic organisation, even going as far as to work with Russian liberals in order to achieve social change.

On 17 November these disagreements bubbled over into a vote over the editorial board of the party newspaper, *Iskra*. The Bolsheviks (from the Russian *bolshinstvo* for 'majority') secured the largest number of votes while the Mensheviks were in the minority. The split soon became permanent, although the Bolsheviks actually remained the smaller of the two factions in terms of membership until the Russian Revolution in 1917.

NOVEMBER
18
1987

The worst fire in the history of the London Underground killed 31 people at King's Cross St Pancras station.

King's Cross St Pancras is a major intersection on the London Underground network. Numerous deep platforms serve the Metropolitan, Northern, Piccadilly, and Victoria lines in addition to the *Thameslink* service. In the 1980s many of these platforms were reached by wooden escalators that had been in place for many years, inside which large amounts of combustible waste had accumulated.

At approximately 7.30pm, passengers reported a fire on one of the Piccadilly Line escalators. The official inquiry later determined that it had been started by a lit match being dropped, which caused the fire to break out beneath the escalator in an area that was difficult to reach with a conventional fire extinguisher. Although water fog equipment was present in the station the staff had not been trained on how to use it so the fire brigade was called instead.

The decision was soon made to evacuate the station using the Victoria Line escalators, and just a few minutes later the fire brigade arrived to find a small fire that soon engulfed the entire escalator. Superheated gases rose to the ceiling of the tunnel, where layers of old paint absorbed the heat and caused a devastating flashover at 7.45pm. Due to the construction of the escalator and the 30° angle of the shaft, a jet of flames and smoke burst into the ticket hall in what scientists now refer to as the 'trench effect'.

The intense heat of the flashover killed or seriously injured the people who were still in the ticket hall, while hundreds more were trapped below ground and were forced to escape on trains. London Underground were later fiercely criticised for failing to train staff effectively on how to deal with fires and evacuate passengers.

NOVEMBER
19
1985

US President Ronald Reagan and Soviet General Secretary Mikhail Gorbachev met for the first time at the Geneva Summit.

The 54-year-old Gorbachev had been elected on 11 March, and quickly began to address the economic, social, and political problems facing the USSR. In terms of foreign policy, his 'new thinking' doctrine moved away from adopting nuclear deterrence and the accumulation of nuclear weapons and instead sought common security. This would demand cooperation with the United States in order to bring about bilateral reduction of nuclear arms.

Meanwhile Ronald Reagan, who had served as President of the United States since 1981, referred to the USSR as the 'evil empire'. Despite adopting a hard line against the Soviet Union, he similarly sought to end the nuclear arms race albeit by the development of the Strategic Defense Initiative (also referred to as 'Star Wars') that would make a first-strike advantage impossible and render nuclear weapons obsolete.

Since both countries wished to reduce their nuclear stockpiles, arrangements were made for a summit conference in Geneva. The first meeting took place on 19 November and, over the course of the next two days, Reagan and Gorbachev spoke at length about nuclear arms reduction and other issues of international diplomacy. Although the two leaders achieved little in terms of formal agreements, they developed a personal connection that led to further meetings over the next two years.

These summits eventually led to the negotiation of the Intermediate-Range Nuclear Forces Treaty. Signed in Washington D.C. on 8 December 1987, the INF eliminated an entire class of nuclear weapons.

NOVEMBER
20
1969

A group of Native Americans occupied Alcatraz Island in San Francisco Bay.

The Occupation of Alcatraz was launched by a group of 89 members of the Indians of All Tribes in an attempt to gain control under the Treaty of Fort Laramie that had been signed in 1868. After the prison closed in March 1963 the federal government declared the island surplus federal property, leading the IOAT to demand that it be returned to Native Americans under the terms of the treaty. A number of previous attempts had been made, although the 19-month long Alcatraz Occupation was the longest attempt to seize control.

A fire that destroyed the San Francisco American Indian Center on 10 October acted as the catalyst for the occupation. On 9 November a group of 14 protesters spent the night on the island and claimed ownership 'by right of discovery.' Less than two weeks later a group of 89 men, women and children sailed across San Francisco Bay from the city of Sausalito to begin the longer occupation.

Although the majority of the protesters were intercepted by a Coast Guard blockade, over 400 people eventually occupied Alcatraz. Citing the Treaty of Fort Laramie, they demanded control of the island in order to build a Native American cultural centre.

At the start of January 1970, the 13-year-old step-daughter of Richard Oakes, one of the occupation's leaders, fell to her death. The family's departure from the island coincided with worsening relations between some of the other protesters and, after the government cut off electrical power and telephone lines in late May, numbers dwindled until only a handful of people remained. The final 15 occupiers were removed by federal marshals on 11 June 1971. Control of Alcatraz was later handed to the National Park Service.

NOVEMBER
21
1974

21 people were killed and 182 were injured in the Birmingham pub bombings.

In the early evening of 21 November, at least three explosive devices were planted in locations around central Birmingham. Two of these were in public houses and, at 8.11pm, a man with an Irish accent called the city's newspapers with a coded warning about the explosives but no specific details about their locations.

Although the Provisional IRA has never formally admitted responsibility for the bombings, they came at a time when attacks on mainland Britain by the Irish republican revolutionary organisation were occurring on average once every three days.

One bomb was concealed inside either a duffel bag or a briefcase and planted inside the *Mulberry Bush* pub on the ground floor of the 25-storey Rotunda office block. It exploded just six minutes after the telephone warning, devastating the building and killing ten people while leaving many others horrifically injured. Ten minutes later a second bomb exploded in the *Tavern in the Town* pub, killing a further 9 people outright while two of the injured later died in hospital.

Within three hours of the bombings, five men had been detained at Heysham Port from where they had intended to sail to Belfast. They had all lived in Birmingham for a number of years but had travelled from Birmingham New Street station that evening. By 23 November, and after being subjected to extreme physical and psychological abuse they, along with a sixth man, had all signed forced confessions admitting their involvement in the pub bombings.

The Birmingham Six were sentenced to life imprisonment in a huge miscarriage of justice. Their convictions were eventually quashed in 1991, but nobody else has since been charged.

The British pirate Edward Teach, better known as Blackbeard, was killed during a battle with British sailors under the command of Lieutenant Robert Maynard.

Details of Teach's early life are so sparse that historians are not even certain of his real name. He only begins to reliably appear in the historical record in September 1717 when he was described in a report by an anti-piracy patrol off the coast of North Carolina as being in charge of 'a sloop of 6 gunns [sic] and about 70 men'. By the end of November 1717, Teach had captured the French slave ship *La Concorde*, which he renamed *Queen Anne's Revenge*. He cruised the Caribbean throughout the winter, during which time the captain of a raided ship gave the first physical description of the pirate that included reference to his 'very black beard which he wore very long.'

Teach was at the height of his power when he lost *Queen Anne's Revenge* after she ran aground on a sandbar. He later sailed to Bath, the capital of North Carolina, to receive a royal pardon that had been offered to any pirate who surrendered on or before 5 September 1718. He and his crew received the pardon from Governor Charles Eden in June but returned to piracy soon afterwards.

News of this soon reached the Governor of Virginia, Alexander Spotswood, who personally financed an operation to capture Teach. Lieutenant Robert Maynard was put in charge, and he attacked the pirates at Ocracoke Island on 22 November 1718. Having hidden many of his men below decks in anticipation of being boarded by Teach's crew, Maynard was able to take the pirates by surprise. Amidst vicious fighting, Teach is said to have taken 5 musket balls and as many as twenty sword cuts before he died. His head was later severed and hung from the bowsprit of Maynard's ship.

NOVEMBER
23
1889

The world's first 'Nickel-In-The-Slot Phonograph' introduced the concept of the jukebox to the public.

Thomas Edison had announced the invention of the phonograph in November 1877 and, within a decade, the technology had found an army of manufacturers and distributors who wanted to exploit its commercial potential.

Realising that the cost of purchasing a phonograph was beyond the reach of most consumers, Louis T. Glass and William S. Arnold of the Pacific Phonograph Company created a device to allow the public to pay to hear a single recording. Their invention featured an Edison Class M Electric Phonograph inside a wooden cabinet, which was fitted with four listening tubes resembling stethoscopes. Customers inserted a five-cent piece in the slot to listen.

The first machine was installed at the Palais Royal Saloon in San Francisco, just two blocks away from the offices of the Pacific Phonograph Company. Although the bar closed within a year, the invention was incredibly successful. Glass boasted that he made more than $1,000 in the first six months of operation and, spurred on by the promise of such high earnings, the concept soon spread.

The first devices were limited to playing back a single wax cylinder. However, following the introduction of recordings pressed on to discs, improvements were made to public phonographs that eventually allowed customers to choose from a broad range of music. In the 1940s these devices, many fitted with carousels to provide a wide choice of records, had become known as jukeboxes. By this time up to three-quarters of all records produced in the United States went into jukeboxes, arguably making the 'Nickel-In-The-Slot Phonograph' the catalyst for the modern music industry.

Joseph Glidden was awarded a patent for the modern version of barbed wire.

Improved fencing systems were vital to the farmers who had headed west to settle in America's Great Plains. The Homestead Act of 1862 allowed honest citizens to claim up to 160 acres if they built a home and worked the land for five years, but the new settlers struggled to erect fences in an area where there were few trees to provide timber. Roaming cattle could push through smooth wire fences and trample crops.

Various early versions of barbed wire had been patented before Joseph Glidden, a farmer from DeKalb, Illinois, developed a form of double-stranded wire that could be mass produced to specifications that are virtually unchanged today. Improving on an earlier design by New York resident Michael Kelly, an inventor called Henry Rose had exhibited a fencing system of barbs mounted on a wooden rail at the DeKalb county fair. Inspired by the idea that a barbed fence would keep livestock away from the boundary, and believing that barbs fixed to wire would be easier to both produce and install, Glidden set about making his own improvements.

Glidden adapted a hand operated coffee mill to create wound barbs that would then be threaded onto a strand of wire. A second strand would be laid alongside, and both were attached to a hook on the side of an old grinding wheel. Rotating the grindstone twisted the two wires together and held the barbs on the first wire in place.

The new barbed wire had a dramatic effect. The expanse of the Great Plains was fenced off, changing the lifestyles of the cattlemen whose herds grazed there and the Native Americans whose already-dwindling territory was now being enclosed by 'the Devil's rope'.

NOVEMBER
25
1491

The Treaty of Granada ended the Granada War and brought about the end of Islamic rule on the Iberian Peninsula.

The Emirate of Granada was established in 1230 by Muhammad ibn al-Ahmar. Ruled by the Nasrid dynasty, the emirate survived as a tributary state under Castile for more than two centuries before becoming the target of a series of military campaigns by the Catholic Monarchs, Isabella I of Castile and Ferdinand II of Aragon.

The seasonal campaigns that constituted the Granada War began in 1482 and led to economic problems in Granada that were compounded by lasting internal divisions over the Nasrid succession. Meanwhile, despite the Christian forces generally being commanded by individual nobles, the army was relatively unified. Their aggressive use of artillery pieces such as bombards and cannons also helped them to shorten sieges and make rapid gains.

Early in the campaign Ferdinand had formed a loose alliance with Emir Abu Hasan's son, known to the Spanish as Boabdil, after capturing him. Boabdil focused his energies on capturing the city of Granada, which he did in 1487, but in 1490 he turned against the Catholic Monarchs due to him allegedly being unhappy with how he was rewarded for his alliance.

The Christian forces began their siege of Granada in April 1491, and by November Boabdil was ready to negotiate. The Treaty of Granada was signed on 25 November and provided a two-month truce prior to the full surrender of the city. The terms were very generous towards the Muslims since they guaranteed their property, laws, customs, and religion. Nevertheless, the Treaty of Granada and the final capitulation of the city on 2 January 1492 marked the end of Islamic rule on the Iberian Peninsula.

The single 'Anarchy in the UK' was released by the British punk band, the Sex Pistols.

The Damned had released what is recognised as the first ever punk single in October 1976. Yet while 'New Rose' may have been the first single by a punk band, numerous groups had already built sizeable followings through chaotic live shows that arguably culminated in the Sex Pistols' own performance at Manchester's Lesser Free Trade Hall on 4 June 1976.

The Sex Pistols were signed to the EMI record label on 8 October and soon entered the studio to record their debut single which they did less than two weeks later on 17 October. Chris Thomas, who had previously worked with such influential bands as The Beatles and Pink Floyd, agreed to produce the single, which sent shockwaves through the recording industry.

In sharp contrast to the traditional rock and roll lyrics of 'New Rose', 'Anarchy in the UK' was rooted in the anger and nihilism of the early British punk movement from its opening line. It reached number 38 on the UK charts, but this fails to reflect the impact the record had on the country.

Less than a week later the band appeared on the *Today* programme broadcast on Thames Television in London. The host, Bill Grundy, later claimed that he and the band were all drunk when he invited them to 'say something outrageous' in the closing seconds of the show. Guitarist Steve Jones responded by calling the host a range of names littered with profanities. The band's appearance was splashed over the national newspapers the next day, bringing both the band and the punk movement to national attention. Within a few weeks EMI ended the band's contract.

NOVEMBER
27
1809

Englishman Theodore Hook orchestrated a practical joke known as the Berners Street hoax in the heart of London.

Theodore Hook was an established writer and composer at the time of the prank. According to contemporary sources he had made a bet with his friend, the architect Samuel Beazley, that he could make a single house the most talked-about address in London.

Hook chose 54 Berners Street, the home of a widow known only as Mrs Tottenham. Whether the prankster had any connection to the address or its inhabitant is uncertain, but he eagerly began preparing the joke by sending thousands of letters to businesses and individuals around the city. Hook and Beazley later rented a room nearby to watch the prank unfold and, at 5am on the morning of 27 November, the first of a stream of visitors began to arrive at Mrs Tottenham's door.

The first was a chimney sweep, who was soon followed by about a dozen more. The roads around Berners Street became impassable as hundreds of tradespeople descended on the house in response to Hook's letters. Newspaper accounts reveal the full extent of the mayhem that included 'waggons laden with coals from the Paddington wharfs, upholsterers' goods in cart-loads, organs, pianofortes, linen, jewellery, and every other description of furniture'. Even dignitaries including the Archbishop of Canterbury and the Lord Mayor of London answered the call.

By nightfall the police had been forced to close the road while across London hundreds of pastry chefs, opticians, undertakers, wigmakers, butchers, clergymen, dentists, brewers and countless other tradespeople sought the identity of the prankster. Hook was never caught, but he won the bet.

NOVEMBER
28
1893

Every New Zealand woman over the age of 21 was able to vote in the world's first general election in a self-governing colony.

The issue of women's suffrage in New Zealand began to gain momentum in the second half of the 19th century. Like in other countries, women in New Zealand had been excluded from political life. Drawing strength from the broader American and northern European movements for women's rights, some of New Zealand's leading suffrage campaigners argued that equal rights for women were necessary for the moral improvement of society.

The New Zealand branch of the Women's Christian Temperance Union was a driving force behind the movement, which was energised by campaigners such as Kate Sheppard and Mary Ann Müller. By the start of 1893 they had secured widespread support for women's suffrage, as shown through the thousands of names that appeared on petitions.

After previous attempts to pass bills to give women the right to vote had failed to make it through Parliament, the 1893 Women's Suffrage Petition led to a new Electoral Bill that would grant suffrage to women of all races. It easily passed through the Lower House, but the Upper House was divided on the issue. However, a late switch by two councillors who had originally opposed the bill led to it passing by 20 votes to 18 on 8 September 1893. Lord Glasgow signed it into law 11 days later, enabling women to vote in the general election. The European part of the election took place on 28 November and saw 65% of all eligible New Zealand women turn out to vote.

Exactly 26 years later, on 28 November 1919, Lady Astor became the first elected British female MP to take her seat in the House of Commons.

NOVEMBER

29

1850

The Declaration of Olmütz was signed between Prussia and Austria, in which Prussia submitted to Austrian dominance.

Austria was the dominant power in the German Confederation during the first half of the 19th century yet, by the outbreak of the 1848 revolutions, the German state of Prussia was preparing to challenge its authority. The revolutionaries attempted to unify the German states under Prussia, but this collapsed after the refusal of the Prussian king to accept the crown 'by the grace of butchers and bakers'. However, the vacuum of power that had been created by the revolution was exploited by the Prussian government to introduce a new German federation under its own leadership.

The Erfurt Union was formed in May 1850 after the *Dreikonigsbundis* or League of Three Kings featuring Prussia, Saxony and Hannover pressured 17 other states into joining together to form a new German Confederation. The significance of this move was that Austria was actively excluded – the Union was effectively attempting to create a Kleindeutschland (or small Germany, one without Austria) as opposed to Grossdeutschland that would have included Austria.

Austria's attention was diverted due to ongoing uprisings in Hungary but, by the spring of 1850, the Habsburgs were ready to reassert their dominance over the German States. This coincided with a dispute over the state of Hesse-Cassel, in which the Prussian king backed down from possible war against Austria and led to the humiliating Declaration of Olmütz in November 1850. Prussia had to accept Austria's dominance by abandoning the Erfurt Union and recognising the restoration of the German Confederation. Although this was a diplomatic defeat of Prussia by Austria, it also signalled the start of an intense rivalry between the two.

NOVEMBER

30

1786

The Grand Duchy of Tuscany became the first modern state to abolish the death penalty.

Pietro Leopoldo, the ruler of Tuscany, came to power in 1765 after the death of his father, the Holy Roman Emperor Francis I. Pietro Leopoldo later became Holy Roman Emperor Leopold II, but in the years immediately after his father's death his mother Maria Theresa co-ruled the empire with his elder brother Joseph II. After five years Leopold successfully obtained a free hand to rule Tuscany as he liked after he travelled to Vienna where his mother agreed to remove her appointed counsellors.

Leopold was an enlightened ruler who revitalised Tuscany's economy through the introduction of new rates of taxation and the creation of public works projects. His habit of spending revenues on improving the state was in sharp contrast to the government of the Medici family who had preceded his father. Nevertheless, it had a broadly positive impact on Tuscany's financial position.

A year before Leopold came to power in Tuscany, the Italian Enlightenment writer Cesare Beccaria condemned torture and the death penalty in his famed treatise *On Crimes and Punishments*. The book, which proposed radical reform of the criminal system, influenced Leopold to stop signing death warrants and after 1769 no executions took place in Tuscany.

On 30 November 1786 Leopold formally abolished the death penalty as well as banning the use of torture. All instruments used for administering the death penalty were also destroyed. The day is now celebrated as Cities for Life Day on which numerous cities around the world show their commitment to the abolition of the death penalty.

DECEMBER

DECEMBER 1
1918

The *National Assembly of Romanians of Transylvania and Hungary* declared the unification of Transylvania and the Kingdom of Romania.

Romania entered the First World War in 1916, having signed a secret treaty with the Entente powers under which they would take control of a number of regions controlled by the Central Powers in which ethnic Romanians lived. This was a nationalist compromise since their ultimate aim was to unite with these regions as well as with Bessarabia that had been annexed by Russia in 1812.

Romania's armistice with the Central Powers in December 1917 had the potential to end the country's nationalist ambitions. However, political unrest in Russia following the Bolshevik Revolution led to Bessarabia proclaiming union with the Kingdom of Romania in April 1918. Encouraged by this, and spurred on by hope for self-determination as laid out in Woodrow Wilson's famous '14 Points', nationalists maintained their call for unification with Romanians in Austria-Hungary.

Romania returned to the war a few days before the fighting ended. Two weeks later, on 28 November 1918, the General Congress of Bukovina voted for unification with Romania. Meanwhile preparations were made for the *National Assembly of Romanians of Transylvania and Hungary* to meet in the city of Alba Iulia. On 1 December the delegates voted unanimously for 'the unification of those Romanians and of all the territories inhabited by them with Romania'. All these proclamations were later recognised under the terms of the First World War peace treaties.

1 December is now known in Romania as Great Union Day and is celebrated as a national holiday.

United States Senator Joseph McCarthy was censured by the Senate for 'conduct that tends to bring the Senate into dishonour and disrepute'.

Joseph McCarthy was elected to the Senate for the state of Wisconsin in 1946. He was thrust into the public eye in February 1950 after a speech to the Republican Women's Club of Wheeling, West Virginia in which he claimed 205 communists had infiltrated the US State Department. Following re-election in 1952, McCarthy became chairman of the Senate's Committee on Government Operations and of its permanent subcommittee on investigations.

McCarthy used his position to launch a series of high-profile investigations of people he claimed to have communist sympathies. Although his tactics were condemned by politicians including President Dwight D. Eisenhower, McCarthy's investigations stretched from the Voice of America news service to the United States Army. Known as the Second Red Scare, the first having begun after the Bolshevik Revolution in 1917, more than 2,000 government employees lost their jobs in what some viewed as a witch-hunt.

Support for McCarthy declined rapidly after the television broadcast of the Army-McCarthy hearings in April and May 1954. The Senator was accused of pressuring the army to give his aides preferential treatment, and the hearings exposed his bullying tactics. The army's chief counsel, Joseph Nye Welch, even interrupted McCarthy to ask, 'Have you no sense of decency, sir?' Meanwhile Edward R. Murrow's popular documentary program *See It Now* ran a negative piece on the Senator that further turned public opinion against him. On 2 December 1954 the Senate condemned McCarthy for conduct 'contrary to Senate traditions' by 67 votes to 22.

DECEMBER
3
1967

Surgeon Christiaan Barnard performed the world's first human-to-human heart transplant.

Barnard was head of the Department of Experimental Surgery at the Groote Schuur Hospital in Cape Town when he performed the pioneering surgery. Having previously performed successful kidney transplants, his team identified 53-year-old grocer Louis Washkansky as a suitable recipient of a donor heart. Washkansky had developed chronic heart disease but had previously been an active sportsman and was said to have displayed a tenacious determination to hold on to his life.

On Saturday 2 December, 25-year-old Denise Darvall and her mother were struck by a drunk driver as they crossed the road. While her mother died at the scene, Denise was transferred to Groote Schuur Hospital where she was diagnosed as being brain dead. A respirator maintained the beat of her heart while doctors approached her father who agreed to their request to donate the organ.

The operation began shortly after midnight. Dozens of specialists made up the team involved in the revolutionary surgery and, shortly before 6am on the morning of 3 December, electric shocks brought Washkansky's new heart into action. Although he regained consciousness, immunosuppressant drugs intended to stop his body rejecting the new tissue contributed to him dying from pneumonia eighteen days later.

Despite this sad end, Professor Barnard quickly gained international acclaim for his pioneering surgery. His technique was quickly adopted around the world, but heart transplants continued to suffer from significant complications until the development of cyclosporine, a more effective immunosuppressive drug, in the 1970s.

The deserted American merchant ship *Mary Celeste* was found drifting in the Atlantic Ocean.

Mary Celeste was launched in 1861 under the name *Amazon* and changed hands several times before being acquired by a New York consortium that carried out an extensive refit. She was then placed under the command of Benjamin Briggs, who carefully chose a crew to sail the vessel to Genoa with a cargo of 1,701 barrels of denatured alcohol.

Mary Celeste departed New York on 7 November, and was followed eight days later by *Dei Gratia*, another cargo ship heading for Genoa. On 4 December, while midway between the Azores and Portugal, this second ship under the command of David Morehouse spotted an erratically moving vessel in the distance. As *Dei Gratia* moved closer it became clear that something was wrong and, on investigation by second mate John Wright, the vessel was identified as *Mary Celeste*. She had been completely deserted by her crew.

The ship's lifeboat was found to be missing and the sails were in poor condition, while two of the hatches were open with an improvised sounding rod to measure the depth of water in the hold lying nearby. The cargo of denatured alcohol was also found to be intact. The last entry in the ship's log was from nine days earlier and placed the *Mary Celeste* nearly 400 nautical miles from the position where she was found.

The crew of *Dei Gratia* successfully sailed the abandoned ship to Gibraltar for salvage hearings. The findings of the court were inconclusive and, although *Mary Celeste* returned to service under new owners, the mystery of the abandoned ship and her disappearing crew has never been solved.

The Great Smog of London descended on the British capital due to a combination of air pollution and weather conditions.

To maximise revenues in the aftermath of the Second World War, the British government had opted to export the country's better-quality 'hard' coal and retain the more sulphurous low-grade coal for domestic consumption. Much of this coal was burned in domestic fires to offset the particularly cold winter of 1952. This combined with pollutants from Greater London's numerous power stations, factories, and public transport to create a thick noxious blanket of smog over the city.

The thick yellow-black smog was held over London for more than four days due to the arrival of a high-pressure weather system. This caused an anticyclone that stopped the polluted air from rising into the atmosphere. Windless conditions, and London's position in a river valley, also meant that the smog was unable to be blown away.

Visibility in the city was reduced to just a few metres, bringing public transport to a halt and forcing schools and businesses to close. Meanwhile, people across the city breathed in the toxic air and began to succumb to respiratory infections. Cattle at the Smithfield Show at Earl's Court reportedly suffocated and, while nobody made the connection until several months after the smog lifted, estimates state that between 4,000 and 12,000 Londoners died as a direct result of breathing the polluted air.

In response the government began to rethink its policy towards air pollution and, in 1956, introduced the Clean Air Act that established 'smoke control areas' where only clean fuels could be burned. This precipitated a shift towards the use of cleaner coals, electricity, and gas as sources of heat.

DECEMBER
6
1969

Meredith Hunter was killed at the Altamont Speedway Free Festival during a performance by the Rolling Stones.

Intended to be a West Coast version of the Woodstock festival that had taken place earlier that year, the Altamont concert should have ended the 1960s on a high. The concert was organised jointly by Jefferson Airplane, the Grateful Dead, and the Rolling Stones but the venue was only finalised two days beforehand due to scheduling conflicts and financial disputes. As a result, the usual concert infrastructure was unable to be installed on time. This meant both the stage and the venue as a whole were ill-prepared for the 300,000 concertgoers who attended.

Members of the Hells Angels Motorcycle Club were given $500 of beer in return for providing informal security for the vulnerable stage. The exact details of the arrangement remain unclear but, as the day progressed, the mood of both the crowd and the Angels themselves began to deteriorate. Even the lead singer of Jefferson Airplane was knocked unconscious when he tried to stop fights breaking out, the Angels by then having armed themselves with sawn-off pool cues and motorcycle chains. Seeing the mounting violence, the Grateful Dead refused to play.

The Rolling Stones began their set after dark. Having already been involved in a fight, 18-year-old attendee Meredith Hunter approached the stage during the song 'Under My Thumb' and drew a gun. Alan Passaro, one of the Hells Angels, disarmed him and delivered at least two stabs with a knife drawn from his belt. Hunter died at the festival, and Passaro was put on trial for murder. He was later acquitted on grounds of self-defence after evidence of Hunter drawing the gun was identified in film footage taken on the day.

The crew of the Apollo 17 spacecraft took the iconic *Blue Marble* photograph of the Earth.

Apollo 17 was launched from the Kennedy Space Center at 12:33 am on 7 December. Around five hours later, when the spacecraft had left Earth orbit and begun its course towards the Moon, the three-man crew all began taking photographs with a 70-millimeter Hasselblad camera fitted with an 80-millimeter Zeiss lens.

By this time, they were approximately 29,000 kilometers (18,000 miles) away from Earth. This was far enough away for the entire planet to be seen through the spacecraft's windows. Since the on-board camera did not have a viewfinder, it was necessary to take a sequence of photographs with slightly different aim to ensure a successful image. Because of this the actual photograph was upside down with Antarctica at the top, but it still captured the entire globe from the Mediterranean Sea to the south polar ice cap.

The image was released by NASA on 23 December, four days after the spacecraft splashed down in the Pacific Ocean. It was seized upon by the press, who printed *The Blue Marble* on front pages across the world. Subsequent analysis of the mission transcript suggests that Lunar Module Pilot Harrison 'Jack' Schmitt took the photograph, but NASA has always credited the crew as a whole while the astronauts themselves were also known to accept joint recognition.

Apollo 17 was the final mission of the program, marking the last time humans travelled beyond low Earth orbit or set foot on the Moon. Consequently, although a number of whole-Earth images have been taken since, these have all been produced by unmanned spacecraft.

The first woman to appear on a professional stage in England played the role of Desdemona in Shakespeare's *Othello*.

Theatre in England had been banned by the Puritan Long Parliament in 1642 but, following the restoration of the monarchy under Charles II, the ban was lifted. The king marked the revival of theatre by granting the dramatists Sir Thomas Killigrew and Sir William Davenant a monopoly on theatre performances.

On 8 December 1660 Killigrew's new King's Company staged a production of William Shakespeare's *Othello* at the Vere Street theatre in Lincoln's Inn. Female roles had previously been played by boys or young men, but this particular performance is known for being the first professional production to feature a woman in the cast. This date is well recorded but, considering the revolutionary nature of this performance, it is somewhat surprising that the identity of the actress herself is not known with any certainty. The majority of commentators believe that the role of Desdemona was played by Margaret Hughes, who went on to become an accomplished stage performer during the Reformation and the mistress of Prince Rupert of the Rhine. However, new evidence unearthed by the British Library in London suggests that it may actually have been Anne Marshall, a similarly well-regarded actress, who took to the stage that night.

Prior to the performance, a prologue composed by the actor and poet Thomas Jordan warned audience members that Desdemona would be played by an actual woman. Contrary to the commonly held view that actresses were equivalent to prostitutes, this prologue said she was 'as far from being what you call a Whore, As Desdemona injur'd by the Moor'.

Thomas Midgeley Jr. discovered that adding tetraethyl lead to gasoline reduced knocking in automobile engines.

Engine knock, sometimes referred to as 'pinging', is caused by the improper timing of fuel combustion in an engine's cycle. By occurring too early, the explosive ignition causes a shock-wave that can cause serious damage to the engine cylinder.

Thomas Midgeley Jr. was a mechanical engineer at the US automobile manufacturer General Motors, where he was tasked with finding a way to prevent engine knock. Although he had already found that mixing gasoline with ethanol would reduce knock by raising the octane level of the fuel, it was a process that was impossible to patent and thus make any significant profit from.

Midgeley continued his search for a suitable additive and on 9 December 1921, after working through thousands of chemicals, he finally identified tetraethyl lead. Ignoring the dangers that this neurotoxin presented, leaded gasoline soon became a standard feature on forecourts across the world while the additive itself became known as TEL under the brand name Ethyl.

A few months after his discovery, Midgeley had to take time away from the laboratory due to lead poisoning. Some of his colleagues were not as lucky. Within a year ten workers at the lead plant had died, while dozens more experienced neurological symptoms including tremors, hallucinations and fits. Despite these evident dangers, leaded gasoline continued to be the standard fuel for automobiles until it was ordered to be phased out in the 1970s.

Midgeley himself went on to develop the first CFCs, making him the creator of two products that have caused serious long-lasting damage to both human health and the environment.

DECEMBER
10
1799

France adopted the newly-defined metric system as the official system of weights and measures.

It is estimated that up to a quarter of a million different units of measurement were in use throughout France at eve of the Revolution in 1789, and that these differed not only from trade to trade but also from town to town. The difficulties in business, science and taxation that arose from these inconsistent systems prompted the French Academy of Sciences to investigate the reform of weights and measurements, although scientists across both Europe and America had discussed the advantages of a universal system of measurement for over a century.

Having decided that units in the new decimal system should be based on the natural world, the Academy defined the metre as one ten millionth of the distance between the North Pole and the Equator. However, since this distance had never been calculated, the astronomers Jean Baptiste Joseph Delambre and Pierre Méchain led an expedition to measure the length of the meridian arc between Dunkirk and Barcelona as a basis for it. They completed their survey in 1798 and presented their findings the following year, having created both a reference metre and kilogram from platinum. The latter was calculated as the mass of a cube of water at 4°C, where each side of the cube measured 0.1 metres. This volume was also defined as a litre.

Although France was the first country to adopt the new metric system, it was abolished by Napoléon in 1812. By the time it was reinstated in 1840, however, numerous other countries had begun to adopt the system. Its universal units soon spread to become the dominant form of measurement around the world.

DECEMBER

11

1946

The United Nations General Assembly established UNICEF to provide help for children in countries affected by World War II.

Six years of warfare on an unprecedented scale had caused widespread devastation, and left countries across the world struggling to provide even basic care for their people. Appalled by the plight of children in these countries, Polish physician Ludwik Rajchman encouraged the United Nations to establish an emergency fund to help them.

Raychman had previously led the Health Committee of the League of Nations, but had been unable to secure a leading role in the newly-established World Health Organisation. Although bitterly disappointed by this, he used his extensive experience of international bureaucracy to create the necessary proposals and lobby the world's governments to vote in favour of establishing the United Nations International Children's Emergency Fund.

UNICEF was formally established with the unanimous approval of UN General Assembly Resolution 57(I) on 11 December 1946. Under the direction of Maurice Pate, its first chief executive, UNICEF immediately began to provide emergency food and healthcare to children in countries that had been devastated by the war.

By 1953 the organisation had renamed itself the United Nations Children's Fund, though it kept the acronym UNICEF. Funded by contributions from both governments and private donors, UNICEF works closely with a team of celebrity Goodwill Ambassadors to promote their work and advocate for UNICEF causes. These continue the organisation's original aim of promoting the health and well-being of children across the world.

DECEMBER
12
1963

Kenya gained independence from the United Kingdom.

Kenya had been under British rule since the 19th century. After formally becoming a colony in 1920 African demands for a greater role in politics had grown. In the early 1950s a group of Kikuyus, the largest ethnic group in the country, formed the Kenya Land and Freedom Army. Better known as the Mau Mau, they began a violent organised campaign against colonial leaders and white settlers that culminated in the Mau Mau Uprising. By 1956 over 12,000 Mau Mau militants had been killed by the British in an attempt to suppress the uprising, although it's important to note that both sides committed ruthless acts of violence.

The revolt did, however, persuade the British of the need for concessions. From 1957 natives could be elected to the Legislative Council and, by 1960, they held a majority of the seats. Britain subsequently worked with the African politicians to prepare the transition to independence and, in May 1963, the Kenya African National Union secured the majority in both houses of the new bicameral legislature.

Independence was formally declared on 12 December 1963 with Queen Elizabeth II as Head of State. Jomo Kenyatta, the leader of the Kenya African National Union, became the country's first Prime Minister despite having been imprisoned between 1953 and 1961 after being found guilty of being a Mau Mau leader. Historians have since cast doubt on his conviction.

Kenya's independence is now marked in part by Jamhuri Day, a national holiday that celebrates Kenya's admittance to the Commonwealth as a republic the following year.

DECEMBER

13

902

Æthelwold ætheling, a claimant to the Anglo-Saxon throne, was defeated at the Battle of the Holme.

Æthelwold was the youngest son of Æthelred I, King of Wessex, who had been killed in battle and was succeeded by his brother, Alfred the Great. When Alfred died in 899 the throne passed to his son Edward, who soon faced opposition from his cousin.

Æthelwold had prepared to oppose Edward at Wimborne in Dorset but, after being unable to raise an army, he fled north where he secured support from the Danes in Northumbria. They sailed together to Essex in 901, and quickly established an alliance with the East Anglian Danes. The following year Æthelwold's new forces began to raid deep into neighbouring Mercia, and even crossed into the northern reaches of Edward's Wessex.

Edward retaliated by launching his own raids into East Anglia, prompting the Danes to return before their territory was completely ravaged. Rather than engage in battle, Edward called for his forces to withdraw. However, the men of Kent were slow to fall back and met Æthelwold and the returning Danes at the Battle of the Holme on 13 December 902.

Although details of the battle are scarce, the *Anglo-Saxon Chronicle* records that the Danes suffered numerous losses while defending their territory. Æthelwold himself was killed, along with several Danish nobles. This removed the threat to Edward's crown and, in 906, he made peace with the East Angles and Northumbrians at Tiddingford in modern Bedfordshire. Nevertheless, Edward's armies continued to harass the Danes and, in partnership with his sister Æthelflæd who ruled Mercia following the death of her husband, Edward continued to expand Anglo-Saxon dominance.

DECEMBER

14

1287

St Lucia's Flood destroyed a sea wall in the northwest of the Netherlands and killed approximately 50,000 to 80,000 people.

In the medieval period the Netherlands, whose name literally means 'lower countries', consisted of large areas of boggy land around the winding estuaries of three of the largest rivers in Europe. Although prone to flooding, the fertile areas close to the sea had attracted many settlers by the 10th century and, by the turn of the millennium, the population began to increase rapidly. The construction of dikes to hold back the sea consequently became an important part of life in the area. Draining the peat bogs that were left behind provided arable land to feed the growing population, but it also made the ground sink by up to a metre every century.

On 14 December 1287, the day after St Lucia's Day, an extreme low pressure system coincided with high tide in the North Sea to cause a huge storm surge that rose far above the usual sea level. The waves battered the dikes built to defend the north and north-western parts of the Netherlands, and the sea poured onto the land below. Numerous villages were destroyed, and records indicate that at least 50,000 people lost their lives. Meanwhile the floodwaters transformed a shallow freshwater lake into the salty Zuiderzee and created direct sea access to what was then the village of Amsterdam. The flood was therefore directly responsible for the development of one of the world's leading port cities.

The English coastline was also severely affected by the storm. Although the number of casualties was considerably lower, other effects were just as significant. Combined with another huge flood that had struck southern England in February numerous ports declined after being silted up, while new ones soon appeared.

DECEMBER

15

1851

Over 14,000 Australian gold miners gathered at Forest Creek in Victoria for a protest known as the Monster Meeting.

Gold had been discovered by shepherds near the modern town of Castlemaine in July 1851. However, it was only after the publication of a letter from John Worley, one of the men who had found the precious metal, in a Melbourne newspaper at the start of September that 'Yellow Fever' seized the people of Victoria on an unprecedented scale.

By December an estimated 25,000 people had arrived in the area to work the river beds and the creeks in the hope of finding gold. The scale of the gold rush had a dramatic effect on society as people left their homes and jobs and headed to Forest Creek in the hope of making their fortune.

To slow the rush, Victoria Governor Charles La Trobe had introduced a thirty shillings Gold License that was payable each month by every digger, irrespective of whether any gold was found. With the area's infrastructure at breaking point due to the continued influx of gold-seekers and their tents, in December he announced his intention to double the fee to sixty shillings from the start of the following month.

Angered by this tax rise, more than 14,000 diggers came together at a rally to oppose what they perceived as an unjust financial burden. Gathering under a new flag, the diggers heard speeches from the demonstration's organisers who addressed the crowd from an improvised stage on the back of a wagon.

On 24 December the Government Gazette confirmed that Governor La Trobe had reversed the tax increase. The Gold License remained at thirty shillings a month.

DECEMBER

16

1773

The Boston Tea Party saw an entire shipment of tea thrown into Boston Harbor by the Sons of Liberty.

The British government had passed the Tea Act seven months earlier on 10 May, partly in an attempt to support the struggling East India Company. The act allowed the company to import tea directly to the colonies, bypassing the middlemen who previously handled overseas tea sales and avoiding the issue of duty and refunds for importing tea into Britain. Tea imported into the colonies would consequently be much cheaper, allowing the East India Company to undercut the price of smuggled Dutch tea.

The problem for settlers in America was that tax was still imposed on tea in a continuation of the three pence duty that came in under the Townshead Acts of 1767. Although tea imported under the new Tea Act would be cheaper than before, a number of colonists opposed the idea that the British government had the right to impose any tax at all on the colonies. Since they did not elect the British parliament they argued that the new Act violated their right to 'no taxation without representation'.

The first shipment of tea to arrive in Boston under the new Act was brought by the *Dartmouth* in November. Colonialists gathered together by Samuel Adams urged the captain of the ship to sail the ship back to Britain without paying the import duty, but Governor Hutchison refused to allow the ship to leave. In the meantime two more ships arrived. Unable to resolve the standoff, on the evening of 16 December a group of up to 130 men, some disguised as Mohawk warriors, boarded the three vessels and threw all 342 chests of tea into the water. This act of defiance served as a catalyst for the American Revolution that broke out less than 18 months later.

The Saturnalia festival was celebrated for the first time in ancient Rome.

Created to mark the anniversary of the Temple of Saturn in the Roman Forum, the Roman festival of Saturnalia was dedicated to the god Saturn who was believed to have ruled over a Golden Age of agricultural abundance. The festival saw the suspension of usual social norms as the people of Rome engaged in lively celebrations.

Saturnalia originated as a three-day festival that began when the wool that was normally bound around the feet of the statue of Saturn was removed. The first day also saw a public banquet, which was preceded by a sacrifice at the Temple of Saturn itself. With the formal elements of the festival complete, the subsequent days – which ranged from three to seven days during the Roman period – were given over to the private celebrations for which the festival is perhaps best known.

The usual social hierarchy was reversed and, for the duration of the festival, slaves were treated to banquets while activities that were usually discouraged became commonplace. Romans from all social spheres were known to engage in gambling and excessive eating and drinking. The hedonism was all overseen by a chaotic King of the Saturnalia who was chosen at random.

The end of Saturnalia saw people exchanging small gifts made of wax or other simple materials. Known as the Sigillaria, this part of the festival saw the more crazed revelry begin to subside ahead of the return to normal social behaviour. Nevertheless, the writer Pliny the Younger recorded in one of his many letters how he preferred to avoid the festival altogether by moving to some of the more secluded rooms of his villa while the rest of the household celebrated.

DECEMBER
18
1898

French aristocrat Count Gaston de Chasseloup-Laubat set the world's first officially recognised land speed record.

Chasseloup-Laubat's older brother, the 5th Marquis of Chasseloup-Laubat, was one of the first members of the Automobile Club de France and bought an electric car from the French manufacturer Jeantaud sometime around 1893. The younger sibling was immediately fascinated with the chain-driven vehicle, and he became his brother's driver.

The first recorded motoring competition took place in 1894 and saw a range of vehicles undertake the route from Paris to Rouen. Focus turned to the raw speed of a vehicle a few years later when the French automobile magazine *La France Automobile* organised a competition in the commune of Acheres in the Yvelines department in north-central France. Situated less than 15 miles outside Paris, the long straight road on the outskirts of the village was deemed the perfect place to conduct a time trial. As a keen advocate of the electric car, Chasseloup-Laubat took the Jeantaud along to compete.

The day was cold and wet, but this didn't stop Chasseloup-Laubat from completing a single flying 1 kilometre run in 57 seconds. The time-keepers calculated that this gave him an average speed of 63.13 km/h or 39.24 mph, and this is universally recognised as the first official automobile land speed record. While this record was broken by the Belgian driver Camille Jenatzy a month later on 17 January 1899, Chasseloup-Laubat regained the title later that day in the same car with which he had set the original record.

The current world land speed record is held by British Royal Air Force fighter pilot Andy Green, who broke the sound barrier in *ThrustSSC*.

DECEMBER

19

1783

William Pitt the Younger became the youngest ever Prime Minister of Great Britain at the age of 24.

Pitt the Younger was the second son of William Pitt, 1st Earl of Chatham, who served as Prime Minister between 1766 and 1768. Educated at home until he was 14, the talented young William graduated from Pembroke College, Cambridge, before securing the patronage of James Lowther, 1st Earl of Lonsdale, through whom he won election to Parliament in 1781.

Against the backdrop of defeat in the American War of Independence, a succession of British governments collapsed. Meanwhile Pitt gained ministerial experience as Chancellor of the Exchequer under Lord Shelburne before resigning the post to develop his reputation as a parliamentary reformer.

In December 1783 King George III dismissed the Fox-North coalition that dominated parliament under the nominal premiership of the Duke of Portland. William Pitt, who was just 24 years old at the time, was instead asked to form a government that many commentators expected to collapse shortly after Christmas. Despite early defeats in the House of Commons, this 'mince-pie administration' gradually eroded the Opposition ahead of a General Election in the spring of 1784 that secured the young Prime Minister a parliamentary majority of around 120.

Pitt's first ministry lasted for seventeen years. During this time he decreased the national debt and reformed taxes, at the same time as dealing with the French Revolution and the Napoleonic Wars. He also engineered the Acts of Union, but Pitt disagreed with the King over Catholic emancipation and resigned in 1801. He returned to the premiership in 1804, but died less than two years later.

DECEMBER
20
1924

Adolf Hitler was released from Landsberg Prison, where he had been sent after being convicted of treason.

In November 1923 Hitler had led an attempted coup against the Weimar Government by trying to seize power in the Bavarian city of Munich. The putsch failed and Hitler was found guilty of treason in the subsequent trial. Sentenced to five years imprisonment, he was sent to the *Festungshaft* prison in the Bavarian town of Landsberg am Lech.

Hitler's 'fortress confinement' provided him with a reasonably comfortable cell when compared to conventional facilities, and meant that he was able to receive mail and have regular visitors. The discovery in 2010 of more than 500 documents relating the Hitler's imprisonment show that more than 30 people were able to visit him on his birthday on 20 April 1924, just 19 days into his sentence.

Imprisonment provided Hitler with the opportunity to dictate his autobiography, *Mein Kampf*, to his deputy Rudolf Hess. It was in this book that Hitler laid out his blueprint for the future of Germany. Although it gained only modest success when it was first published, Winston Churchill later claimed that if world leaders had read it they could have better anticipated the scale and nature of Nazi domestic and foreign policy.

In a memorandum dated 18 September 1924, the Landsberg warden Otto Leybold described Hitler as 'sensible, modest, humble and polite to everyone – especially the officers of the facility'. He was released on 20 December 1924 after serving only nine months of his five-year sentence, and soon set about rebuilding the Nazi Party which had been banned in Bavaria as a result of the Beer Hall Putsch. The ban was lifted less than two months after Hitler's release.

DECEMBER

21

1620

The first of the *Mayflower* Pilgrims landed at Plymouth, Massachusetts, where they established the Plymouth Colony.

The *Mayflower* had departed the English port of Plymouth in September 1620 for the Colony of Virginia. Of the 102 passengers, 37 were Puritan separatists who intended to establish a new settlement in the New World. The rest were servants, farmers, adventurers and tradesmen who were to support the fledgling colony.

After a stormy 66-day Atlantic crossing, land was sighted at the start of November. The *Mayflower* anchored in the large natural harbour of Provincetown much further north than their intended destination, although the area had already been explored by Europeans. Since they did not have a patent to settle in the area, yet had run out of provisions, the Pilgrims wrote the Mayflower Compact that served as a governing charter for the new colony, and began to prepare exploratory parties.

The first expeditions around Provincetown experienced skirmishes with local Native Americans from whom they took corn. The decision was consequently made to search further afield. On 21 December the first landing party stepped ashore at Plymouth, which had been named by John Smith six years earlier. Here they found a village whose native inhabitants had been wiped out by a series of epidemics. The site offered a good defensive position and large cleared areas that would be suitable for building their new settlement.

The first winter was harsh and, by March, over half the settlers had died. However, the next few months saw the colony sign a peace treaty with the leader of the local Wampanoag people, who went on to share their knowledge of the local environment to help the Pilgrims begin to build a successful and self-sufficient colony.

DECEMBER

22

1894

Alfred Dreyfus, a French Jewish artillery officer, was found guilty of treason in one of history's largest miscarriages of justice.

The origin of the Dreyfus Affair scandal lay in the discovery of a ripped-up letter in a waste basket at the German Embassy in Paris. Having been handed to French counter-espionage by the cleaner who found it, it was found to contain French military secrets and was determined to have been leaked by someone within the General Staff.

Alfred Dreyfus, who had been born into a Jewish family in the Alsace region before its annexation by Germany, had been promoted to the rank of captain by 1889. He joined the General Staff in 1893 but, following the discovery of the letter known as the *bordereau*, was arrested after his handwriting was compared to that in the letter.

Dreyfus' trial began on 19 December, but was preceded by weeks of anti-Semitic articles in the right-wing press. The trial itself was conducted in a closed court, where the seven judges unanimously found him guilty of treason after being handed a secret dossier during their deliberations. They declared their verdict on 22 December, and sentenced him to life imprisonment preceded by military degradation. This involved the insignia being torn from his uniform and his sword broken, before being paraded in front of a crowd stirred up by the press shouting, 'Death to Judas, death to the Jew.'

Dreyfus was transported to Devil's Island in French Guiana, but in France new evidence began to emerge that another officer was the real traitor. With support from the 'Dreyfusards' that included the novelist Emile Zola, a retrial in 1899 reduced the sentence while the President of the Republic granted a pardon. However, it wasn't until 1906 that Dreyfus was finally exonerated and readmitted to the army.

Benjamin Franklin, the American polymath, accidentally electrocuted himself while attempting to kill a turkey.

Benjamin Franklin began experimenting with electricity around 1746, and conducted a series of well-documented scientific experiments to explore its properties. His letters reveal that by 1750 he had already applied the terms 'positive' and 'negative' to electrical charge, and had performed numerous investigations using Leyden jars to store static electricity.

Franklin first expressed his intention to use electricity to cook a meal in a letter to his friend Peter Collinson on 29 April 1749. However, it wasn't until the following year that he successfully killed a full-size turkey by using electricity stored in a number of 6 gallon Leydon jars. His earlier attempts had only resulted in the birds being knocked unconscious and, in a report by English scientist William Watson, it is revealed that Franklin was consequently forced to increase the shock by using more jars.

In a separate account Franklin himself recorded how, on the evening of 23 December 1750, he hoped to demonstrate his experiment to an audience. The letter, written on Christmas Day, describes how 'I inadvertently took the whole [charge] through my own arms and body'. His audience reported hearing a loud crack accompanied by a great flash, while Franklin himself was rendered senseless. While the shock wasn't enough to kill him he felt numb for a while afterwards, and his chest was sore for the next week. This prompted him to warn his friend James Bowdoin to take care in his own experiments with electricity. However, the experience didn't put Franklin off experimenting with electricity as he reportedly conducted the famous kite experiment two years later.

The Eggnog Riot broke out at the United States Military Academy in West Point, New York after more than three gallons of whiskey were smuggled onto the campus.

Earlier in 1826, the academy's strict superintendent Colonel Sylvanus Thayer had banned the purchase, storage and consumption of alcohol due to concerns about drunkenness among the cadets. However, the new rules were ignored by cadets who sought to continue the annual tradition of drinking homemade eggnog on Christmas Eve.

Late on 22 December three cadets crossed the Hudson River and bought whiskey from Martin's Tavern. Having paid the security guard at the academy to ignore their smuggling efforts, they hid the alcohol in one of their rooms in the North Barracks while another cadet successfully obtained another gallon from another local tavern.

The party began at around 10pm on the evening of 24 December in North Barracks room No. 28, followed by another party in room No. 5. Jefferson Davis, who was later elected President of the Confederate States of America, was one of the cadets in attendance.

The party continued without much incident until around 4am, when noise from the increasingly drunken revellers woke teaching officer Captain Ethan Allen Hitchcock who went to investigate and ordered the cadets back to their rooms. Incensed, at least 70 drunken cadets instead launched a riot in which they brandished weapons, broke windows, and assaulted two officers.

Of the rioters, only 19 of them faced disciplinary action. Beginning on 26 January 1827, the trials resulted in guilty verdicts for all the defendants although eight of them were saved from expulsion.

DECEMBER
25
1914

The Christmas Truce saw soldiers on the First World War's Western Front take part in a series of unofficial ceasefires.

Autumn 1914 saw Germany's advance into France grind to halt as successive attempts by both sides to outflank the enemy resulted in a stalemate. By December 1914 the armies had constructed a continuous line of trenches stretching from the North Sea to the Swiss border where they waited to mount offensives in the spring.

With soldiers confined to their trenches, the 'Live and Let Live' system developed in which some of the quieter sections observed periods of non-violence. These unofficial breaks in the fighting were strongly discouraged by the military leadership, who later rejected Pope Benedict XV's calls for a formal period of peace at Christmas. In the end, therefore, the individual breaks in the hostilities that have become known as the Christmas Truce were largely spontaneous unofficial events.

As the ceasefire had no central organisation, it is unclear exactly where the Christmas Truce began. Evidence points to the front around Ypres in Belgium, where numerous accounts from both sides report the singing of Christmas carols as night fell on a frosty Christmas Eve. As the morning fog cleared the next day, some troops ventured into No Man's Land to exchange small gifts and Christmas greetings. These meetings often conjure up the popular image of troops playing football but, while there is evidence of at least one game being played, these were a rare exception.

Up to 100,000 men on both sides took part in the Christmas Truce, making it one of the largest examples of the 'Live and Let Live' system. While this is a significant number, it also shows that hostilities continued along the majority of the Western Front.

DECEMBER

26

1973

The American supernatural horror film *The Exorcist* opened in cinemas.

The Exorcist is one of the highest-grossing films of all time, but originally opened in just twenty-six American cinemas. Famed for its ground-breaking special effects, the film terrified audiences and was nominated for ten Academy Awards of which it won two.

The film, directed by William Friedkin who had previously had success with *The French Connection*, was adapted from William Peter Blatty's 1971 novel of the same name. This was itself inspired by reports of the real-life exorcism of an anonymous boy known by the pseudonym Roland Doe that emerged in the late 1940s. Blatty described his novel as 'an apostolic work' that sought to prove that if supernatural evil existed then so too must supernatural good.

These themes came through in Friedkin's film, but for many audience members it was the sight of the twelve year-old Regan's spinning head, levitation, vomiting and other extreme behaviour that proved both shocking and memorable. With newspapers reporting cases of people fainting at screenings, *The Exorcist* quickly became a social phenomenon.

The film went on to sell 6 million tickets within just three months of its release in the United States despite a mixed response from the critics. While *Variety* praised its 'expert telling of a supernatural horror story', the *New York Times* criticised it as 'a chunk of elegant occultist claptrap'.

Such negative responses failed to affect the film's success, however. *The Exorcist* was the second most popular film of 1974 and, once gross earnings are adjusted for inflation, remains the ninth highest-grossing film of all time.

DECEMBER

27

1929

The Soviet dekulakisation campaign began when Joseph Stalin announced the 'liquidation of the kulaks as a class'.

The kulaks were a class of wealthy peasants who had been powerful members of their communities in the years before the Russian Revolution of 1917. In the aftermath of the communist victory the kulaks were portrayed as capitalist class enemies of the new socialist state from whom surplus grain was requisitioned. Despite this, the introduction of Lenin's New Economic Policy in 1921 saw the abandonment of forced requisitioning in favour of allowing individuals to sell their surplus for profit in return for paying high taxes.

The NEP was abandoned under Stalin, who accused the kulaks of hoarding grain to exploit price rises. In response he introduced forced agricultural collectivisation, which prompted some peasants to burn their crops and barns and kill their animals rather than surrender their property to the collective farms. Angered by this active resistance to collectivisation, on 27 December 1929 Stalin called for the 'liquidation of the kulaks as a class' as part of an official policy of dekulakisation.

By the end of the following month the Politburo had formalised Stalin's decree and begun preparations for mass political repressions. Over the next three years kulaks were categorised into different groups, leading to millions of people being arrested, deported, or executed by the secret police, and their property confiscated.

Together, collectivisation and dekulakisation were significant factors in causing the Soviet famine of 1932–33 that resulted in the deaths of millions of people, particularly in the main grain-growing regions of Ukraine and Kazakhstan.

DECEMBER

28

1895

German physicist Wilhelm Röntgen published a paper detailing his discovery of X-rays.

Röntgen was experimenting with vacuum tubes at the University of Würzburg when he discovered the new 'invisible light' on 8 November 1895. Although his lab notes were burned after his death in 1923, Röntgen's biographers describe him noticing a faint glow from a screen covered in fluorescent material about a metre away from his apparatus. This was despite the vacuum tube itself being covered with black cardboard that stopped all visible light.

Having reasoned that the tube itself must be giving off these invisible rays, Röntgen conducted a series of experiments over the next few weeks in which he found that they could pass through certain objects but not others. Due to his uncertainty over the exact nature of the new rays, he adopted the mathematical designation 'X' to reflect their mysterious nature.

As his experiments continued, Röntgen began to notice that the rays were able to penetrate the soft tissues in his body but were stopped by bone. After subsequently replacing the fluorescent screen with a photographic plate he made the first ever X-ray image clearly showing the bones of his wife Bertha's hand and her wedding ring. On seeing the image she is said to have remarked, 'I have seen my death.'

Röntgen published the paper 'On a New Kind Of Rays' on 28 December 1895, and news of his discovery spread quickly. Within a year X-rays were being used as far away as the United States as both a diagnostic tool and for treating cancers. Röntgen refused to take out a patent on X-rays in order to allow the entire world to benefit from them, and was awarded the first ever Nobel Prize in Physics in 1901.

DECEMBER

29

1890

More than 150 Native Americans from the Lakota tribe were killed by US soldiers in the Wounded Knee Massacre.

The 19th century saw white settlers move westward across North America, in accordance with the disputed ideology of Manifest Destiny. The resulting forced relocation of Native Americans led to a series of conflicts collectively known as the American Indian Wars. Yet, by 1890 settlers and gold miners had begun to encroach on the new reservations while the bison on which the people of the Great Plains depended had been almost wiped out. In desperation the native peoples began to turn to performing the Ghost Dance that promised to bring about a revival of their pre-European existence.

White Americans, fearing that the Ghost Dance might be a prelude for war, decided to act. In a botched attempt to arrest the Lakota Sioux Chief Sitting Bull, he was shot and killed. This raised tensions in the community and resulted in hundreds of people, led by Chief Spotted Elk, opting to head for safety at the Pine Ridge reservation.

Having been intercepted by a detachment of US 7th Cavalry, the Lakota set up camp near Wounded Knee Creek on 28 December. The next morning Colonel James Forsyth ordered the Native Americans to surrender their weapons. The majority of the weapons were reportedly collected in without any problems, but a young Lakota named Black Coyote allegedly engaged in a scuffle after he refused to give up his rifle, possibly because he was deaf or he didn't understand the order to disarm. In the commotion a rifle discharged, prompting a frantic gunfight in which at least 150 and possibly as many as 300 tribespeople were killed, most of whom were old men, women and children.

DECEMBER
30
1993

Israel and the Vatican City signed the Fundamental Accord that established diplomatic relations between the two states.

Relations between Catholicism and Judaism cover a long, complex and violent history in which Christians revered the Jewish scriptures yet held Jews collectively responsible for the crucifixion of Jesus. However, the murderous anti-Semitism of the Nazi Holocaust led to moves for reconciliation between the two religions in the second half of the 20th century.

A key milestone in relations came when the Second Vatican Council published *Nostra aetate*, ('In Our Time') in 1965. This document formally rejected the idea of collective Jewish responsibility for the crucifixion. Two decades later, John Paul II became the first Pope to visit a synagogue where he called Jews 'our beloved elder brothers' and condemned anti-Semitism.

Despite these positive steps towards reconciliation, the diplomatic negotiations between Israel and the Holy See in the 1990s were still enormously complex. In particular, the Vatican maintained its call for Jerusalem to have 'international status' due to its unique position as a holy site for Christians, Jews and Muslims. Property rights and tax exemptions for the Church in Israel also featured heavily in the discussions.

The final agreement was signed by Monsignor Claudio Celli, the Vatican Undersecretary of State, and Israel's Deputy Foreign Minister Yossi Beilin. However, it has never been ratified by the Israeli Knesset due to ongoing economic disputes over the legal status of church properties in Israel. Despite this, the Vatican appointed an apostolic nuncio to Israel in 1994 while Israel appointed an ambassador to the Vatican.

Arthur Guinness signed a 9,000 year lease for the derelict St James's Gate Brewery in Dublin.

Arthur Guinness was the son of the land steward to the Reverend Arthur Price, the Archbishop of Cashel. In 1755 he began brewing ale in Leixlip in County Kildare approximately 17 km north of Dublin. Four years later, at the age of 34, he negotiated with the descendants of Sir Mark Rainsford, the former Lord Mayor of Dublin, to rent the abandoned 4-acre site of the St James's Gate Brewery in Dublin at £45 per annum. Much is often made of the lease lasting for an incredible 9,000 years. However long leases were reasonably common at the time to avoid full transfer of the freehold, since questions over land ownership posed serious political and social questions.

Having replaced the existing brewing equipment Arthur Guinness initially continued to produce ale at the new site, and within a decade had built a thriving export business shipping his beer to England. However, the business really began to flourish following the decision to begin brewing porter in 1778. Its popularity prompted Guinness to make the decision in 1799 to focus exclusively on darker beers. This set the business on the road to developing the signature stout with which the name is now most commonly associated.

Arthur Guinness died in 1803, by which time the brewery was producing over 20,000 barrels a year. The business then passed to his son, Arthur Guinness II, under whose control it continued to expand. In 1838 the St James's Gate Brewery became the largest in Ireland in terms out of output and soon began to expand beyond the original 4-acre site. However, the original lease stayed in place until the 1980s when it was eventually bought out for an undisclosed sum.

INDEX

Armistice of Mudros, 161
Armistice of Thessalonica, 311
Armstrong, Neil, 290
Arras, 122
Articles of Confederation, 55
artillery, 83, 122, 168, 180, 225, 299, 367, 396
Asimov, Isaac, 170
assassination, 68, 69, 136, 187, 210, 221, 224,
    236, 247, 262, 272, 278, 321, 348, 354
assembly line, 14, 157
Aston, Ken, 178
Astor, John Jacob, 118
Astor, Nancy, Viscountess, 370
astronomy, 58, 73, 170, 224, 253, 317, 384
Atatürk, 161
Athens, 135, 199
Atlantic Charter, 256
Atlantic Ocean, 30, 73, 83, 104, 132, 149, 211,
    223, 256, 257, 258, 264, 267, 282, 301, 378,
    395
Attorney General, 63, 119, 300
auction, 297
Augustus, 13, 185, 321
Auschwitz, 166
Australia, 41, 94, 112, 131, 150, 163, 204, 234,
    336, 389
Austria, 28, 129, 180, 197, 227, 236, 261, 315,
    328, 349, 371
Austria-Hungary, 106, 107, 162, 180, 194, 236,
    273, 315, 375
Austro-Prussian War, 315
automobile, 31, 41, 91, 121, 155, 157, 186,
    187, 195, 233, 249, 383, 392
Aventine secession, 186
Avery, Tex, 235
Aykroyd, Dan, 319

Baden-Powell, Robert, 34
Baghdad, 238
Bailey, Guy, 140
Baisakhi, 123
Baker, Sir Benjamin, 80
Bal des Ardents, 38
Balkans, 162, 194, 315
Balliol, John, 101, 247
balloon, 17
Baltic Sea, 169, 284
Baltimore, 210
Bampton, John, 172
banking, 11, 26, 287
barbed wire, 366

Barbie (toy doll), 85
Barcelona, 95, 384
barcode, 202
Barents Sea, 338
Barère, Bertrand, 281
Barnard, Christiaan, 377
Basel, 19
basketball, 53
Batista, Fulgencio, 127
Battle of Actium, 278
Battle of Arnemuiden, 299
Battle of Bannockburn, 101
Battle of Berlin, 144
Battle of Bogesund, 350
Battle of Britain, 283
Battle of Cable Street, 312
Battle of Cannae, 244
Battle of Castillon, 225
Battle of Falkirk, 101, 247
Battle of Fishguard, 66
Battle of Fukuda Bay, 326
Battle of Gravelines, 237
Battle of Halys, 170
Battle of Hastings, 15, 304
Battle of Jena, 32
Battle of Lincoln, 117
Battle of Monte Cassino, 27
Battle of Naseby, 190
Battle of Río de Oro, 83
Battle of Santiago, 178
Battle of Saratoga, 50
Battle of Stirling Bridge, 247
Battle of the Atlantic, 211
Battle of the Baggage, 306
Battle of the Bogside, 254
Battle of the Coral Sea, 150
Battle of the Holme, 387
Battle of Zama, 327
Bavaria, 133, 143, 255, 328, 394
Bay of Cádiz, 139, 237
Bay of Pigs Invasion, 127, 322
Bayreuth, 255
Beatles, 24, 250, 368
Beaumont, William, 182
Beccaria, Cesare, 372
Bedford, James Hiram, 22
beer, 16, 133, 380, 405
Beer Hall Putsch, 40, 114, 394
Beijing, 105, 120, 217
Beilin, Yossi, 404
Belfast, 31, 363
Belgium, 91, 129, 145, 155, 168, 181, 297, 320,

407

419

Pompey, 20
Ponche Verde Treaty, 296
Pony Express, 113
poppy, 145
Port Arthur, 52
Port Elizabeth, 288
Porto Alegre, 296
Portsmouth, 299
Portugal, 26, 32, 66, 96, 139, 282, 326, 378
Powell, Jody, 12
practical joke, 369
Praetorian Guard, 185
Pragmatic Sanction, 328
Prague, 156, 165, 317
Prague Astronomical Clock, 317
Prague Spring, 156
Pravda (newspaper), 147
prejudice, 198
Presley, Elvis, 24, 90, 285
Pretoria, 288
Priestley, Joseph, 324
Prince William Sound, 100
Princess Louise, 295
Princeton, 325
Princip, Gavrilo, 236
printing, 18, 87, 102, 118, 147, 153, 202, 293, 349, 381
prison, 63, 114, 148, 152, 222, 230, 239, 262, 288, 320, 353, 362, 394
privateer, 139
Prohibition, 195
Project Mogul, 216
propaganda, 235, 262, 290
Prospero (satellite), 336
protest, 45, 94, 146, 179, 254, 266, 346, 357, 389
Protestantism, 36, 48, 69, 129, 139, 165, 192, 239, 243, 254
Provincetown, 395
Provisional Government, 126, 134, 218
Prussia, 32, 129, 223, 227, 328, 351, 371
Punch (magazine), 145
punk, 286, 368
Puritanism, 382, 395
Pyréolophore, 228

Qin Shi Huang, 105
Quaker movement, 259, 314
Quang Duc, Thich, 187
quarantine, 46, 103
Qumran, 59

Race to the Sea, 122
racism, 62, 93, 114, 140, 198, 245, 288, 318, 333, 355
radio, 39, 83, 111, 187, 218, 265, 283, 286, 301, 336
radioactivity, 130
radium, 130
RAF Scampton, 159
Ragamuffin War, 296
railway, 80, 258, 291, 310, 344, 360
Rainsford, Sir Mark, 405
Rajchman, Ludwik, 385
Raleigh, Walter Sir, 337
Ramsay, Vice Admiral Bertram, 168
Ramsey, Alice Huyler, 249
rape, 144, 189
RCA (record company), 24, 90
Reagan, Ronald, 188, 335, 361
Realpolitik, 315
Réard, Louis, 213
rebellion, 69, 243, 346
Reconstruction, 68, 355
Recording Industry Association of America, 90
Red Army, 97, 144, 262, 265, 284
Red Baron. See Richthofen, Baron Manfred Albrecht Freiherr von
Red Guards, 105
Red Rum, 112
Red Scare, 376
referendum, 93, 263
Reformation, 36, 48, 345, 382
reformed Egyptian, 102
refugee, 325
Regent's Park, 160
Reich Ministry of Aviation, 70
Reichstag, 40, 144
Reign of Terror, 281
Reinheitsgebot, 133
Reinsurance Treaty, 194
Renaissance, 51, 128, 163, 289, 343
Republic of Korea. See South Korea
Republican National Committee, 210
Republican Party, 55, 68, 263, 348
revolt, 15, 63, 126, 172, 185, 192, 264, 292, 306, 350, 351, 371
Revolución Libertadora, 292
Rhapsody in Blue, 56
Richard I, 92
Richard II, 172

420

421

ABOUT THE AUTHOR

Scott Allsop is an experienced history teacher and graduate of the University of Cambridge. He began the daily www.HistoryPod.net podcast in 2014, and continues to run an award-winning educational website for history students at www.MrAllsopHistory.com.

He currently lives in Romania with his wife and two children. This book is dedicated to their grandpa, who provided unquestioning support for every hare-brained scheme and project.